PENGUIN BOOKS

Tim Hanna is the author of *John Britten*, the best-
selling biography of the late New Zealand motorcycle
engineering legend. Hanna himself still rides the same
Norton Commando Fastback he's owned for the last
twenty years and wouldn't consider any other bike –
although if he ever makes any money he might allow one
of those new Nortons garage space as a backup. He is
completing the restoration of a 100-year-old, 45-foot
motorsailer sometime soon.

This book is dedicated to Max,
the best boy in the world

ONE GOOD RUN
THE LEGEND OF BURT MUNRO

Tim Hanna

PENGUIN BOOKS

PENGUIN BOOKS

Published by the Penguin Group

Penguin Group (NZ), cnr Airborne and Rosedale Roads, Albany,
Auckland 1310, New Zealand (a division of Pearson New Zealand Ltd)
Penguin Group (USA) Inc., 375 Hudson Street,
New York, New York 10014, USA
Penguin Group (Canada), 90 Eglinton Avenue East, Suite 700, Toronto,
Ontario, M4P 2Y3, Canada (a division of Pearson Penguin Canada Inc.)
Penguin Books Ltd, 80 Strand, London, WC2R 0RL, England
Penguin Ireland, 25 St Stephen's Green,
Dublin 2, Ireland (a division of Penguin Books Ltd)
Penguin Group (Australia), 250 Camberwell Road, Camberwell,
Victoria 3124, Australia (a division of Pearson Australia Group Pty Ltd)
Penguin Books India Pvt Ltd, 11, Community Centre,
Panchsheel Park, New Delhi - 110 017, India
Penguin Books (South Africa) (Pty) Ltd, 24 Sturdee Avenue,
Rosebank, Johannesburg 2196, South Africa

Penguin Books Ltd, Registered Offices: 80 Strand, London, WC2R 0RL, England

First published by Penguin Group (NZ), 2005
9 10

Copyright © Tim Hanna 2005

The right of Tim Hanna to be identified as the author of this work in terms of
section 96 of the Copyright Act 1994 is hereby asserted.

Designed by Mary Egan
Typeset by Egan-Reid Ltd
Printed in Australia by McPherson's Printing Group
Front cover photograph Marty Dickerson. Back cover Norman Hayes.

ISBN 0 14 301974 0
A catalogue record for this book is available
from the National Library of New Zealand.

www.penguin.co.nz

CONTENTS

I don't panic. I can get scared and feel the adrenaline and feel the butterflies, but I don't panic. I think how to get out of a bad situation and the worse it gets the faster I think. Fear is your friend because it ensures you'll be cautious, but you can't let it overwhelm you. You tuck it in your pocket and it rides with you.

CRAIG BREEDLOVE, LAND SPEED RECORD CHAMPION

I can't wait to get here to race. When I get here, I can't wait to leave, and after I've left, I can't wait to come back

ART ARFONS, LAND SPEED RECORD CHAMPION

If it blows up before the line it's too hot. If it blows up after the line it isn't hot enough. If it blows up *on* the line it's just right.

BURT MUNRO

INTRODUCTION

I must first commend George Begg's earlier book *Burt Munro – Indian Legend of Speed*. George's meticulous research was of enormous assistance in writing my own version of Burt's life and times. I also commend the works of the late Florence Preston, Burt's literary sister, whose novels, gardening books and travel books are beautifully crafted. Her research proved a rich resource in writing this book. In particular her novel *Who Rides the Tiger* gave me an invaluable insight into the expulsion of fine Scots families like the Munros from their homeland.

This work is a dramatic recreation of Burt Munro's life. It is not a history. I have used the available research to create an account that fits the facts and reflects his character and personality, such as I have come to understand them, mainly through conversations with those who knew him best. I have been careful to avoid bold assumptions. I have not invented any major characters and I have not altered the chronology of events or otherwise tampered with reality. Readers will notice that Burt begins life as Bert; this is deliberate, as he only adopted the former spelling after his first journey to America.

I must thank Finlay Macdonald, my publisher, and Alison Brook, my editor, who did not once let my tardiness visibly irritate them. Thanks also to John and Margaret Munro for all their help and hospitality. This book would be the poorer without Marty Dickerson's wonderful photographs from Bonneville, and I am indebted to him. Finally my gratitude to the late Norman Hayes, perhaps the best-natured gentlemen it has ever been my privilege to meet.

Tim Hanna, September 2005

CHAPTER ONE
SALT

How the old buzzard came to be on the salt was difficult to comprehend. Under its quaintly old-fashioned fairing his machine was a battered heap, generations old and looking every day of it. He was in similar condition, an elderly codger wearing baggy suit pants that might have been fashionable once, with the cuffs tucked into his grubby socks, not-quite-worn-out tennis shoes and a weathered, black leather biker jacket. If you asked him a question he was likely to react with the kind of loud and guttural exclamation the aged and crusty use to indicate both deafness and indifference.

Even the black, humpbacked sedan with which he towed his equally peculiar home-made trailer looked like the kind of decrepit menace that should have been dragged off the highway by the authorities in the name of public safety. He was an obvious danger to himself and to anyone unlucky enough to be standing within a couple of country miles of him, judging by the dinky little brakes at each end of his machine, even if he was only capable of the highway speed limit. What could he possibly hope to achieve other than embarrassing and possibly killing himself, and wasting a lot of time for a lot of people with better things to do?

He was a joke, and that should have been the end of it. But

it wasn't. Somehow he had permission to run his motorcycle in front of a carload of officials – who would presumably putter along behind until they'd seen enough to order him off the salt.

There was something spooky about the way he stood beside his red, goldfish-shaped machine, one hand resting on its dull flank as if it were alive and in need of reassurance.

And then he was climbing into it, or onto it, with his back sticking out the top like the goldfish's fin breaking the surface. A team of like-minded misfits was preparing to give him a push start while he yelled instructions at them in some incomprehensible patois. They should have known better than to encourage such stupidity. It was bound to end badly and when it did they would be at least partially responsible.

And then he was off, his helpers pushing like maniacs until the thing suddenly caught with an unholy racket and leapt away like the demented fish it so resembled, leaving one of the pushers sprawled flat on his face in the Bonneville salt. The car full of officials was off after it, accelerating hard to catch up with the red machine until both car and bike settled at about ninety miles an hour, running smoothly across the shimmering salt.

The machine was obviously a bit faster than might have been gathered by looking at it in repose. The officials nodded their Stetsons at one another and agreed that, surprisingly enough, everything seemed under control ... when suddenly the red oval in front lurched while its rider groped about in its innards for something – a gear lever as it turned out – and changed up a cog.

The machine slewed slightly as the rear tyre spat a shower of salt back at the following car, giving them a brief view through to the nose before it straightened up and hurled a further shovel load all over the car's windscreen. The salt landed with a solid thump that made the car's occupants duck, and the suddenly bellowing machine in front lit out for the horizon like a stone out of a slingshot. It simply disappeared.

There was no catching him, and that was the end of the story until they found him at the other end of the run, standing beside his streamliner, which once again had its little landing wheels extended.

Earl Flanders, the American Motorcycle Association (AMA) steward for Utah's legendary Speed Week, got out of the car and strolled over. The old guy was looking a bit flustered but, considering he must have been going over 140 miles an hour by Flanders's educated reckoning, that was hardly surprising. Flanders nodded at him with a puzzled smile that belied a certain new-found respect and which made him look a lot friendlier than he had when he first spied the ancient combination an hour or so earlier. He said something like, 'The old girl seemed to run pretty good.'

'You think so, Earl?' replied the old guy. He seemed as surprised as everybody else.

Earl Flanders nodded again. 'She really took off when you changed into top!'

Once more the old guy looked puzzled. 'Top,' he repeated, shouting like the old deaf coot he was. 'I never got her out of second.'

Earl Flanders chewed that over for a moment or two, seeming to be a little lost for words. When he eventually located his vocal chords he told the old guy that he could run the bike in qualifying and after that, well, it was up to him. If he could hit a higher speed on a one-way run than the record he was after, a record he could only subsequently establish with a two-way average, he could try for it – same as everybody else.

He called him Bert and shook his hand, welcoming him for the first time to the 1962 Speed Week. The old fellow returned the handshake with a numb expression. Most of the guys thought it was probably a reaction to the speed – and the fact that he had travelled about halfway around the world from a place few had even heard of. It was bound to have taken it out of him.

But they were wrong.

Bert Munro loved to travel. He loved to see new places and meet new people. He loved to gas on to them about all his adventures on motorcycles and he especially enjoyed meeting women. He was, where they were concerned, as agreeable as he could be whenever the opportunity arose. He always pushed every possibility as fast and as far as he could, most often being rejected with equal promptness and sometimes with anger. On rare occasions, as he frankly admitted, his wide-cast net landed a prize, a likelihood he maintained by casting continuously. He would sweep women into his arms with the slightest encouragement, his larrikin good humour charming all but those most mindful of their dignity. A world full of rejections, he would say reflectively, was worth the occasional visit to heaven. He had a T-shirt he often wore that read: Even dirty old men need love!

What he loved most of all, however, was to run his Indian motorcycle. He'd bought it new in 1920 and tuned and rebuilt it ever since to go faster and faster, until he was sure that with 'just one good run' he could achieve at least 200 miles an hour.

What he did not like were high-speed accidents. He'd survived enough of those to last several lifetimes and he hated the sight of blood, especially his own. And the way his new streamline shell had encouraged the Indian to weave from side to side in the most violent and wayward manner as he approached 150 miles an hour had scared three kinds of crap out of him. He was sure the officials following must have decided there and then to ban him forever.

All this way and the son of a bitch just wanted to trip over itself and smear him all over the salt.

He looked at the curious faces gathered all about him and squared his shoulders. Having not realised that he had left the officials so far behind by the time his Indian got the wobbles, it was only just dawning on him that they'd missed it. Whatever the reason, they had given him the green light. He had come to run, so he supposed he'd better just get on with it.

For the past forty years he had worked with an almost insanely single-minded determination toward this point. Certainly there were many, and Bert knew a few of them in the tight community he came from, who thought him as mad as a meat axe to have squandered an entire lifetime on such an unlikely and unproductive pursuit. Uncounted hours, tens of thousands of them, had been consumed in a workshop lit by just a solitary, bare 150-watt bulb, carving parts on an almost completely worn out lathe, melting old pistons into home-made moulds to machine new ones.

'One of Chev,' he'd intone as he placed them into the crucible and prepared to run his blowtorch over them, 'three of Ford, for the hint of titanium Henry puts in them. One of Bedford truck for a bit of British pig-headedness. We'll see how that brew goes.'

Or he might have been machining down discarded cast iron agricultural pipe to make cylinders, all the better because they had been spun rather than extruded at the ironworks and were therefore of consistent density. Good for the lathe.

He regularly lay awake at night in his narrow little bed in the dampest corner of his dark, clay-floored workshop with his hand resting on the Indian's tank, thinking about the way gas might flow in a different-shaped combustion chamber. He made overhead valve heads for his machines out of other people's discarded rubbish. He could make almost anything.

It wasn't dank in his one-windowed shed, but it could be dark during the day if the sleet was driving and the garage doors were shut. At night it was pitch black except when the moon was really bright. It never shone directly through the window. He'd been careful when he built the shed to ensure he'd be left alone by the moon as much as possible. He found it hard enough to sleep at the best of times.

A wood stove with a chimney that angled right across the width of the shed to exit on the other side surrendered all the heat it had before trickling cool smoke into the air. No point wasting coal.

Sometimes he filed or hacksawed for days – making a conrod, maybe, out of a bit of bulldozer axle he'd had stamped flat at the local heavy-engineering shop, which had not charged him because everyone from the boss to the apprentices liked him and knew he had no money other than his pension.

Sometimes he tapped away for days with a hammer. The

aluminum shell alone, the thing that now threatened to kill him, had taken him five years to patiently knock into shape.

Gazing back down the preceding seasons he could no longer remember the number of runs he had made, with the machine going flat knacker on the beach beside the cold Southern Ocean, trying to find out if months of work had been a complete waste of time or had yielded just a few more miles an hour. Or racing furiously under a blazing summer sun against a determined bunch, who were hard to beat, with the smell of salt and seaweed and sausages in the air.

He had grinned at the cracks and holes occasioned by the hundreds of blow-ups that had so often reduced his engine to mangled wreckage; loud and terminal bangs that he'd always endured with the same stoic and even cheerful equanimity he'd handled his dozens of accidents. A significant number of those had knocked him unconscious for varying lengths of time and some pile-ups had left him badly injured.

To be honest the accidents had quite often seriously worried him, especially while they were happening. It was a sickening thing to have the ground and the sky suddenly go spinning and tumbling, and to have the wind thumped out of your body as a prelude to the sudden, horrible world of pain and that final white flash of pure kinetic energy that turned the lights off. But there had been no point in dwelling on such incidents and he hadn't.

Finally he had survived the loss of his family, a family he loved dearly but which had nonetheless abandoned him when it was clear he had virtually abandoned them to attend to the never-ending demands of his machine. He'd had to acknowledge that they were either old enough to have absorbed most of the gifts he had to give, or young enough to adjust to other arrangements. He'd never considered that they might be better off without him. They knew he cared; he had been a patient and loving father in his own way. The God of Speed, he thought, was a cruel and pitiless master to his disciples, demanding everything and granting precious little in return. And he had never asked for much.

Why anyone would want to take a 1920 Indian Scout, a fine machine in its day but no rocket, and turn it into an alcohol-burning fire-breather to attack international speed records almost half a century later, at speeds almost four times those it had been capable of when new, was not a question the old rider had ever bothered with much. In fact, the idea of breaking records was fairly extraneous to the exercise. He did what he did mainly because meeting the challenge gave him more satisfaction than anything else, with the possible exception of an encounter with a willing woman.

All he really wanted was one good run to prove his life's work, and the person he wanted to satisfy was none other than himself. He just wanted to go as fast as the machine could go. Since he'd literally run out of room back home he'd come to the salt flats at Bonneville, Utah, where the vast, dead-flat bed of an ancient lake provided the perfect track for petrol heads like him to let rip.

However, it was now clear that his rather humble objective would take all the skill he possessed to achieve. Although his ability on a motorcycle was in fact a lot greater than anyone in the small crowd might have imagined, the way the thing was handling made the outcome disturbingly uncertain. Maybe the weave would go away as he went faster, maybe it would not. He hoped it wouldn't get worse, but maybe it would. He could not possibly know until he got there, wherever *there* might be, and by then it might easily be too late.

Ah well, he thought, faint heart ne'er did win a flipping thing. He was going to get back on when his turn came, get the old thing up into third, its top gear, and crack the throttle wide open until it ended one way or another. It might be death or glory but if it ended up neither he could always come back the next year.

He shuddered. Bert Munro was a brave man but he was not stupid. There was just no anticipating what might happen.

CHAPTER TWO
DISPOSSESSION

Bert Munro was a stubborn old miser who cadged, cajoled, whee-dled, charmed and occasionally begged for anything he needed to make his old machine go faster. Actually there were two machines; a 500cc 1936 MSS Model Velocette kept company with the 1920 Indian Scout in the dark shed they shared with Bert. In fact, you could hardly call the Indian an Indian, considering all the changes Bert had made, and he didn't. He called it the Munro Special. The Velocette was similarly removed from its origins and he called that the Five Pound Special, the price he'd paid for the wreck when he pulled it out of a chook shed. Of course, that had been seven years ago and now the Velo was a 138-miles-an-hour job it probably deserved a better moniker. But Bert got a kick out of doing every-thing on a shoestring, positively rejoicing in the transformation of trash to treasure he managed nearly every day.

In some ways he was simply carrying on a tradition that recog-nised the simple wisdom of the phrase 'waste not, want not'. It would be uncharitable to say that the extremes to which he took this philosophy were characteristic of those boasting Scottish ancestry, but there are some who claim this to be largely true. If they say it as an insult, however, they do so only out of ignorance. The

Scots who landed in New Zealand in the middle of the eighteenth century and begat the likes of Bert were survivors of long hardship. The Highland Scots in particular had suffered since Queen Elizabeth of England knocked down the forests of Scotland to build her navies, the first salvo in a war of unconscionable exploitation that would go on for hundreds of years.

The final ignominy was not soldiers but sheep, and the perpetrators of what would come to be known innocuously as the 'clearances' were the very people whose responsibility it was to look after the best interests of the largely rural population. With the invention of the mechanical loom, mostly absentee landowners realised that large flocks of sheep needed few shepherds while their wool was needed in ever-increasing quantities to feed the booming mills in the north of England. The entire society of rural Scotland and Ireland became an impediment to progress, thrown off the land and left to starve.

In the case of the Irish the situation was hugely exacerbated by the blight that ruined their subsistence potato crops. To encourage this exodus some landlords resorted to the simple remedy of burning down their tenants' dwellings. The more enlightened types sometimes compensated their faithful servants with the few pounds needed to secure a passage on a sailing ship to somewhere else – Australia, America, Nova Scotia or New Zealand.

Emigration, like the transportation of criminals to Australia, was almost inevitably a one-way journey, as those who waved and called out from the docks, and those who crowded the rails of the departing windjammers, knew.

Beannachd, beannachd!

Goodbye!

James Robertson Munro was a brawny three-year-old with just one cloud peeking over an otherwise clear horizon, had he but known it. His family had farmed the smallholding on which his father's house was sited for generations. The local *sennarchie*, a weathered old body who lived in a tumbledown croft at the head of the valley, could trace the history of James Munro's family in his sing-song Gaelic, relating as he did a tale of battles, betrayals, marriages and murders, back to when the Scots had arrived from what later came to be known as Ireland, conquering the Pictish people in the process.

Munro's ancestors had originally been known by the name O'Ceanns but their racial make-up, now modified by marriage with the peoples they had dispossessed, had been further changed by the arrival of Norse people, who had raped and pillaged their way inland some centuries later. The *sennarchie* believed that at about the time King Duncan was murdered by the usurper Macbeth the O'Ceanns had taken the name of their clan leader and become Munros. They had been living in Glencalvie ever since, farming peacefully but always ready to take up arms under command of their laird to defend their homes and hearths. For the most, however, they worked, assiduously tithing part of their crops of potatoes, barley, oats and kale to the laird, and more latterly paying rent to his factor.

There were almost a hundred people, members of some ten families, who sub-rented their plots from the three tenants-in-chief, making a living from the eight flat hectares of fertile land where the rushing waters of the Cuiliannach, Alladale and Calvie burns met to form the River Carron. The cloud that shadowed James Munro's future cast a pall over all in the glen and already things had changed significantly for the worse.

Over the preceding decade the laird, who had forsaken the grand pleasures of his castle outside Dingwall to live in London, had slowly withdrawn the traditional privileges that offered his crofters more than mere subsistance lives. Ancient rights, like the taking of salmon from the river, the gathering of firewood from the birch and oak forest, and the grazing of a few sheep, cattle or goats on the unfenced moorland above the glen had been withdrawn one by one. Wealthy Englishmen now rented the rights to fish the river, to hunt deer in the forest and to shoot grouse on the moors, arrangements that excluded the locals and made their lives immeasurably harder.

Many of the young men had left to work the fisheries on the coast or to labour on the roads and canals being pushed toward the Highlands. However, the gravest fear held by the villagers was that the laird would soon revoke their grazing privileges altogether and as a final blow evict them from their cottages.

When it happened it did so with a cold finality that brooked no argument and shattered the community in one fell swoop. One afternoon the three tenants-in-chief returned sadly over the little bridge linking the glen with the outside world. They came from a meeting with the laird's factor in Tain, to which they had been summonsed, and were carrying writs of eviction and some cash in coins to give to all who agreed to leave without being physically forced. They could remove their personal effects and the timbers from their houses. They would also receive compensation for any animals they might find more convenient to leave behind. The money on offer was seven guineas for an adult and five for a child, the price of a passage to somewhere else.

James Munro's father took the money and made arrangements to hire a horse and four-wheeled wagon. They took everything including the timbers from their now destroyed home, attended a service on a grassy knoll near the old cemetery, crossed the little bridge across the river and left the glen for ever.

They would all follow the track to Drumnadrochit, passing through the village, to follow the Great Glen to the crossing at Fort Augustus before carrying on to the bridge at the mouth of Glen Spean. From there they would slowly make their way around Loch Leven and through Glencoe to the Rannoch Moor, taking great care to avoid the bogs, thence through Glen Falloch and the Trossachs and Campsie Fells to the mighty River Clyde. Some would end up in Glasgow, a city teeming with resentment, poverty and filth, trying desperately to find work among the pressing crowds of unemployed. Others would cash in their coins to board the next available ship to somewhere else.

James Munro's father took his little family to Foulis Point where they used their old home's timbers to erect a shelter in a sandy hollow behind the beach. As the days shortened he laboured long and hard to cut and build up the thick peat walls. He prayed it would prove sturdy enough to survive the coming winter. James's mother planted potatoes in the thin coastal soil for the following spring. They were reliant on the grain they already had in storage from the last crop out of the rich black earth of Glencalvie. How they all survived the winter must finally have been a matter of faith, for they had little else to sustain them.

They spent most of the winter days in the bed, huddling together to stay warm as cripplingly cold gales clawed at the roof and pounded on the door. There was little driftwood to burn on this hard coast and no money to spare for coal. Ice and snow lay on the ground until the spring when they discovered that the blight had come to Scotland. The hopeful crop of potatoes withered.

With things now desperate for all who had been driven from the Highlands, there were riots in the towns when starving people discovered the bumper crop of wheat and oats produced by early spring in the Highlands was being shipped directly to the Lowlands or to England. Even money could not save them from hunger when there was nothing to buy with it. Grain wagons were mobbed and ships seized by crowds who flung the contents of the holds onto the docks to be shared among the starving. It did no good. Soldiers used their rifle butts to break heads before reloading the ships.

It was only the early arrival of the herring shoals that saved many. Once more there was work and food and James's father was able to keep his family healthy but thin. A quantity of dried herring was salted away for the winter and the garden finally yielded a quantity of poor oats. But such an existence held no promise for the future, and he looked far and wide for better work.

His luck picked up when he was hired as a labourer building the Caledonian Canal. Even if he was away from home for months at a time there was now some money. Naturally skilled, he worked on stone viaducts to carry the canal across the valleys, and stone bridges to carry traffic across the canal. He went from there to build stone culverts on the roads being driven into the Highlands and finally learned to work with iron, becoming a supervisor on several important bridge constructions.

The work suited a determined and practical Highlander and indeed there were many like him who rose quickly, in spite of their almost total lack of formal education, to become quite prominent engineers. James's father never quite acquired the position to guarantee a reliable income, but he was able to move his family into Glasgow. Here they rented a small tenement that if not luxurious was at least solid and dry.

James attended school and learned to read and write. He grew up hale and strong. On the day he turned twenty his father gave him his passage money to New Zealand and a large part of his life savings, about twenty pounds in all. With the gifted money and the fifteen pounds he had managed to save himself he looked forward to buying a piece of land and making a new beginning. James's parents well appreciated that once his ship had sailed they would never see their son again, but the Highlands were finished and the boy deserved a better future than to graft in a shipyard or on roads alongside his father, as he had from the age of fourteen.

The Otago Association had founded a successful and profitable settlement in the southern extremity of New Zealand, with a fine new town called Dunedin as its port. It was largely a free kirk settlement and many more displaced Highlanders would be going there now that Prince Albert himself had set up the Highland Emigration Society to pay a large part of the passage money to those affected by the clearances. The English were on the way, too, with The New Zealand Company paying two-thirds of the passage to those travelling on its ships to take up land it owned, though the Scots of Otago were determined to maintain the character of their settlements against such cultural encroachment.

As James's parents watched and waved across the widening stretch of water separating the creaking *Lady Egidea*, they drew at least a little comfort from the promise that no Englishman or treacherous laird would ever lord it over their son again.

CHAPTER THREE
REDEMPTION

When James Munro finally took his grateful leave of the rolling, heaving, rat-infested ship that had been his home for the last four long months and took his first unsteady steps into Dunedin, he found an impressive and graceful city already boasting significant civic buildings. It was a most welcome change.

The voyage had been hard. Four hundred and thirty souls had embarked and thirty had been consigned to the deep en route. One had been a seaman. James saw him topple from the end of spar thirty metres above the water as the ship rushed along under a full spread of canvas. He had survived the fall and could be seen waving in the ship's wake, but by the time the vessel was stopped and a boat lowered he was several kilometres behind. The ship resumed her course after only a few minutes of what to James seemed the most perfunctory search.

Most of the victims were children who had succumbed to the dysentery that spread quickly in the fetid conditions below deck. James had lost no opportunity to get himself above, often joining in the sailors' work to avoid being sent back below, the captain apparently believing it more convenient to keep his cargo secured.

He breathed a silent prayer of thanks for his safe deliverance and shouldered his sea chest. It was 1862 and Dunedin was in the grips of gold fever. Panhandlers and hustlers from the goldfields of California and Australia had arrived in their tens of thousands to seek their fortune in Central Otago, and many had done exceptionally well. The city bustled, its pavements cramped with chatter and activity, and James was briefly tempted to try his luck with shovel and pan, too. But his Highland prudence was too deeply ingrained and he was soon stowing his chest in the cabin of a small coastal steamer that slugged its way through rough seas along a rocky and inhospitable coast reminiscent of home. First south then west, he arrived two days later at Bluff, a small port serving the town of Invercargill, which had the distinction of being the most southern point of the South Island.

James Munro was, like his father, a practical Highlander and used to both punishing hardship and the frustrating perversities of life. He found his servings of both in this new country were less than daunting and his progress was steady and assured. He worked for an already established Highlander as a shepherd for several years, saving every penny he could, until he could buy a forty-hectare parcel of land some fifty kilometres to the north of Invercargill. He chose carefully and wisely and set about creating a farm.

It was flat and gently rolling land blessed with rich soil and a clear stream. He called it 'New Field' and it was from the beginning a blessed venture. He saw nothing of the fierce natives he had been warned about, although the newspapers carried stories of open warfare in the North Island between Maori warriors and the colonial army.

The few Maori he did meet mainly wanted work and were prepared to do it for reasonable rates, carving out the land by removing the massive rimu and totara trees that grew there. Munro's first money came from selling pit-sawn planks, many produced with the help of local Maori, needed to build houses in the rapidly growing cities of Southland. In just a few years he had transformed a rolling woodland reverberating with birdsong into a patchwork of green paddocks as bare of trees as the Highlands themselves. He was well pleased.

He used his profits to buy stock from which he bred good-quality herds of cows and sheep, and benefited from the beginning of wool exports to England. When he felt his prosperity was assured he built a fine house and went looking for a wife, finding her in the person of Margaret Grant, the daughter of a couple who had been among the first to settle in nearby Oteramika District. It was said that Margaret was the first white woman born in the South Island and it may well have been true, although she considered it both immodest and a little less than respectable to make the claim. The couple had talented, good-looking children.

In 1882 a business founded at Totara Estate, to the north of Dunedin, commissioned the conversion of a ship to carry the first refrigerated cargo to England, changing at a stroke the nature of farming in the colony. Many farmers turned to meat and dairy production, James among them, and with the establishment of regular refrigerated shipments of meat to Britain and Europe they experienced something of an economic boom. It was just as well, because by now the family had grown to include six boys and six girls, and it wouldn't be cheap to settle six sons on their own farms and provide six daughters with adequate dowries.

Even though New Zealand would suffer quite gravely in the depression that hammered the economies of the industrial world through the late 1870s and well into the 1880s, the Munro clan did indeed prosper. When William Munro's time came to leave home he was able to buy another fine forty-hectare farm where he milked cows and ran sheep. The establishment of a large dairy factory at nearby Edenvale underpinned his success and he built his own graceful house, married his own beautiful bride, Lilly, and set about establishing a family. They were soon blessed with a son, Ernest, and when the boy was still less than a year old Lilly fell pregnant once more with twins. Sadly, on 25 March during the last year of the century, she gave birth to a stillborn baby girl and a weak baby boy whom the doctor pronounced would be dead too in a matter of months.

But Herbert James Munro was made of stringier stuff; he would live to witness, and be fascinated by, an era of extraordinary change – even if his own survival would always remain a matter of some uncertainty. Because Herbert James Munro would grow up worshipping the God of Speed. Born during the dawn of the age of flying machines and automobiles, the fantastic inventions of men with boundless dreams, he would become a true believer, willing even to offer his life to this most demanding of deities.

The very first recorded land-speed record had been documented just four months before his birth, in December 1898 when Gaston de Chasseloup-Laubat raced his electric Jentaud Duc at 39.24 miles an hour. Early in 1899 Camille Jenatzy of Belgium raised the record with his electric dogcart to 41.42 miles an hour. By the end of the century it would be broken another four times and would stand at 65.79 miles an hour. The race without end had started.

CHAPTER FOUR
FARMING

For as long as he could remember Herbert Munro had always hated farming. He especially loathed getting up in the dark on a blustery, cold day to gather the cows for milking, a chore he attended to every morning without exception once he turned eight. The farm was a pleasant enough place and his family was generally a picture of harmony. Ernest, or Ernie as his family called him, was a proper elder brother who took the lead and looked out for Herbert, or Bert as his family soon named him. Of course, Ernie could not guard his young brother against every eventuality and when he dived straight off his bed onto his head at the age of three there was nothing Ernie could do other than run to fetch their mother. Several anxious hours passed before young Bert finally groaned and opened his eyes, and afterwards he could not say why he had taken the dive. His mother would later wonder if he had been conditioning himself for a lifetime of crashing onto his head.

The children all worked hard before and after school but still found time to climb trees and explore. Three sisters followed the boys: Eva, Ruby and Florence. The big house swallowed them all up without complaint. The girls grew up and attended school and variously developed their musical and artistic talents with keen parental encouragement, although this was never allowed to over-shadow their domestic education. While the boys learned to plough behind horses, milk cows, make wooden gates, tighten wire fences, deliver calves and lambs, shear sheep, sort fleeces, stack hay, shoot rabbits, fix leaking irrigation pipes, maintain machinery and all the other skills a farmer had to master, the girls learned how to be farmer's wives; to sew and cook and clean house. They learned to produce immaculate, white, crisply starched laundry and to make everyday domestic necessities such as soap. They learned how to cook appetising, filling meals and how to bottle fruit. They learned to keep a large vegetable garden, a responsibility they shared with the boys. They were taught to be good hostesses, able to look after guests with gentle and self-effacing deference. The farm thrived and all was well with the world at Edenvale until one fateful afternoon when Ernie was killed by a falling tree.

It was a dreadful accident. The boys and their father had chopped down a gnarly old pine that had become hung up in the branches of another. They left it there while they retired to the house for lunch, before returning to finish the job. Ernie, always keen to get on with things, climbed onto the leaning tree and jumped up and down on it. Before William could order his son off the doomed tree it ripped loose from its neighbour's embrace and crashed to the ground, spinning as it fell and crushing Ernie beneath.

Lilly took it so badly that fears were held for her sanity. The doctor recommended she have another child as soon as possible, which she did. It was another boy and they named him Charles – soon of course to be known as Charley. Charley was on his own a lot, being so much younger than the other children, so Lilly had Rita to keep him company.

Bert was now the eldest and it was not a welcome change. He missed his brother badly and his sadness was compounded by the growing realisation that the farm would now inevitably become his prison. Not for him grand adventures in distant, romantic places, the dreams he had always imagined one day becoming real. Now he was duty-bound to stay home and help his father, eventually to take over the farm and run it as his own. It was a detestable thought.

If asked he would have found it hard to articulate his feelings about the farm. He had nothing specific against the place except perhaps that the pace of life was so slow. His father refused to buy a tractor, instead relying on a team of massive Clydesdale horses to operate a shed full of machinery. There was horsedrawn hay-making equipment: a cutter, rakes and a bailer. There was a big, formal carriage and a number of tipping drays in addition to several sturdy four-wheeled wagons. There was a combined seed sower and top dresser made by Bert's Uncle Jim in his factory in Winton. The Munro Seed Sower and Top Dresser was a tremendous success and it was being shipped off all over the world. Uncle Jim had recently completed his new model, which was designed to be towed behind a tractor.

Tractors seemed a wonderful thing to Bert but his father's opposition to them was absolute. The horses would see them right. On the few occasions Bert managed to wrangle a ride he tried to choose Tommy. Dolly, Nellie, Bessie, Frankie and Gertie were all good horses but Tommy had spirit. He liked to go! If his father was not looking Bert would kick the huge beast into action and get it up to full steam. Tommy was surprisingly quick and quite agile for an animal his size, and he would pound over the farm, clearing gates with his ears pinned back as if it was the best fun in the world. For Bert that was precisely what it was, and the rushing wind filled him with the most exhilarating sense of freedom he had ever known.

His father strongly disapproved of such shenanigans, however, and he always found out. Later, having survived a tongue-lashing, Bert would lie in bed and imagine he was flying across the countryside again, free to go where he pleased, to carry on, to go faster and faster. And then, just after he'd fallen asleep it always seemed, it was time to get up and fumble into his rough working clothes before stumbling out into the dark early dawn to gather the cows again.

He was not riding Tommy the day he took the tumble that knocked him out cold for the second time in his life. He and his father were shifting cattle and Bert was astride one of the mares.

It was a silly fall, caused by some irritation that made the mare suddenly rear up. Bert had been carelessly leaning down to latch a gate and was caught off guard. His father saw him arc through the air to land with a tremendous thump to his head on the sun-baked earth. Once more the family waited anxiously while Bert took his time coming back to them; this time a full twelve hours, after which he seemed no worse for wear.

His dissatisfaction at the pace and monotony of farm life was not helped by the incredible stories that would make their way to Edenvale from the world outside. One of Bert's first memories was of a conversation between his father and a visitor who had spent time in a place to the north called Temuka. The man claimed to have seen a flying machine, built by a local farmer of bamboo and cloth, fly through the air with a motor-driven fan dragging it along. His father had expressed disbelief but the visitor was adamant. It was only a year later they heard of Richard Pearce and his attempts to build a flying machine.

It was rich fantasy material and even the sight of washing billowing on the line could find young Bert daydreaming of soaring effortlessly through the air. The newspaper finally reported that two brothers had flown a motor-powered aeroplane – in America. Pearce was never mentioned. Bert's father conceded then it had happened, but saw little to commend such activities. There was enough rushing about to no useful purpose in the world and flying would only increase it.

Automobiles were viewed with similar disdain. Although rare, the Munro family had seen a number of them by the time Bert was five. As early as 1904 some families were using them to attend church and they made a stark – and to Bert wonderful – contrast to the collected traps and buggies. William had complained for a while that the chattering, backfiring machines would upset the horses, but they had quickly learned to ignore the contraptions. Cars found an early and enthusiastic following in prosperous Southland and by the time he was ten Bert was familiar with dozens of different makes. It was a source of keen disappointment that his father still refused to even entertain the idea of acquiring one.

On rare occasions Bert was taken to Invercargill by his father. Travelling by steam train for fifty glorious kilometres was the greatest excitement in his young life. Seeing the train pull into the platform, steam curling around its wheels like the breath from huddled horses on a cold morning, made his heart sing. He would take his seat by the window and wait for the wheels to spin on the rails as the engine heaved into action.

It was great to watch fences flit past the window so quickly they registered only as a rising and falling blur, and to feel the train rocking as if impatient to go faster. Arriving was the worst part, but there was always the return journey to look forward to. Back home, though, he would feel a pang of loss for days.

One rail trip took him and his father just a little further, to the end of the twenty-kilometre line that went to the port of Bluff. They were to take delivery of a chest for Lilly, sent by an aunt in London who obviously felt her niece had been exiled long enough to deserve a few luxuries from home.

Bert loved every moment of the visit. Tall ships with masts that seemed to scrape the clouds lay next to the docks, bowsprits thrusting. Steam cranes and donkey engines hissed and puffed, unloading the ships' holds while sailors watched from the rails.

There were steamships too, dark and squat with massive iron hull plates lumpy with rivets and streaked with bright rust like freshly dried blood. They smelled of hot oil and coal, like the train that had brought them here. The grassy scent of coir rope and the ripe smell of fish from a line of trawlers mixed with a sharp aroma from a big, black whaler and wafted on the ocean breeze. A steam tug set out, leaving whirlpools of boiling water astern as she surged into the harbour, her tall funnel billowing black smoke.

It was a doorway into another world and Bert stood at it completely transfixed.

On one train journey, while his father was in another part of the carriage, Bert slid the wood framed window up and put his head out into the rushing wind. When his father returned and ordered

him to pull it in, with a grim warning about tunnels and decapita-
tion, he instantly obeyed. But nothing could wipe the smile from
his face. He had sensed something profound beyond the raging air
tearing past his head. He had glimpsed for the first time the blurred
face of the God of Speed.

The farm was thriving and William was able to install a large water
wheel to generate electricity to light the house and power various bits of domestic and farming equipment. Water for the wheel
was carried in an iron pipe from a small stone weir William had
constructed across their stream. Installation of the system was a
consuming fascination for Bert, as were the machines the new
electric power drove. The Munros had an electric washing machine,
the first for many years in the district and an object of admiration
and even jealousy. William finally relented and bought a car, though
for the rest of his life he continued to abhor tractors. The car, a
black Model T Ford, was kept in a special shed he built for it,
and it only came out on Sundays for church – and then only if it
was fine.

Bert left school when he was fourteen to take his proper place
alongside his father on the farm. Life was now fixed in place and
the days merged with one another, some fine, some wet, all pretty
much the same. His feelings of futility and boredom grew keener,
but there was nothing for it but to pocket the shilling his father paid
him every week and carry on.

Occasionally something happened to remind him that the world
he still dreamed of was out there and waiting, but this only added
to his gloom. Once, while fixing a fence on a corner of the property,
a distant drone drew his attention to the western sky. It was late in
the afternoon with the sun already low and shining in his eyes, but
he picked up a small dot heading his way. It had to be an aircraft!
He dropped the wire strainer and shielded his eyes. The dot drew
nearer until he could make out two wings and a skeletal fuselage
with a man sitting in it. The engine grew louder and then the thing
was sweeping overhead with a roar, waggling its wings awkwardly

in response to his wild waving. He watched it disappear over the
low hills, the beat of its engine fading into the afternoon's silence,
then picked up the wire strainer and turned back to his work. The
world was carrying on without him.

Nothing of any significance happened for two years, except that
Bert grew taller, finally ending up an inch shy of six feet, which
annoyed him. Then he began to build a glider.

He had noticed a stand of large bamboo growing on the roadside
near the front gate to the McLean's property a mile or so down
the road. One Sunday afternoon he set off with a saw and after a
few trips had enough poles for his purposes. That evening he spent
several hours in the big shed happily cutting up old kerosene tins
to make fastenings and fittings from which to run fencing wire that
would hold his project together. He made no drawings but had
already determined in his head exactly how the aircraft would look.
His father tried to dissuade him but without any real conviction,
having decided that an early failure might be good for the boy.
When Bert returned to his task the next evening he was left alone.

After a month he had made considerable progress. The craft now
sported a skeletal frame, much like the one he had observed on
the aircraft that had flown over him, suspended beneath a single
main wing. Three bamboo poles, triangulated with shorter lengths,
formed the fuselage, joining under the tail which was shaped like
the feathers on a dart. The sixteen-foot wing was made up of two
thick bamboo spars, one of which formed the leading edge, with
split bamboo ribs every two feet. These were fastened to a trailing
edge planed from a single piece of one-inch by three-inch beech
laid on its edge. Bert had spent nearly a week of evenings carefully
cutting this out of a well-seasoned fallen trunk with the same
handsaw he had used to cut the bamboo. Each part of his craft was
fixed with a combination of kerosene-tin fastenings and lashings of
heavy, waxed string his father kept for general purposes.

Bert had determined the cross-section shape of his wing after
reading an article in the *Otago Daily Times* that gave a reasonably
detailed description of the general principles of modern aero-

dynamics – although the wing's final form owed as much to the willingness of bamboo to bend as it did to theory. Similarly, the shapes of the rudder, rear elevator and ailerons, which he intended to hinge straight off the trailing edge of the wing, were determined by the available materials and conformed only approximately to the plan in his head. He had, however, a very good idea of how he would control the craft, employing an arrangement of wires running to a single control stick.

In spite of the somewhat arbitrary nature of its design the machine had begun to manifest an almost threatening presence in the gloom of the shed. Bert approached William to ask if he could use a bolt of old canvas, kept mainly to fix horse tack, to cover his machine. William walked out to the shed with his son and was finally forced to acknowledge that far from showing signs of defeat Bert was in fact forging ahead. He thought for a moment and then delivered a prohibition on further work, demanding instead that the monster be dismantled immediately.

It was the most devastating moment in Bert's life.

The young man pleaded in vain with his father to let him finish the glider, if only to see if it would fly unmanned, but William was adamant. Bert then asked his father to let him fly it down a sloping cable, strung from the top of one tree to the base of another. William quite reasonably pointed out that such an activity would prove nothing beyond the willingness of an object to slide down a slope and smash itself against a solid object – hardly worth the price of a bolt of good canvas.

Bert knew then that his cause was lost. Many things had survived the long journey from distant Glencalvie, but of all of them a father's right to expect absolute obedience from his family was paramount. It was the way the world was.

Bert set about taking his creation apart with the same care he had used putting it together. The lashings were carefully untied and unravelled and the string wound back onto the ball. The fencing wire was looped back into a coil of 'shorts' for fencing repair work. The bamboo poles were lugged back up the road and returned to

McLean the farmer, who had not noticed their absence and was nonplussed by their return. The carefully cut and shaped kerosene-tin fastenings were placed in a wooden box of odds and ends to be used for some future purpose. Nothing was wasted.

There was never time for self-pity on the Munro farm and so Bert swallowed his biting disappointment and got on with life. It wasn't all work and solitary dreaming – Lilly was determined her children should grow up with all the social advantages and at least once a week she instigated musical evenings when she would play the piano. Her three older daughters were expected to contribute, sometimes with a song, on occasion with a recitation. Such performances might be solo but Lilly also expected the girls to shine when singing in part, and their excellent harmonies often entranced Bert, something he found surprising, as he had never considered himself musical. To his relief he was generally allowed to stand with his father in passive support, neither having much of a singing voice.

All this changed when a player piano arrived, along with several dozen music rolls. Lilly had lobbied for the piano with quiet persist-ence for several years. Now that she was free of the keyboard, with the piano automatically playing tunes selected from the perforated paper rolls, she could teach her children to dance. Bert discovered that he liked it, even if it was with his mother and then later with his sisters, and he became accomplished at the waltz, foxtrot, quickstep and polka. The highlight of these musical soirees, as Lilly called them, came at the end of the evening when the children cleared the floor and William danced with his wife. The sight of his parents gliding effortlessly together, while the piano played away by itself, was pure enchantment. They never spoke of it but Bert knew his sisters felt the same.

Shortly after the arrival of the magical piano Bert saw yet another wonderful new invention. It was a strange little contraption called a motorcycle. He had heard of such a thing and had marvelled at the idea of a bicycle that did not need pedalling, but the sight of one far exceeded his most vivid imaginings. It was really just a bicycle with a noisy little engine, but it intrigued him in a way that even the aeroplane had not. He watched it thread its way through the traffic cluttering the wide main street of Invercargill, most of which was still horse-drawn, trailing a thin stream of oily smoke.

In spite of it being high summer the rider was wearing heavy boots, oilskins, gauntlets, a tight-fitting leather hat and goggles. Bert felt an uncharacteristic moment of resentment. With that machine and that get-up he could ride to the ends of the earth! Why should one man be so free while another was shackled to a herd of cows? After that, the gentle pop, pop, pop of the motorbike's motor kept intruding on his thoughts.

Motorcycles became popular very rapidly in Southland, partly because bicycles had been almost universally adopted since the 1880s. There were any number of local manufacturers of the modern safety bicycle, with the new low frame and chain drive, and there were few people in the area who had not mastered the art of riding them.

Automobiles remained the province of the very well heeled, but there was a new and growing middle class that aspired to personal transportation. The motorcycle, and particularly the sidecar outfit, was the perfect solution. Machines were imported from England and America and by 1914 there were dozens of different brands puttering about, all of which young Bert knew by sight and, more often than not, by sound.

He took every opportunity to go to town with his father. If William suspected his son was feeding further fantasies of flight and freedom he did not let on. Of course, the new mechanical contrivances were no longer the only attractions in the town. For some time Bert had been aware of a growing fascination with girls. In fact *attraction* hardly seemed the word for the feverish, compulsive need he felt for their company as he worked alone on the farm, conscious more than ever of a world oblivious to his presence in it.

Later that year, on 4 August, when the world descended into the maelstrom of war, fifteen-year-old Bert was little affected. His parents received visits from neighbours whose sons had signed up proudly. Some were scarcely older than Bert, and he knew there were boys his own age who were volunteering and lying about their age, no questions asked.

His father made it clear, however, that as far as he was concerned his son's duty lay at home. Now, more than ever, he intoned, the Empire will need food. As the only grown son on the property there was little danger any draft board would seek out Bert, even when he came of age. The same neighbours who had so willingly sent their own sons to the trenches understood and accepted the need to keep farm production up and that many able-bodied young men had no choice but to stay. There would be no white feathers for them.

The Munro family went to town the day Invercargill's main street was festooned with bunting and men in tall, black hats made speeches, before a brass band struck up 'Now is the Hour' and over 300 young men marched off to the special train waiting for them at the city's grand wooden station. Bert waved and cheered with everybody else and then went home to carry on with the endless cycle of work, resigned to the fact that war was just another adventure he would probably never experience.

CHAPTER FIVE
SHOOTING

The war had been going for a year when Eon McLean acquired a motorcycle. It was an English Douglas, which he called a Duggie, and its two cylinders ran fore and aft. It was also a proper motorcycle, rather than a bicycle with an engine, with a full 2.5 horsepower to motivate it. McLean was proud of his investment for the economies it offered over his big Darracq car, which he had laid up for 'the duration'. Douglas, he said, was a good, solid Scottish company, the founders being members of the Douglas-Hamilton clan. Like most of the farmers around the district he was proud of his Highland origins; in spite of the general sabre-rattling jingoism on behalf of Mother England, he was not overly inclined to support British products if he could avoid it.

Bert was captivated. His enthusiasm for the machine prompted many questions beyond his neighbour's competence to answer. William rescued McLean by inviting him in for a cup of tea, instructing his son to find something useful to do. Naturally, Bert began inspecting every detail of the motorcycle, imagining himself astride it, bouncing along gently on the rich chestnut leather saddle. It was beautifully built with a proud acetylene lamp mounted above the nickel-coated spring controlling the girder front suspension.

Bert found this particularly interesting and it took him only a few minutes to figure out how it worked. He also admired the large exposed flywheel and the leather belt driving a big pulley on the rear wheel.

He was still on his knees in the dust peering at the engine, his hands running over the still warm alloy as if to divine what wonders might lie inside, when the two older men emerged. McLean brushed William's apologies aside and assured Bert that he was welcome to come by some time and try it out. William was equally quick to decline on his son's behalf but McLean repeated the invitation before he left, assuring William that his son would be most welcome. And then with a gentle kick of the starter he was off, the Douglas spitting a little rooster tail of gravel as he accelerated down the drive.

A chance to take up the invitation came sooner than Bert had dared hope. Visitors were coming to stay, a rare occurrence in the Munro household. Lilly had not seen her cousins since she had visited them in Dunedin some years before and they had never been to the farm. William had arranged to meet them at the turnoff from the main road to escort them the fourteen kilometres along a narrow metal road to the Munro farm. But when the day came the Ford T refused to start.

William, who had dressed carefully for the occasion, was reduced to sweat-soaked mortification after swinging vainly on the T's crank handle for twenty minutes. When Bert suggested a solution he was, for once, inclined to listen. The boy offered to ride a horse over to the McLean's place and take up the offer of a ride on the motorcycle. There was still time and after thinking about it for a moment William agreed. Bert had a halter on Tommy and was away over the paddocks at a good gallop before his father had time to change his mind.

When McLean heard about the emergency he immediately wheeled the Douglas out and showed Bert the brake, throttle, choke, fuel cock and starting technique. Douglases were easy to start and Bert soon had the hang of it. After a couple of loops of the circular driveway he was off down the road on the most exciting adventure life had yet granted him.

The day was warm and he could hear the drone of cicadas and smell the fresh scent of the roadside bracken as he gradually opened the throttle wider and wider. Soon he was flying along, the gentle blat of the Douglas's engine bouncing back at him whenever the road went through a cutting. He remembered McLean's warning not to speed through the several fords as the shock of the cold water could split the hot engine, and he eased the machine through the first with hardly a splash. Then it was back up to full speed, leaning the machine into the steeply banked corners and laughing out loud for the pure joy of it.

His exhilaration lasted only a couple more kilometres, however, before the machine suddenly chugged to a halt. He carefully rolled it onto its stand and stepped back to glare at it, hoping for inspiration. None came. A careful examination of the wires and leads revealed no obvious fault and the tank was still brimming with petrol. He climbed back on and began kicking it over. After about ten minutes the machine suddenly burst back into life and he was off again, though the engine now sounded a little less sure than it had.

When it stopped again he again kicked it over until he was exhausted. But a few minutes rest followed by a gentle prod on the starter saw it burst back into life. The next time it stopped he simply waited ten minutes when once again it ran faultlessly. In this manner he made the rendezvous in time. After giving precise instructions to his uncle and aunt he led the way home until the machine once again took a rest. He waved them on and waited happily for the bike to get its breath back, which it duly did. When he eventually made it back to McLean's he found the farmer looking concerned. 'I forgot to tell you about the bloody oil pump,' he exclaimed. 'You have to give it a pump every now and then or it will bind up!'

Bert explained that he'd given the machine plenty of rest each time it stopped and as it was still running sweetly they both agreed it was unlikely any harm had been done. Riding Tommy home Bert reflected upon how nothing would do now except that he have his own bike. How to achieve that was another matter. One shilling a week's income was obviously insufficient. In the two years he had been working he had saved nearly every penny but still had only a few pounds to show for it. Unless something changed, owning a motorcycle would remain a daydream.

He leaned forward and laid his head on the horse's neck, speaking softly into its ear, 'Two and a half horsepower Tommy,' he murmured. 'That little egg of a thing contains two and a half of you!' He sat up and slapped the horse's rump. Tommy shambled into a gallop and then seemed to catch the boy's spirit, lengthening his strides until he was pounding across the fields, throwing up clods of wet earth.

His father would complain when he saw those deep divots, especially since they had obviously been made on the way home, after the emergency was over. Bert would handle it with his usual mumbled apology and all would soon be forgotten. Unlike the memory of a fine morning spent riding a Duggie. That would remain in sharp focus for the rest of his life.

Confident hopes that the war would be over by Christmas were now forgotten. As 1915 dragged on the casualty lists published daily in the newspaper began to grow longer. In March the name Gallipoli had appeared and it was soon evident that this previously unheard-of peninsula on the Turkish coast was becoming a mass grave for the Anzac forces sent to invade by sea. By the time the operation's failure had been acknowledged by the British commanders and the last troops withdrawn in early January the next year, one in four of the 7500 New Zealand troops taking part had been killed. Worse would follow when the surviving troops arrived at the Western Front. Every week, it seemed, the newspaper would publish a name well known to the Munro family. And once a week, Lilly would sit at her desk and write a letter of condolence to a relative, a neighbour or a friend.

Bert, stuck on the farm and unlikely to go anywhere, felt the need to contribute. The same newspapers that carried the casualty lists and continued to trumpet the need for further sacrifice also regularly warned of the danger of invasion. How or why the Germans should wish to attempt this was not explained, but the need to be eternally vigilant was constantly stressed and Bert was more than willing to take heed. His response, finally, was to build a cannon.

Quite how his cannon was to be of any material use in the event the dreaded Hun should suddenly spill onto the beaches of Southland was not a matter that overly concerned Bert. It was likely that his decision to build it in the first place had more to do with his discovery of some discarded heavy iron water pipe than any sincere military ambitions. William allowed Bert to devote his evenings to the production of the cannon and did not complain when he commandeered a significant length of number-eight fencing wire for his project.

Bert was quite familiar with the power of blasting powder, his chosen propellant, as he and his father regularly used it to blow apart the old tree stumps that dotted the farm, and he knew the pipe might not be strong enough to withstand a good explosion. He therefore wrapped it in wire, using a Spanish windlass to ensure the wire was tight, employing progressive wrappings to increase the number of windings as he worked his way down the barrel, ending with about a dozen windings around what would eventually be the breach.

Bert had threaded the inside end of the pipe to take a matching threaded cap, which, when screwed home, sealed the bottom of the barrel. He achieved this with the help of McLean, who owned a comprehensively equipped workshop. Using a hand drill – several evenings' work – Bert made a hole just above the plug, into which he could insert a fuse. The weapon was mounted on a pair of old buggy wheels by lashing it to the axle with yet more wire. A wooden tail for the cannon to rest on was secured – with a set of heavy U-bolts retrieved from a derelict wagon axle – in such a way that by tightening and loosening the nuts the barrel could be elevated or depressed. The gun achieved a certain menace that finally began to make William nervous.

Bert's next task was to produce a suitable projectile to feed down the fifty-millimetre bore and he did this by hacksawing the end of an old wagon axle and filing it down over many nights until it finally slid up and down inside the pipe with a satisfyingly slick metallic sound. He then patiently filed a point on one end and the gun was ready to fire.

At first William refused to give Bert any of his precious blasting powder. He relented only after imposing a peculiar and somewhat macabre condition – the cannon could be fired once and once only, and it was to be used to dispose of an old sheep-dog, saving William the expense of a bullet.

So keen was Bert to test-fire his gun that he agreed without a second thought, hoisting the weapon into a vertical position, with the assistance of a block flung over a handy tree branch, in order to pour his allowance of blasting powder down the spout. He lowered the gun to the ground as William fetched the unsuspecting animal. After being tied to a stake the old kelpie obliged by lying down and dozing off while Bert pushed the projectile home with a long manuka stick. He then depressed the barrel until he had the dog lined up and made sure everything was properly secure before striking a match. He had allowed plenty of time to retreat behind a nearby tree with his father, who had insisted they remain out of sight.

The loud explosion set up a rolling echo that must have been audible for several kilometres and the effect, when they looked, was mercifully complete. All that remained of the dog was a bloody mess. The cannon had done its job.

Bert was ordered to bury the dog and so he dug his projectile out of the ground before shovelling the remains of the animal into the hole and filling it over. The day would come, he thought, when he would fire his cannon into the air. The effect of this would be no more spectacular than firing it into the ground but he strongly suspected it would be a great deal more satisfying. For the moment, however, his gun was effectively spiked. As luck would have it, though, he discovered a new diversion from the boredom of farming that also involved shooting animals – although this time he was doing it for profit.

Rabbits had been introduced by English settlers to New Zealand in the middle of the nineteenth century to provide sport and to remind the new immigrants of home. By the 1880s they had become a plague and many farmers, particularly sheep farmers on the vast high-country stations, were forced to walk off their land as their sheep starved for want of grass. Hillsides seemed to move as the rabbits fed – only a dozen could consume as much as one sheep ate. The same hillsides, once stripped of all vegetation by the voracious pests, really did move in heavy rains. The erosion was so bad in parts that the landscape began to resemble a lunar desert. At that point farmers introduced ferrets, weasels and stoats to eat the rabbits, but these proved to be at least as partial to native birdlife and made little difference to the rabbit population. Cats were also released into the high country in the hope they would prey on the young rabbits, but they too proved ineffective and just as disastrous to the wildlife.

Bert had been shooting rabbits since he was nine, usually at twilight when the animals emerged to graze. He was allowed the use of the .22-calibre rifle and all the ammunition he could get through. It was boring, since the rabbits simply sat about waiting to be shot, but he had a good eye and seldom wasted a bullet. And his lonely rambles at least got him out of the house.

One evening while he was drawing a bead on a foraging rabbit he heard a shot from a shallow gully half a kilometre away. His target scampered off unharmed. A little irritated and considerably curious Bert trotted to the location of the shot and found a young man down on one knee skinning a rabbit, his rifle slung across his shoulder. He looked up surprised when Bert challenged him, but calmly completed his task and stood up, the rabbit carcass gleaming wet and pink at his feet. He carefully folded the bloody pelt and placed it in a bag hanging from his belt and only then looked directly at Bert. 'You'd be Bert Munro,' he said.

Bert demanded to know what the stranger was doing on his father's land. The fellow was about the same age as Bert and a little stockier. Like Bert he was dressed in working clothes and he had a pleasant, open look to him. He told Bert politely that his name was Jack Murdoch and that his father owned the property on the other side of McLean's place. He apologised for being on the Munro property without permission but said he didn't think anyone would mind him shooting a few bunnies. Murdoch shrugged his rifle into a comfortable position and held out his hand.

'I'd like to stay and chew the fat,' he said, 'but I have a bit of a tramp home.'

Bert shook his hand. 'You're the first bloke I ever saw out here apart from my father. I won't say anything but he probably wouldn't appreciate you being here.'

Murdoch paused and seemed to come to a decision. 'There's a rooster who buys my pelts and pays me good money,' he said. 'I could show you how to prepare them if you want. We could do a bit of shooting together and you could make a bit of extra money. Interested?'

Jack Murdoch was as good as his word. He showed Bert how to make simple frames to stretch the pelts and how to treat them with rock salt. He took all of Bert's finished skins to his buyer, presenting Bert with the receipts and paying him exactly what he was owed. Bert enjoyed the company and they met very nearly every day just before dusk. They did very well.

William seemed happy with his son's sudden enthusiasm for shooting but insisted Bert pay for his ammunition now that it was a financial proposition. At the end of the first month Bert had made almost a pound, a stunning success. Hunting with Jack quickly became a big part of his life and it seemed the time went by faster. He still greeted each dark morning with a groan but getting the cows in seemed a little less onerous with the prospect of hunting with Jack to look forward to.

The passing seasons brought little good news from the war and more and more young men left the district to fight, and more and more families grieved for the ones who didn't come back. In spite of the dire reports from the front, Bert and Jack talked about walking off their fathers' farms and joining up when they turned eighteen. Bert was some nine months older than Jack and he agreed to wait until the other was of age so they could walk off together. The truth was that Bert was more nervous of defying his father than he was of being blown up on the Western Front. The prospect of having a companion to share the experience with was comforting. But it was not to be.

On 10 November 1918, with just a few weeks to go before Jack's eighteenth birthday, the paper reported that Germany had signed an armistice and the war was over. The news came as something of an anticlimax. Bert and Jack had spent most of their teenage years with the war raging somewhere over their horizon, always expecting that one day it would reach out for them. Now, as mysteriously as it had started, it had finished. There were celebrations but they were muted, for the losses were still massive and raw while the victory seemed vague and inconclusive.

Bert and Jack carried on shooting together for a couple of months when something else dramatic and unexpected happened. When William made the announcement, without fanfare during dinner, Bert could not believe what he had heard. He asked his father to repeat it, which William obligingly did. He spoke slowly and firmly so that there could be no confusion: 'I have sold the farm.'

CHAPTER SIX
ESCAPE

William did not bother to inform his family of the reasons for his actions and they did not think to question him. He had made a decision and, as always, that was the end of the matter. It may have been that William had held on to the farm longer than might have suited him in order to prevent his oldest son becoming embroiled in the war. If so, he didn't say, only telling Bert that he was free to consider his own future, at least for the time being.

This was almost more than his son could comprehend – free to leave, to travel, to see the world and shape his own destiny! He had managed to save nearly £10 from his meagre wages and had salted away another eight from the rabbit business. It was a good start. That evening he told Jack the news. His friend vowed to accompany Bert on his travels, at least as far as Christchurch. More than 500 kilometres to the north and the largest city in the South Island, Christchurch was the hub of the rich Canterbury Plains and a romantic destination for two lads whose only previous city experiences were day-trips to Invercargill.

When the day came to leave, Bert said his goodbyes in a daze, hardly hearing his mother's warnings about the dangers of consorting with the baser types he was bound to encounter. His father said little as he drove his son and Jack, rescued en route from a weeping mother and glowering father, to Invercargill. William shook both boys by the hand with a solemn finality and left them at the train station without a backward glance. He had issued a stern list of prohibitions the previous evening in the privacy of the barn, which included bans on drinking, smoking, gambling and a vice he called womanising. Bert had no argument with the first three, indeed he held quite strong views on the subjects. Drinking was the occupation of wasters and gambling was for idiots, while those who smoked had to be a mixture of both. Womanising, on the other hand, was not something he was prepared to condemn before he'd had a chance to study the matter in more detail. But it was politic to agree with everything his father said and he was careful to keep his thoughts private.

Their train took them first to Dunedin where they were to change to the powerful express. Their view of the city was fleeting and limited to what they could see as they approached the station, but it was clearly a more substantial place than sleepy Invercargill. For a moment they were tempted to break their journey and have a look around, but the lure of even greater marvels to the north persuaded them to stick to their plan: that and the uncertainty that they could cash in their tickets.

The Dunedin railway station itself left both completely speechless. A delicately ornate, gleaming white, pressed-tin ceiling floated above rich mosaic floors. High stained-glass windows depicting onrushing trains streamed white light into the interior though their subjects' headlights, a magical effect that held both young men spellbound. If Bert could travel just a few hours and find something this wonderful, what wonders might the rest of the world hold? As the express accelerated into the sunlight he made a vow to find out.

Christchurch was a lot of fun, no doubt about it. Within half an hour of arriving Bert and Jack had located a comfortable and clean little boarding house next to Cathedral Square in the middle of the city. They paid fifteen shillings a week each for a shared room with two comfortable beds plus a very acceptable breakfast and dinner. They walked all over the city, exploring everything open to the public, visiting some places such as the museum nearly every day for three weeks. On hot days they caught the trolley bus to Brighton and swam in the surf and had sandwiches for lunch. Every night they found a dance where Bert could demonstrate his prowess on the polished floor – to Jack's initial surprise and enduring envy – with a constant stream of young ladies. They discussed the 'womanising' situation at length but there seemed no answer to the seemingly inevitable presence of a large brother or equally daunting dowager riding shotgun for each prospective partner. Even dancing close, as Bert's mother had taught him to do, had on a number of embarrassing occasions resulted in unseemly interventions by those who felt it their duty to break things up.

The young men's money lasted the better part of the summer before both were finally forced to look for work. They were sitting on the grassy bank of the river Avon, the clear ribbon of water that ran through the city, when Jack announced his intention to catch the train to Banks Peninsula where there were apparently many dairy and sheep farms. He was confident he and Bert would find work, experienced as they were.

Bert lay back with a sigh and closed his eyes.

'Jack,' he said, 'if I never saw another farm in my life it would be too soon. It's taken me eighteen years to escape one and I'm blowed if I want to just give up and go back to another. I've had a gutsful of cows and that's a fact.'

Jack assured Bert that farming would be just a temporary thing until they were back in funds and could move on. Maybe Australia! But Bert remained uncharacteristically silent, clearly unhappy at the prospect of cows once more ruling his life.

'Bugger it, Jack. If we have to we have to but I'd rather pull my own head off and drop rocks down my neck!'

That night as the two boys were having dinner for the last time at their boarding house a new man joined them. He was a nuggety fellow with a full beard and large, heavily calloused hands. He drank freely from a little hip-flask that he kept in his waistcoat and became increasingly loquacious throughout dinner, regaling them with tales of his time working on the Otira Tunnel.

Everybody knew about the tunnel, of course, at 8.5 kilometres it was the longest in the Empire and now more than twelve years in the making. Driven through wet shale and rotten rock in the mighty Southern Alps, it was intended to provide a rail link between Christchurch and Greymouth on the West Coast. Valuable West Coast coal could then be railed to the port of Lyttelton near Christchurch to feed local industry and for shipping around the country and abroad.

The original construction company had gone broke, victims of a long-standing campaign by union radicals to cripple the project, forcing the government to step in. After the public works department had taken over work had proceeded, albeit at a desultory pace for the duration of the war, with both ends of the tunnel finally meeting just a few months before the armistice. Of course the bore still had to be turned into a proper railway tunnel and work continued on enlarging the headings to full tunnel profile with the concrete lining being poured in sections as the work was completed. There were still years to go before the first electric train would run through it.

Workers lived in a village on a flat bit of ground above the Otira River's flood level. The collection of single and married men's quarters was called the Island and, according to the bearded man, it was a grand place with drinking clubs and two-up gambling schools. It was also, he added, a shining example of workers' solidarity. In all the time he had been there, and that was many years now, there had never been a complaint to the solitary policeman of a theft. It was that sort of place.

He asked what his two young companions did for a crust. Jack told him that they were off in the morning to find work on a farm. The man scoffed. Farming was all right for those who owned the farm, he opined, but the devil of a job for those who did not.

Working all hours, paid a pittance and fed tough old mutton! If you were going to be stuck in the middle of nowhere, he said, you might as well make some money. Two strong blokes like them could be making two-and-a-half quid a week in the tunnel.

Bert leaned forward eagerly and questioned the man at length. Two pounds, ten shillings a week was almost as much as he had earned in a year at home. That night he could not sleep.

Jack had made it clear that he was not interested in being a troglodyte for a living and if Bert wanted to he was on his own. In the morning they argued about it over breakfast until Bert at last proposed that they toss a coin. 'Heads for the tunnel, tails for the cows,' he said laughing. Jack shook his head. He wasn't going underground on the toss of a coin or anything else. Bert flipped a penny anyway. It was heads.

An hour later they were at the station. Jack was going east, Bert west. The departure of the train for Little River was announced and Jack hefted his bag. Bert's train would be another hour. They shook hands solemnly and Jack shook his head sadly.

'I wish you'd change your mind,' he said. 'We could still do a bit of shooting.'

Bert hooted. 'If I went back to a farm I'd probably shoot myself!' He clapped his friend on the shoulder. 'I'll say hello to any bunnies I come across down there and tell them to keep an eye out for you.'

The whistle sounded and Jack swung up the steps as the train began to move. He turned back to wave and then he was gone. It was the last time Bert would ever see him.

CHAPTER SEVEN
LOVE

Working on the tunnel turned out to be a great adventure and the pay, miraculously, was exactly what Bert had been told it would be. It was always cold and usually wet and the Stygian darkness inside the mountain range was relieved only by the dull glow of feeble electric lights strung from the dripping ceiling. But it wasn't cow farming and for that Bert was willing to overlook a great deal of discomfort. He also enjoyed living on the Island, even if the huge mountains all around shut out most of the sunlight.

The deep aqua of the Otira River tumbling down its rocky channel, the grey shadowed scree slopes eternally slipping toward the valley floor and the dark, jagged, snow-spattered ridges thrusting into the clouds could form a desolate picture, but he was seldom unhappy. Even when a bitter southerly blew up the valley, freezing everything in its path, he remained cheerful. It was true that many of the men liked to drink and gamble, but they also looked out for one another and there was seldom any real disharmony. The union was as strong as ever but Bert's refusal to join was treated more as a joke than anything else. His vague but forthrightly conservative political views, formed after his father's, were to most of his fellow workers an amusing curiosity and tolerated with good humour.

The single men liked nothing better than to catch the train on Saturday evenings and head down to Greymouth for a night on the booze and in search of some serious womanising. Bert was always pleased to join them, and although they teased him and sometimes called him the Laird, he was accepted and made welcome. The West Coast was a rugged place, populated by an eclectic mix of miners, farmers, foresters, fishermen and all manner of coves more difficult to categorise but who shared a certain preference for anonymity.

The gold had mostly given out by then but there were still hardy souls to be found wrangling with a publican on a Saturday night over the value of a careful measure of dust gleaned in the pan from a mountain river. A deal would be struck and the panhandler would be set for the night.

And there were women to make just such an evening complete. The atmosphere in the wild little pubs that served illegally distilled whisky late into the night, long after the law deemed they should have thrown their last punters out, was quite different to Christchurch. It was as if the rain that always seemed to fall on the West Coast had caused a certain sagging in the ladies' moral stays. On Saturday nights, at any rate, things seemed looser.

Bert's tall frame and big grin appealed to quite a few of the women he encountered, even though he remained as careful with his money as ever. Growing up in a house full of sisters under the influence of a mother who insisted scrupulously on the observance of gentlemanly courtesies, had also given him a certain sensitivity that many found refreshing, especially compared with the coarse behaviour they usually encountered. It was not long before Bert was finally able to make an educated judgement on the merits or otherwise of womanising, which he found, in fact, to be much to his liking.

Altogether the life suited him. His new cobbers ribbed each other constantly, forever pricking each other's little vanities and conceits. It would have been churlish to take offence and few ever did. Bert discovered that he possessed a well-developed sense of his own inadequacies and that sharing such thoughts promoted much laughter and little in the way of ridicule. Self-deprecating humour, he found, had the effect of removing barriers and building friendships. He would probably have been happy to carry on like this for years but fate had other plans. After only a year and a half his freedom, which had been granted so precipitously, was taken away in like manner.

During his time on the tunnel project Bert had received a letter every week from his mother telling him the news, of which there seemed little of real significance, and he had tried to write back at least once a month. It seemed the family had been happily living with his grandparents and that William had resumed farm work for his own father. It seems not to have occurred to Bert to wonder why his father had taken what, on the face of it, looked like a backward step, though he did wonder what might come next.

When he was called to the engineer's site office and handed an urgent telegram from his father he was not surprised to read that William had bought another farm and that his assistance was required immediately. Nor did he consider for a moment that he could refuse to go. Instead he asked for and signed a resignation form, arranged for his outstanding pay to be forwarded, packed, made his farewells and departed. He had £150 in the bank and he was leaving a job that paid £125 a year to return home to work for a miserable shilling a week.

Being home was not all bad news. It was wonderful to see his family again, although they would not move to the new property for some time, and it was surprisingly easy to fit back into the old routines. Elston Lea, as the farm was called, was on the outskirts of Invercargill on Tramway Road. The road had been named after a rail line used to transport logs from the tall forest but its tracks were long buried under the shingle road that followed its course. The forest had also disappeared years before, the land being productive pasture for half a century.

Bert's first task was to help his father with the construction of a new homestead, a building William clearly intended to be something very special. The house when it was finished was a fine bungalow: large, graceful, with airy rooms and generous verandahs – altogether a perfect family home.

Building the house gave Bert considerable pleasure as he had always enjoyed working with timber and liked demonstrating to his father the skills he had learned erecting staging and scaffolding in the Otira Tunnel. Now, with the family together under their new roof and farming proceeding as usual, Bert finally had time to contemplate his future.

While there were no immediate prospects of escape, he did not feel the same desperate sense of entrapment he had on the old property. The trolley to town stopped within a kilometre or so of their gate, and he had money in the bank, enough at least to give him a sense of independence. His new social confidence had also subtly changed his relationship with William. He could cheerfully obey him when building the house and working on the farm, but he no longer regarded his spare time as anything other than his own. Hungry for company and as eager as ever to meet girls, he took the trolley to town most nights to go dancing.

There was a bacchanalian element to dances in those days. A generation of men still in their twenties who had survived the bloody harvest of the trenches sought little more than to forget the experience for a while and make up for lost time. Those who had endured the enforced and joyless austerity of 'the duration' at home were just as keen to see the revival of simple pleasures.

Many became drunk and some became legless, but it was mainly good humoured. Violent, troubled drunks were thrown out and were not welcome back. The dancing never stopped and it was often of a high standard. Traditional dances like the waltz remained popular, especially near the end of the evening when the lights might be turned down and the entwined couples could generate a little extra heat. But it was the new dances – the Blues, the Charleston and the Black Bottom – that raised spirits the highest. People fell in love, in lust and into every other degree of attachment as local halls all over the country heaved and shuddered to the stamping of feet.

Bert regularly missed the last trolley home and cheerfully walked through the night, humming a flat tune under his breath, his coat turned up against the cold. As his nocturnal activities seemed to make no difference to his reliability on the farm William seldom challenged him.

If women were Bert's primary interest he also made many new friends among the young men thronging the dances. Some of whom owned motorbikes. At the time, motorbikes were enjoying record sales in New Zealand and there was always a good collection gathered outside a hall. Local importers brought in a variety of models from the many English and American manufacturers, and Bert slowly gained a passing familiarity with most of their products.

Marques such as ABS, Ariel, AJS, Arno, Bat, Blackburn, Bradbury, BSA, Calthorpe, Chater Lea, Clyno, Connaught, Cotton, Coventry Eagle, Douglas, Big X, Excelsior, FN, Harley Davidson, Henderson, Hogart, Humber, Indian, James, Matchless, New Imperial, Norton, NUT, OEC, Panther, Premier, Reading, Royal Ruby, Royal Enfield, Rover, Rex Acme, Rudge, Scott, Singer, Standard, Sunbeam, Torpedo, Triumph, Velocette and Zenith were all to be found chattering about the streets of Invercargill, many with sidecars attached.

Ever since his experience with the Douglas, Bert had dreamed of having another ride and his opportunity came at last when one of his new friends offered him a spin on his almost brand-new silver Norton. He and another mate were going to a dance at a small country hall in Fortrose, about seventy kilometres out of town. If Bert was keen he could ride the Norton on the way up while the owner pillioned on his mate's Matchless. They would swap for the return journey, which would be in the dark and therefore somewhat more hazardous.

It was a generous offer and Bert was quick to accept. The ride up to Fortrose, a small country backwater, was a further revelation. The Matchless took off like a startled hare and Bert had to keep the Norton's throttle wide open most of the time to keep up. They were travelling faster than he would have thought possible and at every corner he expected the lovely Norton to slide onto its side.

But it tracked through the gravel with its front suspension jiggling up and down while Bert bounced in the saddle like a jockey on a trotter. As he banked the bike through the corners, the exhaust alternatively cackling and roaring, exhilaration flamed through his body. By the time they got to the dance he had made up his mind: he had to have a machine of his own.

There was quite a selection to choose from. Not knowing too much about it Bert relied on his friends for advice. Unfortunately they all disagreed and, in the end, Bert bought his first bike mainly because he liked the colour – a bright, blood red. It was a Clyno, manufactured in England since 1910, with a well-engineered 750cc V-twin, six-horsepower engine mounted in a low and comparatively light frame, and featuring a three-speed gearbox.

Clyno manufactured their own sidecars, which were welded rigidly to the motorcycle frame rather than simply clipped on, and their solid performance in sidecar trials in England had commended them to no less than Winston Churchill. With the outbreak of war Churchill had encouraged collaboration between Clyno and Vickers, manufacturers of, among other things, the famous machine-guns. The result had been a curious creature called a Vickers-Clyno Machine Gun Motorcycle Outfit, the utility of which was never really demonstrated, although the army ordered significant numbers.

Bert's machine was a 1913 model, similar to the machines the company resumed manufacturing after the war, and it cost £50 – including sidecar. By now, though, Bert had set his mind on racing. Since the sidecar was superfluous he simply cut it off and sold it, banking the £10 he got for it.

At home William was deeply disappointed and made no effort to disguise it. He regarded the motorcycle as a frivolous and dangerous indulgence; the kind of thing only a spoilt, rich wastrel would squander his time and money on. He berated Bert for weeks, telling him he had hoped his oldest surviving son would grow up to be more responsible, especially with his money. He refused to even look at the machine and would not hear a word spoken in its defence.

This suited Bert quite well for, in truth, he barely heard his father's complaints. He was happier than he had ever been. The big, elegant Clyno was quite a capable machine when it came to tearing up the metal roads, especially without the sidecar, and he had many memorable dashes around the countryside with his growing band of motorcycling mates. He continued to attend dances every night, except that now he had the Clyno to come and go on. He wasted no time inviting every available woman he met for a ride, making sure the few who actually accepted hung on good and tight by going as fast as he could. He adopted a favourite expression of one of his motorcycling mates: 'There are two speeds in life – flat out and faster!'

Lilly made few complaints about her son's constant absences until one Tuesday night, as he was pushing out the door, she asked if he might spend just one night at home with his parents. Something in her tone caught Bert's attention and he sat back down at the kitchen table. He spent every Tuesday night at home from that evening on.

Bert accepted many invitations to roar about the country with other motorcyclists on expeditions that would be mounted for the flimsiest reasons. One fine summer day he was part of a small group that set out to visit a sick friend. Somehow the invalid was forgotten in the rush to get there and the group zipped by his gate and into the hills, finally rolling to a stop to admire the view from a peak.

On the way home Bert was keeping company with yet another Munro, a distant uncle named Hugh, who was just a few years older than Bert. Hugh's New Imperial had developed a misfire and he was struggling to keep up. Bert fell back to make sure he made it home. From time to time he slowed right down to allow Hugh to catch up and amused himself by practising stunts. As they were clearing the foothills Hugh came around a corner to see his nephew wheeling briskly down a gentle incline with the bike in neutral, standing on the seat with his arms outstretched.

Hugh nursed his ailing machine alongside and yelled at his grinning nephew. 'Who the hell do you think you are? Jesus Christ on a bloody motorcycle?'

Bert grinned, flipped him a smart salute and then fell off, landing heavily on top of his head. Certain that the fall must have broken Bert's neck, Hugh skidded to a stop, switched off, dumped the New Imperial on its side and scrambled back to the figure stretched out on the road. He vaguely heard the Clyno, which had rolled on for a considerable distance, finally crash over. Bert lay there as if fast asleep, his breathing deep and even. A careful examination revealed no blood or obvious injuries, so Hugh pulled him over onto the grass verge and rolled up his coat to make a pillow. The Clyno puttered away happily in the background until it finally coughed and stopped and the afternoon was suddenly, awfully quiet.

There was little Hugh could do except to make himself comfortable and hope another vehicle came along. He retrieved both machines and placed them on their stands, grabbing a picnic blanket out of his saddlebag to cover Bert. Dusk began to fall and it was getting dark before Bert groaned and wearily sat up. He eyes slowly focused on the two machines standing in the gathering gloom. He gave a puzzled sigh and then suddenly noticed the worried Hugh.

'Oh, hello Hugh,' he said. 'It was good of you to wait.' He rubbed his head and then calmly stood up. 'Well come on. We need to get home.'

As well as these impromptu tours, organised motorcycle races took place quite frequently and Bert went to every one he could, soon becoming an accepted figure on the scene. Motorcycle racing had been conducted in Southland since 1911 when races were first held on Invercargill's Oreti and Otiti beaches, part of the same horseshoe sweep of coast that ends near Riverton. Through some peculiarity of local law the beaches were controlled by the city council, as opposed to every other beach in the country that fell under the mandate of the marine department.

This anomaly made it easier to obtain official sanction to race, which was one of the main reasons for the popularity of both beaches with local motorcyclists. Just as importantly, the beaches also offered firm, flat sand with long runs uninterrupted by streams or river mouths. For much of the year both beaches were clear of driftwood and seaweed, with cars and motorcycles racing around courses defined by a simple marker at each end. Various lengths were achieved, from sprints to full hundred milers, simply by varying the number of laps raced.

The beach courses were augmented by grass tracks at local horse-racing ovals and country fairs, with occasional racing taking place at more exotic venues like Rugby Park, the famous sportsfield in the middle of the city. New Zealand had a sound claim to being the home of grass-track racing, with a demonstration performed as early as 1908 by one Bill Hyslop, who barrelled his Triumph around Cornwall Park in Hastings. By 1919 it was popular around the world but never more so than in New Zealand. Crowds as large as 20,000 turned up to watch the thrills and spills, of which there were always plenty, far more than the numbers attracted by the hay-burners.

Racing at the southern country fairs became something of an institution, with an annual two-week pilgrimage to fairs at Winton, Gore and Wyndham, as well as a big two-day event back in Invercargill. Whether racing on horse tracks or at show-grounds the competition was fierce and by the time Bert joined the fray average laps of over seventy miles an hour were common.

At those speeds the bumpy surfaces were lethal and it was uncommon for a race to be completed without at least one rider being tossed off, the greatest danger being that a following rider might spear into him. Competitors roared broadside into the oval turns, stacked one outside the other with their throttles wide open and their rear tyres spitting a wake of stones and torn up grass. If one fell it would inevitably involve all those outside him in a tangle of tumbling wheels, arms and legs.

Serious injuries were rare but they did happen, and to the crowds it always looked likely to occur at any moment. On the only occasion Lilly saw grass-track racing, during the Invercargill Country Fair, she was so horrified she begged her son to give up riding altogether. Bert grinned and promised to always be careful, but they disagreed about all forms of motorcycling from that moment on, Lilly loathing it as much as Bert loved it.

Bert enjoyed the Clyno but he was not besotted with it. It took another bike to give him a bad case of love at first sight. He was passing the Criterion Hotel car park and saw her sitting there. She was red but not an obvious red like the Clyno; a more subtle shade for a more seductive creature. The elegant script on the side of her shapely tank proclaimed her to be an Indian and at her heart was a neat and compact, narrow-angle V-twin.

Bert's eyes wandered all over her, noting the way the soft glint of nickel plate contrasted magically with that lustrous red paint. He patted the rich, tan leather seat, testing the spring and smiling as the saddle bounced back against his palm. His gaze lingered on the multiple leaf-spring suspension, admiring the simple and solid design, before he got down on one knee like a suitor to gaze upon the shape of her cast alloy primary case. Like everything about her it was beautifully executed.

He stood and walked back a few paces, never taking his eyes off her. She was a beauty all right but she was no angel. She'd go, he reckoned. No doubt about it. Within minutes he was a goner and he knew it. He realised she already belonged to someone else and he knew he would not have her secondhand; that would never do. But all was not lost. There would be a twin sister somewhere and by God she would be his!

One of his new friends, Archie Prentice, was the man to see and Bert reluctantly dragged himself away from the beauty in the car park and made his way to Archie's modest showroom. Voluble Archie was as pleased to see him as ever and became even more pleased when he learned the nature of Bert's visit.

Red was it? Ah yes, that would be the brand spanking new, 600cc Indian Scout. Just a few in the country but there were a couple more on the water from the United States. A lovely thing, there is quite a call for them. Anyone wanting one would need to put down a deposit.

Oh very good value – £150 all up. Well you get what you pay for, don't you. Of course, the electric headlight adds £10 to the price over the acetylene unit. No, nothing wrong with acetylene lights. Done the trick up till now, haven't they? Always got us home. One hundred and forty pounds then. And you want the exact same colour. Indian Red!

William would be furious, but he'd get over it. And besides, Bert was twenty-one years old now. Old enough and ugly enough to spend his own money on anything he liked.

Bert's new Indian took only a month to arrive, but it had been a long time in the making. The company was an old one by motor-cycle standards, turning out its first machines in 1902, which were designed to assist in training racing bicyclists by running in front and carving a path through the air. This training method was sufficiently popular to sell three units in that year, and the company quickly became a mainstream manufacturer, selling 143 machines the next year.

The two founders, George Hendee, himself a champion bicycle racer, and Swedish immigrant Oscar Hedstrom chose the name Indian Motocycle for their Springfield, Massachusetts enterprise, leaving the 'r' out of motorcycle to establish a unique trademark.

Their greatest rival, Harley Davidson, appeared in 1903. By then Indian was well on the way to becoming the largest motorcycle manufacturer in the world, with stylish and reliable products boast-ing better than average performance. This was amply demonstrated in the 1911 Isle of Man Tourist Trophy (TT) competition when Oliver Godfrey won it on an Indian followed by Charles B Franklin and Arthur Moorhouse, both also Indian-mounted, the first time one company had managed a 1–2–3 finish.

Performance remained an Indian byword and in 1916 Hedstrom's former assistant Charles Gustafson developed the 1000cc Powerplus, the first engine not designed by Hedstrom (who, with Hendee, had left the company after continuing differences of opinion with its board). The Powerplus was to remain a favourite with sporting motorcyclists for many years, but the zenith of Indian design was reached shortly after the war when the company offered race bikes with overhead valve heads and four valves per cylinder, very advanced specifications at the time.

These machines were supplied without brakes, suspension, lights and fenders – items not required on the board tracks that had sprung up all over the United States. They could manage a staggering 125 miles per hour, and several had been imported into New Zealand where, with riders like Percy Coleman, they proved winners on grass.

The racer was, of course, an expensive and exclusive machine, and by 1920 the company needed a new model to tempt the every-day motorcyclist. The Scout provided an effective answer. The same Charles B Franklin who had run second in the 1911 TT had conceived of it in 1912 after studying evolving motorcycle design. His approach was markedly different to the somewhat haphazard attitude of most designers at the time, including Hedstrom and Hendee, and marked the beginning of a more academic approach to motorcycle design.

Born in Ireland in 1886 Franklin had attended the Dublin College of Science. After graduating in 1908 he worked for the engineering department of Dublin's municipal government, where he soon distinguished himself. However, his real passion lay in motorcycling, both as a designer and a rider, and he had raced a variety of machines before purchasing his first Indian in 1910. His success on the Indian in local competitions attracted the attention of the British agent for the Indian Motocycle Company, an exuberant, larger than life character named Billy Wells.

Wells made Franklin part of the team that went on to triumph at the TT in 1912 and then ensured that the Irishman was offered a job by Indian, which he joined formally in 1914 after emigrating to America. He was the first trained engineer to be employed by the company, although the war meant the company was kept busy churning out existing designs for the army. It was not until 1919 that Franklin was able to build a prototype of the machine he had first envisaged back in 1912, derived in large part from the Powerplus.

Tests of the prototype showed it to be an outstanding design and in September it was put into production, the first machine out of the plant being number 5OR001. When Bert's bike was eventually delivered it was 5OR627, making it number 627 off the line. By the time the Indian had been carefully broken out of its wooden ship-ping crate in Archie's modest workshop the discarded Clyno had gone to its proud new owner, the local blacksmith – for exactly the same money Bert had paid for it when it had a sidecar. He counted out the balance owed to Archie from a thick wad of cash and was left holding just a few limp notes. He was now almost completely broke. But as he carefully checked over his new machine he felt like the richest man in town.

The design of the Scout was fairly conventional – no bad thing at a time when many manufacturers offered questionable design features simply to be different. But it was also technnically right up to date. The engine was a simple but effective 600cc forty-two-degree, V-twin and, like the Powerplus, it was a side-valve design. Unlike the Powerplus, it featured semi-unit construction, with the transmission being bolted to the engine. This was driven by an efficient helical-gear primary drive housed in an oil-tight, cast alloy case. The three-speed, hand-change gearbox was operated by a foot clutch, a normal arrangement for the time, and gear selection was smooth and positive. The final drive to the wheel was achieved with a chain, a far superior system to the leather belt drives still used on many English bikes.

Like the rest of the machine, the frame represented the best con-temporary thinking. It had been designed to provide a comfortable and reliable ride over the rugged roads still common outside city limits. It was a double down-tube cradle unit and it was solidly engineered without being unduly heavy. Although there was no rear suspension, the elegant, leaf-spring saddle gave a comfortable ride, with a generous fifty-millimetres of travel in the front girder forks' suspension.

It took only a few minutes for Bert to confirm his first

impressions. The machine might be a silky smooth operator but she also loved to get up and go.

By the end of the week Bert had covered several hundred kilometres and was infatuated with his new bike. He had also met a girl who impressed him as different to every other woman he had met or was likely to meet. Her father ran a successful accountancy business and kept a tight reign on his only daughter. But as Bert constantly reminded her, love will always find a way. They began to see each other regularly, meeting several times a week at the dances in town, slipping away for brief moments when the ever-present watchdogs weren't looking.

It was more difficult to meet during the day on the weekends, but she was resourceful and with the help of a girlfriend was able to steal a little time to go riding. She loved clinging on behind him and for once he did not feel the need to deliberately terrify a female. He wanted her to enjoy every moment she was with him and it seemed she did. They would find a private grove beside a quiet river and spread the old blanket he now carried. She would arrange a selection of food she had packed carefully and they would have a picnic.

Bert was most solicitous and for once did not try to move too fast, even though the circumstances often seemed most propitious. Instead he studied her serious grey eyes as she talked to him, and tried not to be distracted by the gentle curve of her mouth and the soft movement of her body as she shifted about on the blanket. He was, he supposed, in love.

He could think of little else and the days when he could not see her became a torment. Even the Indian was insufficient distraction. Finally one day he told her in a rush that he loved her with all his heart and he wanted to marry her. She said she felt the same way and that she would, but how would they live?

Bert visited her father at his office, after formally requesting an appointment by mail, and found the man in such a high fury that veins throbbed visibly on his temples and his face turned an unhealthy puce. He seemed to know a great deal about Bert, including that he swanned about on a motorcycle like a man on holiday and that he worked for his father as a farm labourer – a farm labourer, furthermore, who, having no qualifications, lacked any immediate prospects of earning more than the shilling a week his father paid him!

He also now knew that Bert and his daughter had been sneaking around unchaperoned for months and that his daughter's reputation was therefore sullied. He ended the meeting by assuring Bert that if he ever, ever attempted to see his daughter again he would personally horsewhip him from one end of Queen Street to the other and back again.

It was not, on the whole, a successful interview.

Bert was far too gone to heed these threats and tried for months to see the girl. His only reward for his time and effort was an occasional glimpse on Sundays of her distant face, pale and strained, in the midst of a scrum of family galloping in and out of church. In time he gave up and returned his attention to the only thing that could give him comfort. On nearly every evening, except Tuesdays, he fired up the Indian and headed for a dance where he met his friends and did his best to cut one of the young ladies out of the herd, if only for a few minutes outside. They were high-spirited evenings with endless practical joking, and even though Bert remained mostly a non-drinker he was always at the heart of the party.

Like many such fraternities, Bert's motorcycling mates enjoyed giving one another nicknames and Bert was soon had one of his own. Lilly had always taken care of her children's teeth and Bert had a number of gold fillings, some of which were quite prominent. He became the 'Flying Goldtooth'.

More often than not there was a motorcycling adventure at night, some of them expeditions to quite distant destinations. One night Bert agreed to ride pillion behind his mate Bert Martyn, who rode a 350cc Indian Prince, to Riverton, twenty-eight kilometres out of town. The dance there turned out to be a dud and when the handful of young ladies who had turned up left at about ten o'clock it was time to go home. Unfortunately, the little Prince was struggling under the extra weight and about halfway home, at Wrights Bush, a small hamlet with a hall and little else, the clutch gave up. The two friends pushed the machine into the weak pool of light from a single naked bulb hanging over the hall door, and spread out the tool roll every biker carried. Inside the desultory tinkle of a badly played piano struggled to be heard over the clomping of feet. Clearly a better dance was in progress here.

The pair very quickly stripped the clutch and decided that it might just get them home if they could pack it out with some suitable spacer. Bert slipped into the hall foyer and returned with a smart trilby. Taking his clasp knife he deftly cut off the brim and handed it to a surprised Martyn.

'Hell's bells, Bert. Someone's going to be pretty annoyed when it's time to go home!'

Bert chortled. 'Well, it could have been worse.'

'How?'

'It could have been us!'

Martyn shook his head and began reassembling the clutch with the new packer in place, shooting nervous glances at the door. They were soon ready to continue, but only after Bert had insisted on returning the remains of the trilby to its hook. The Prince carried them home without further trouble and the hat brim was still giving good service some months later. Martyn must have related the episode to a mate because the next time Bert walked into the public bar at the Criterion, where his friends gathered, someone yelled out above the hubbub, 'Hold on to your hats, boys, the Flying Goldtooth has arrived!'

Considering Bert's enthusiasm for speed it was surprising he did not come unstuck regularly, particularly with the law. Yet he was only once pulled up by the constabulary, when a Sergeant Stopford issued him with a ticket for exceeding fifteen miles per hour on the North Road, an offence that earned him a £1 fine with seven shillings costs. It was hardly enough to deter him and it did not slow him down for a moment.

The fact was that riding motorcycles flat out was the only high spot in Bert's life. Cow farming continued to occupy most of his time and one year after another was slipping by. In 1925 he married Bert Martyn's sister Beryl and sold the Indian. Bert was suddenly determined that his days working for a shilling a week at a job he detested were over. There were frequent sailings by tramp ships from Bluff to Australia and a ticket to Melbourne travelling supercargo, in one of the few cramped little cabins such ships had available, cost just £5. The couple was soon aboard a small steamer heading into the Tasman Sea. It was time for a new beginning.

CHAPTER EIGHT
RACING

Australia was booming. There was plenty of work for a handyman to get his teeth into and the wages were good. Bert was soon employed as a carpenter and with many new buildings going up in Melbourne he was seldom short of work. At his first job, constructing a power station, he was quickly made a gang supervisor, with twenty men working under him. They were mostly occupied building gantries and erecting scaffolding, work Bert had plenty of experience with from his months in the Otira Tunnel. The responsibility gave him an extra shilling a week and he enjoyed the work, being quickly accepted by his workmates.

It was a turbulent time, with the trade unions flexing their muscles and the conflict frequent and boisterous. As always, Bert favoured the bosses, but again his good-natured and forthright defence of such views somehow placated his fellow workers, who might normally have dragged him into the nearest alley and given him a good kicking.

One of those in his gang was a late middle-aged, diminutive, bald firebrand named Tommy Casey. Bert and Tommy were soon friendly despite being diametrically opposed over labour relations. Tommy, a committed communist and well-known union activist, organised a strike which rapidly became a lockout, with some 1200 striking workers being shut out of the site. Among the 200 left on the inside was Bert.

The strikers gathered to march on the town hall some kilometres away, and noisily set off with Tommy leading the way. But it was a hot day and only a dozen tired men arrived, the rest having fallen away to grab a restorative beer or two at one of the many pubs en route. The next day Tommy was standing on a plank atop an oil drum kept beside the main gate as a rubbish bin, haranguing the strikers for their general lack of commitment, when someone surreptitiously flicked a match into the drum. Bert was on the inside looking out and it was only his shouted warning that saved Tommy from a decent singeing. Tommy might have been redder than corned beef, but he was a mate. And with Bert that always came first.

With the completion of the power station in 1925 Bert and Beryl moved to Sydney, where she gave birth to their daughter June. From the first Bert doted on his little girl, and was a caring and involved father. His devotion to family did not extend to devotion as a husband, however, and although he was fond of Beryl and wanted her happy, the marriage wasn't strong. He was never a bully and was always respectful. There were no rows. But Beryl found herself in a difficult situation. Bert may have moved on from the time 'when he worked all day and danced all night', but he had not settled down. He was restless at home, always seeking greater satisfaction and fulfilment in his life. Marriage had not provided it and neither had a child. He still carried the easy, cheeky charm that women had always found attractive and was soon unfaithful. Even though he was careful to keep his dalliances separate from his domestic life, Beryl knew that all was not well.

Bert moved his family often, following various construction projects around the country. With constant upheaval the marriage seemed always to come second, to be attended to when there was time to draw breath. When bikes returned to the centre of Bert's life those opportunities were pushed even further away.

In Melbourne he had become a speedway fan, regularly attending the mile-long, hard-surface track at Aspendale. This unusual concrete circuit had a big banked corner at one end and two sharper corners at the other, with two reasonably long straights where riders could really open up their machines. It was a dangerous place and typically attracted up to 10,000 spectators to thrill at the many accidents.

Bert made himself known to the racers and met the local Indian agent, who supplied bikes to various riders. Bert proved his usefulness by helping out with tuning and spanner work, and was eventually offered machines to race at the speedway and in hill climbs, timed speed events and economy runs – events where agents could demonstrate the quality of their machines to the public. Sales of motorcycles were at an all-time high in Australia and the old axiom about racing on Sunday and selling on Monday was never truer. A useful, capable and utterly fearless man like Bert was bound to thrive in such a scene. There were opportunities to race and to pick up extra cash doing all manner of little deals. He took full advantage of them all.

Sometimes there was beach racing and in 1927 he took an Indian Scout to Inverloch Beach to win a gold medal at 90.01 miles an hour, equal to the time put up by a very determined air-force pilot on a Chicago 61 Harley Davidson.

Of course, racing was an uncertain proposition and there was always the possibility of things going wrong. Things did so spectacularly for Bert just a week after his beach triumph when he was racing in front of the usual large crowd at the Aspendale Speedway. Travelling flat out down the straight at more than ninety miles an hour he reached down to give the oil pump a squeeze. The momentary distraction was enough; he suddenly found that the straight had run out and he was on a collision course with the murderous post-and-rail fence that ran around the track. His oversized twenty-nine inch front wheel hit a deep gutter and the bike launched into the air, landing with the handlebars pulled around, causing a horrendous speed wobble. Bert knew it was time to bail out. He

rolled off and he and the bike began to cartwheel. The crowd
oohed and finally aaahed as machine and rider eventually slid to a
halt, both lying silently beside the track.

Later he would tell the ambulance men that he clearly remembered blacking out four times as he was cartwheeling. For the
moment he was completely dazed as they lifted him onto a stretcher
and carried him to the ambulance room. He came to as they put the
stretcher down and jumped up to go back to the track and pick up
the bike, babbling with urgency. It took both men to subdue him
and he was eventually carted off to hospital to be diagnosed with
severe bruising and concussion. Although he was allowed home
almost immediately it took weeks in bed before he was able to get
back to business.

At the other end of the spectrum he won an economy run by
coaxing 116 miles to the gallon out of a Scout, proving that he could
ride sensitively if he wanted to. In spite of his success it was not a
form of competition he felt any desire to persue. He continued to
race in hill climbs, and often did very well. At one event the climb
was waterlogged after heavy rain, which casued traction problems
on the mostly grass track. Bert thought about the situation for a few
moments and then borrowed a length of rope, winding it tightly
around his rear tyre. The hotshot favourite scoffed loudly at Bert's
impromptu modification but was left in a distant second place when
Bert scorched up the hill. The local star's humiliation was complete
when Bert returned the rope – to the beaten man's own highly
embarrassed crew.

In Sydney he continued riding at speedway events at the Penrith
track, another mile-long course set out in a big D-shape. He
competed on the very wide track as a solo rider and occasionally
with a partner in frantic sidecar events. Although it had only been
opened in 1924 the Penrith track attracted a huge number of fans,
elevating some riders to the kind of celebrity normally reserved for
rugby league stars. Riders like Billy Conoulty and Les Weatherby
established big followings and were mobbed by young fans for their
autographs. Although Bert was not to achieve their level of celebrity

he was one of the better-known riders and enjoyed the attention it brought.

He also rode in a miniature TT, the very first scrambles event in Australia. The course had been hacked out of the bush at Chatswood in North Sydney and the mile-long circuit crossed a creek. All the roots and stumps from the cleared bush had been left in the ground and as there were numerous jumps, including the big one out of the creek bed, the course was extremely hazardous. Undeterred, a large field of heavy motorcycles attacked the race with gusto. There were numerous accidents, some more painful than others, but Bert was not among them. He kicked and cajoled his Scout around the course to finally finish second to Les Weatherby, winning not just a place in the race but a place in a little bit of history.

When Bert had first arrived the main competition had been between Indians and Harley Davidsons, both favoured by Australian motorcyclists for their ruggedness. However, by the mid-twenties things were changing. Many of the lighter, overhead valve English machines were making inroads in both general sales and in racing. A number of American stars, like Ralph Hepburn, had come over to race in Australia and were impressed by Nortons, Triumphs, BSAs and other British imports. The one that impressed Hepburn most was the AJS Big Port B4. In turn Bert was impressed by Hepburn and took note when the American, who at home raced only Harleys and Indians, bought an AJS and used it to great effect.

Bert spent a lot of time looking over these machines, noting particularly the way the exposed, cast aluminium rockers were simply located by two steel brackets screwed onto either side of the head. As soon as he had an opportunity he also examined the internal layout of the heads, something he was able to do as other competitors quickly appreciated his skills as a mechanic. He was soon familiar with the interior of the engine as well as the history of its development.

He learned that Jack Stevens, one of the founding brothers of AJ Stevens, or AJS as the marque became known, had designed the first AJS overhead-valve engine in the early twenties, modelling the head on that used in the 1921 grand prix Fiats. Fiat's highly competitive engine featured an overhead camshaft operating two large valves per cylinder inside a hemispherical combustion chamber. The hemi head provided sufficient surface area to house the big valves, which operated at right angles to one another, and also allowed an efficient inlet port shape, encouraging a good flow of air–fuel mix into the chamber. The engine was a cross-flow type with the fuel flowing in from one side of the head and the exhaust flowing out the other. It was an altogether a potent recipe for deep breathing and good power. Bert appreciated its beauty from the moment he saw it.

When AJS introduced their new engine it proved its superiority over existing overhead-valve engines – which then all had their valves mounted vertically – by winning the Isle of Man Junior TT three times and the Senior once, the last in 1921 when their 350cc machines beat all the 500s. The AJS Big Port of 1923 carried on this racing tradition in a production motorcycle with massive inlet and exhaust ports, the exhaust port and pipe being two inches in diameter, twice the size of most production motorcycles.

In 1924 they had further refined the arrangement in the machine Hepburn was now riding by making the inlet valve even bigger, setting an average lap time at the TT that year of a then highly respectable sixty-four miles per hour. It was little wonder the visiting American, accustomed as he was to heavy Indian and Harley Davidson twins, found the light and snappy AJS so worthy. Or that Bert Munro from New Zealand would file away all he had learned from the machine for later use.

By 1928 Bert was working regularly as pit crew for Eddie Darke, then the acknowledged Australian sidecar racing champion. Sidecars were raced in a variety of different ways, including road races, and in one such race, over a notoriously dangerous mountain pass, Bert borrowed a Scout and sidecar plus passenger and succeeded in beating Darke, who as always was riding his extensively modified 1200cc Harley Davidson outfit.

Bert also returned to Inverloch where a fast quarter-mile track with extensive banking and an asphalt surface had been built. Once more mounted on an Indian he managed to win a fiercely contested five-mile race at a highly credible average of 90.1 miles per hour, taking away a special gold medal as his prize.

Another recent development in Australian racing was the quarter-mile, cinder-surfaced speedway track. This new kind of racing rapidly became the most popular form of motor sport in Australia and the idea soon found favour abroad, particularly in the United Kingdom. Riders could maintain spectacular slides right through the corners, often three or even four abreast, and the crowds loved it. Accidents were frequent and sometimes serious, adding tremendously to the spectator appeal. Men who raced speedway knew they were putting their lives on the line.

The loose surface favoured the lighter English machines and Bert was able to test a number of them, riding for various import agents. Among them was a AJS Big Port and it took him only a few laps to confirm his already high opinion of it. It was indeed a superior machine.

The Australian speedway scene was now quite international and some of the most talented tuners in the world were to be found trackside. Bert wasted no opportunity to pick their brains and most were pleased to answer his questions. He drank it all in, aware that he was in the ideal place at the right point in history. Unfortunately, history was sprinting toward yet another catastrophe.

In October 1929 the stock market in America collapsed, converting about $30 billion dollars worth of stock to worthless paper and plunging the world into depression. Australia was particularly hard hit, being reliant on primary exports and not yet having an industrial infrastructure robust enough to stand on its own. Suddenly there were no building projects to work on and no motorcycle sales to encourage agents to supply bikes for racers like Bert. He decided not to wait for the prosperity that politicians assured a panicking world lay just around the corner, and booked tickets for his family on a steamer home. By now he had two daughters, his second girl Margaret being born in Sydney in 1928.

Fate had decreed it was time to get back to cow farming.

Before he left there was time for just one more race. This time it would be on 950 kilometres of the worst roads in Victoria, a marathon that would determine the Victorian Hill Climb champion. In spite of being mounted on yet another Indian, which fellow racers and fans alike all agreed had little chance, Bert surprised them all and won his class. It was a good note to bow out on.

Back at Elston Lea much had changed. With Bert's sisters and brother now grown up Lilly had begun to take in abandoned children, or State children as they were known. Of course William was complicit in her plans but it was Lilly who drove them, although all her 'children' called her 'Mum' none called William 'Dad'. Most, however, would take the name Munro.

Altogether she would foster about a dozen such youngsters, acquiring them at various ages between infancy and early teens. Some were ill or handicapped. One unfortunate young man had suffered rheumatic fever; a condition that eventually killed him when he was just twenty-four years old, after he had lost his arms and legs. Another, John Baldwin Munro, had been crippled by polio. He would grow up to become a long-standing member of parliament for the Labour Party and later the chief executive of the Intellectually Handicapped Children's Society. Eventually Lilly's dedication to these children would lead to her receiving a letter of commendation from the Queen, but for the most part she worked quietly and privately.

Bert was always wryly supportive of his mother and regarded her good works fondly, extending to his new half-brothers and -sisters a generous measure of fraternal affection, which they were universally pleased to return. It was clear, however, that Bert's family could not permanently share the old house with this growing number of new siblings, especially when his third daughter Gwen was born in 1930. So he decided to take time off from farming to build a house almost half a kilometre away from the homestead.

June and Margaret often watched him at work in the fields from their attic bedroom; it was a happy time for the family with the five of them getting together for lunch every day on the building site. The house took shape very rapidly. When finished it was a comfortable, warm home with all Bert's trophies from Australia displayed in the living room in an imposing glass-fronted cabinet. His final project was to convert a rickety old hay barn into a proper shed by installing a wooden floor and a workbench, his workshop for when he returned to motorcycling. With the house finished and his family comfortably installed he took up farming again.

With his days once more dominated by the job he liked least, Bert's thoughts turned inevitably to his old Indian. Shortly after returning from Australia, on 18 March 1929, he had joined the Southland Motorcycle Club, which had been formed in his absence. The club organised rallies, grass-track races, beach racing, scrambles, hill climbs, and socials. The annual Bluff Hill Climb, a race up the twisty road leading to the historic old signals station, was already very popular with competitors and spectators. Naturally Bert was keen. When he ran into the man to whom he'd sold the Indian and learned that he had in turn sold it to someone in Riverton, he decided to track it down.

A few weeks later one of Bert's motorcycle mates gave him a ride up to the little coastal community and he soon found his old machine. It looked the worse for wear. Grass had grown up through the wheels, which sported two flat tyres. It was slumped out in the open against a fence at the back of the beachfront property, the once supple leather saddle a hard black lump. The paint had faded, the chrome was pitted with rust and the machine looked washed out and lifeless. Bert felt a surge of excitement but was careful to betray only a certain distaste at the sight of the wreckage before him.

'Cripes,' he said to the embarrassed owner, 'this thing looks about as useful as tits on a bull.'

The owner nodded apologetically. 'Yep, she's pretty far gone.'

Bert scratched his head. 'It might be good for parts, I suppose.'

The owner agreed.

Bert thought of a small number and then halved it. The Depression was biting hard and it was unlikely anyone would want the ruin leaning against the fence. Anyone except him. 'I'll give you a quid for it.'

The owner did not even haggle and Bert had his bike back.

It took about an hour to fix the punctures and get it going again. It ran, as he had known it would, with the same old sweet, even beat. The man who had just sold it watched, puzzled, as Bert gunned it up the road, the back tyre fish-tailing under power, spraying gravel and leaving a cloud of dust in the air. Bert grinned as he snicked the hand-change gear lever into second and spun the back wheel on the loose metal again. No doubt about it. There were still a few good parts in there!

Now that he had transport again Bert was able to contemplate a change of occupation, and it was not long before an offer came in. It came from his new brother-in-law, a man called Jim Farrelly. Bert's sister Ruby had married Farrelly a few years back when he had been a bushman with an eye to the main chance, and his ambition and cunning had subsequently seen him rise to run a timber operation in the Catlins, a mountain range to the south east.

Farrelly was a tough customer, a hotheaded Irishman with a propensity for trouble and the bloody-minded gall to always push his way out of it. He habitually wore an old belted gabardine coat and he was always shadowed by Sodestrom, a huge Scandinavian known to one and all as Scandy. Scandy was a big drinker but never to the point he could not slap a man unconscious with a single swipe from his ham-like paw. He was Farrelly's man.

Farrelly had been in charge of a mill called Fortification but he had used the opportunity to set up a rival timber company he called Niagara. He took many customers with him when he left, causing much acrimony with his former employers. They nevertheless joined forces with him when Niagara took over a third company and allowed Farrelly to assume the role of supervisor of the lot. The quality of his management was a matter of some contention and on several occasions the board demanded his resignation. He always gave it and then continued to run things anyway, ignoring the replacements the board hired until the man became dispirited and left. One of the most frequent complaints was that he freely made promises that he could not deliver.

A few days after Bert got his new job he witnessed Farrelly in action at the company's married man's camp. He had promised two women that he would get them a tin bath; when only one arrived they argued over who should have it. Farrelly dismissed both by observing that one was too fat to fit and the other was so grubby she looked as if she never took a bath anyway. He gave the bath instead to a third woman. Bert was a little stunned by the episode. It would never have occurred to him to treat a woman with such disrespect, let alone two at once, and he was never quite at ease with Farrelly after that.

The company used Wilson Brothers GM-powered twelve-wheel-drive tractors to take logs from the bush to the mill on tracks the company laid down, and Bert's job was to drive and maintain them. He was also responsible for the company's jiggers, lighter vehicles used to carry men. Bert soon tired of the pedestrian pace of the jiggers and hopped them up with the result that they started to regularly derail. He was ordered to return them to their old sluggish state, which he did with great reluctance.

One of the best things about the job, other than the fact that it paid well at a time when this was rare, was that he got to ride the Indian to work. It was a good long haul over twisty roads and took several hours. He always made a point of detouring at speed along the front verandah of the Waimahaka store. There was a considerable drop at the end of the board verandah and Bert would sail over it, trying to extend his jump each time. Anyone lucky enough to witness Bert's passing enjoyed a free and quite spectacular show. For the storekeeper, however, the sudden burst of the engine and the thudding progress along his verandah was a constant irritation. He complained loudly that he could never catch the silly bugger who was bound to break his neck. By the time he bustled from the counter at the back of his shop to the door to give the bastard a piece of his mind, Bert was always disappearing around the next corner.

His hot pace also annoyed many closer to home. One neighbour on Tramway Road finally came stomping around to tell Bert that if he continued to spray gravel and dust all over his house every time he went past he would stretch fencing wire across the road at head height. Bert took no notice and the man's house continued to wear a grey mantle through the summer and a spattering of mud in the winter. Bert Munro slowed down for no one – although he did take to ducking behind his big acetylene light when he went past the neighbour's property.

With Farrelly on his side he was able to organise his life to attend as many racing events as he liked. One of the first was a quarter-mile grass-track meeting held at Rugby Park. Bert had told his mates all about the fantastic new cinder tracks he had raced on in Australia and about how the riders would drag a foot along the ground to steady the bike as it slid around corners. He was keen to demonstrate the technique, but grass is a very different surface to loose cinders and the track around Rugby Park far bumpier. Grass also provided relatively good traction, making it a lot harder to slide.

In spite of this Bert attacked his race with gusto, sticking his inside leg out and trailing his foot as he poured on the power to provoke a two-wheel slide. The crowd loved it and cheered him on, especially loudly when he eventually bit the dust. In the end he finished dead last, but he had earned an honorable mention in the local newspaper, the *Southland Times*.

'Munro,' the paper recorded, 'provided the thrills in this race. His control of the bicycle as it advanced crab-like was certainly good but after one very prolonged side skid he made a spectacular crash in front of the grandstand. Amidst applause, he immediately remounted and despite further skidding finished the race at good speed.'

On 21 April he was at Oreti Beach and again the newspaper recorded his attendance, reporting that he finished second in a six-mile handicap event. The paper later mentioned his participation in a reliability trial in June and a second beach race in December. At the latter event Bert won two of the four races, placing second and third in the other two and taking away £15 10s in prize money – an outstanding haul. His victories that day were hard fought, with a more modern Daytona Indian and an exotic OEC to race against, both of which were much faster machines.

He managed to beat them through his perseverance with the power slide, always a difficult proposition on anything other than a loose surface. Oreti Beach was hard-packed sand, so it was only possible to slide at high speeds and with the application of a fistful of power. This was definitely not something for the faint-hearted. Most competitors were content to slow down at the markers and simply ride around them. Falling off on the beach was not a good idea, either, as the sand was terribly abrasive. But if Bert feared being flayed alive he didn't let it influence the way he rode. The idea of slowing down was always anathema.

Moreover, heavy braking wasn't much of an option as his machine was sadly deficient in that area. In 1920 the Indian factory had equipped the Scout with a tiny little front drum brake that worked reasonably well on a machine that was not intended to go over fifty-five miles an hour flat out, and to usually cruise along a great deal slower. Repeated braking from higher speeds just overheated the drum and caused the brakes to fade away. Performing a lurid slide was one way to quickly scrub off speed.

The shows Bert put on sliding the Indian on sand, gravel and grass were much appreciated by the crowds that turned up to watch in ever-increasing numbers. Once again the newspaper recorded his efforts at a grass-track meeting early in 1930. 'H. J. Munro took a second and can be relied on for a fair turn of speed. He is an expert at correcting a broadside.'

The *Southland Times* had by now realised that Bert was always good for a column inch or two, even when he did not compete. On 1 February 1930 they reported his non-participation in the Bluff Hill Climb: 'H.J. Munro was unfortunate in blowing one of his cylinder heads off, which prevented him from racing throughout the meeting.'

The next day they were able to report his attendance on a rebuilt machine at a grass hill climb, held about sixty-five kilometres out of town at Hokonui. He had adapted his old rope trick by winding chain around his rear wheel and many others at the meeting had apparently followed suit. Bert battled with another determined competitor called George Winton and at the end of the day they had recorded equal best times. On the subsequent run-off Bert threw what little caution he normally retained to the wind and went all out, knocking a full second off his previous best time and taking the win. The paper commented on the recourse to wrapped chains for traction by congratulating 'riders on their use and especially to Munro who mounted the hill running on his back wheel only'.

With as much motorcycle racing as he wanted and with a job that paid for it Bert was content. He still got on well enough with Jim Farrelly and would have been happy to stay with the job indefinitely. Unfortunately both the company and Farrelly personally were always sailing close to the wind financially, and one day the job evaporated.

In the end, it didn't matter. There was a better job waiting for Bert Munro, a job that came close to being ideal. He was about to become a travelling motorcycle salesman.

CHAPTER NINE
ON THE ROAD

Tappers was the leading motorcycle shop in Invercargill. It was run very capably by two Tapper brothers and a sister. The company had thrived during the boom in the twenties and at the end of the decade made the bold decision to import machines directly from manufacturers. Unfortunately, while the shipments were still at sea, the market collapsed and the company faced ruin. It was not alone. Many businesses had been hit by the suddenness of general economic collapse. The great majority ended up closing their doors. Not so Tappers.

While the Depression wiped out many jobs in Southland, as it did everywhere, there was still one thing in this part of the world that an energetic person could fall back on – they could go after gold. The goldfields of Central Otago had been among the most spectacularly productive in the world and, like all such fields, they had absorbed countless fortune seekers. When the easily won gold was gone the prospectors tended to drift away again, looking for the next big thing, and most had left by the end of the 1880s. But they had not by any means exhausted all the gold. It was just harder to extract.

Gold, the one metal that never degrades, remained a certainty in a world full of terrible uncertainty. During the Depression it became more valuable than ever, adding to the attractiveness of scratching for colour among the tailings left by the previous century's miners. A new rush was on, albeit it one that provided steady but unspectacular returns. It was a lot better than the government work schemes, then the only response to the crisis. These schemes split fathers from their families and put them to work on hard graft schemes, often in primitive conditions and for less than subsistence wages. They were miserable, mean-spirited solutions from an unimaginative and arrogant conservative government, and did little more than breed further misery.

Searching for gold alongside the wild rivers that had scoured it out of the mountains, on the other hand, provided a living. With hard work it could be a very reasonable one. It was tough, of course. Central Otago, beautiful in summer, was an icy hell-hole in the long winter and only the most determined stuck it out.

These were the resourceful people the canny Tappers decided to target. They had cash, they were usually young and they were adventurous. A motorcycle was just the thing to get them to and from town on the cart tracks that wound through the mountains where their primitive cribs nestled. Bert was ideally suited to the job. He was a natural salesman who relished the challenge of hawking motorcycles to prospectors who probably could not think of anything they needed less. Neither would he be put off by kilometres of appalling road, often running beside spectacular drop-offs to raging rivers far below. If some resistant gold panner protested that the roads were too bad for a motorcycle, he'd simply point to the one he had just ridden in on.

Bert took his orders primarily from Alf Tapper and once they got to know each other Alf gave him a great deal of licence. Deals would depend on slashing prices and tempting free extras, such as complimentary crash helmets and pannier bags. Anyone who even glanced at a machine would be offered a ride, for the duration of a weekend if they wished. There were no phones in most places to call Alf for guidance, but Bert knew the bottom line – and that the returns had to cover his own wages. Whenever he picked up a new machine to sell, Alf Tapper would exhort him not to bring it back.

Bert carried a small set of accurate scales everywhere he went, often taking payment in gold, and he always asked where the next camp was before leaving. Getting home after selling the machine he'd been riding could be tricky. Usually he could cadge a ride with the new owner, though Bert would insist on riding himself, just to show the client the ropes. Back in civilisation he would pick up the Triumph that the Tappers had given him to ride. If the new owner couldn't leave his diggings Bert would simply walk out. He quite often slept rough and as often went hungry. A replacement for the machine he'd sold would be dropped off by another salesman, a younger man named Jim Lawry, who Bert would then return to Invercargill on the back of the Triumph.

It was a clumsy arrangement but with little public transport running into the country there was little choice. The return trips were a trial for Lawry, who simply hung on with his eyes closed as Bert hammered along the loose metal roads. Sometimes they would break the trip to grab something to eat. Bert particularly favoured a little diner in Edendale where he had formed an attachment to the waitress. Once while leaving, Bert had turned completely around on the saddle to wave back at her and, with the throttle wide open, was so engrossed in his farewells that he failed to hear Lawry's increasingly panicked warnings. Suddenly he found he was heading straight for a train on a level crossing. Luckily it was stationary, but both men were bruised and scraped when Bert instantly dropped the bike and they skidded into one of the big driving wheels with a solid wallop.

On other occasions Bert and Lawry would ride into the country on the Triumph to recover push-bikes when payments to the Tappers had fallen behind. They would rest the bike between them on the seat, a wheel on either side, for the trip home. As always Bert kept the throttle wide open, while Lawry waited for a push-bike wheel to catch on the road or in the scenery as they banked into the corners. Had it ever happened he would have been wrenched violently off the back of the Triumph. Somehow it never did, but he grew to dread these recovery missions. It was only the fact that his job was on the line that saw him climbing on again behind Bert, with a final despairing plea to his grinning pilot to take it easy. He never did.

The job was made for Bert; its only drawbacks being that he was often away from his family for weeks at a time, and that it greatly reduced the time he could spend on his own Indian. With a number of English manufacturers now offering high-performance overhead-valve engines in comparatively lightweight frames, the now ten-year-old Indian was showing her age. Considering that her design went back to before the First World War this was hardly surprising, but she remained Bert's favourite machine, even though he could now buy higher performance bikes for loose change.

Few bothered at the time with old machinery if they could afford something new. There was no vintage car or motorcycle movement as such, and even Edwardian machines were regarded as worn out and mostly useless relics. Old was just old, and the scrap heaps were full of exotic machinery that had once been the envy of all. For some reason that he would never even try to articulate, the Indian Scout was special to Bert. He would soon buy a number of different machines to tune and race, but the Scout remained parked securely in his shed long after the others had been moved on.

To stay competitive, however, he needed to increase the bike's power. He had organised his shed with a ramp, onto which he could push a bike and work on it without bending over. He had also acquired an old Myford lathe, a small unit, more suited to hobby work than serious engineering. It was also almost completely worn out, which was why he had got if free from an engineering company. Curling metal shaving, evidence of Bert's efforts to teach himself the art of machining, now surrounded the lathe's feet. He had also installed extensive shelving and laden it with old Indian parts, bought from various agents who no longer wanted to keep them.

He was ready to begin. If ever there was a pivotal moment, this was it. By taking the first step to keep the Indian competitive, when he could easily have bought a newer machine, he was committing himself to a lifetime of such work. The Indian would soon cease to be an Indian – it would become the Munro Special. And when that happened the task was no longer simply to win races and go faster. It became a matter of building the machine to do it.

To keep his hand in when he was not riding for work or racing, Bert built his own track. He hitched up his father's Clydesdales, which William had steadfastly refused to replace with a tractor, to the front of a grader and hacked out a quarter-mile oval on the farm. The track was a convenient place to test bikes and to develop riding skills, and soon a number of other riders were turning up to use it. William, as always where motorcycles were concerned, remained frowningly disapproving. But he still said nothing, having long accepted that his oldest boy would never fulfil the promise of his ancestry by becoming a frugal and dedicated farmer.

Bert continued to help on the farm when time permitted and took some responsibility for his end of the property. If an animal died, for example, he would, without complaint, retrieve the body, dig a hole for it in the orchard he had started, and plant a tree over it. Asked by a curious motorbike mate why he bothered, when the weather would soon enough strip a carcass to bleached bones, he said it was his business to keep the land pure. The ancient Celtic wisdoms of Glencalvie were not entirely lost to him.

One of those who turned up to race and to chew things over afterwards was a slender, clean-cut young man named Johnny Checketts. He was completing a mechanics apprenticeship for the local Ford dealer but his first love was motorcycles. Norton, Velocette, Rudge and Triumph had all tried to build machines to challenge Douglas when the new speedway craze arrived in the late twenties. None were destined to last, but Tappers had imported one of the dozen Triumphs made. Checketts had bought it for £45 and enjoyed immediate success. He was now one of Bert's main rivals, but Bert always left his rivalries on the track. As he and Johnny shared a fascination with tuning engines, they had become friends.

Bert had identified a number of areas he could profitably investigate in his quest for more power, but he was constrained by the fact that the Indian had a side-valve engine. By 1930 it had become accepted that race engines needed to be not only overhead-valve engines, but overhead cam as well. Still, Bert was convinced he could get a lot more power out of it than it had when it left the factory. He was encouraged by the fact that he was still almost competitive on the Indian. It would not take a great deal more, he hoped, to return the bike to its winning ways. It did not occur to him that he might also improve his performance if he could slow the machine down better, and so the dinky little brakes stayed just the way they had always been – virtually useless.

He began by modifying the engine's cam profiles and raising its compression, both objectives being inherently difficult because of the design of the engine. Its single cam controlled both inlet and exhaust valves by acting on the two legs of the inverted L-shaped cam followers. These in turn motivated the pushrods that then acted on the valves. It was a good arrangement for a trouble-free, relatively low-performance tourer, but entirely wrong for a high-performance unit. The big problem was that a race engine tuner needed to vary the inlet and exhaust timing relative to one another and this was, with a single cam, extremely difficult.

Bert's only option was to either extend or truncate the legs of the cam followers and to file and grind a radius curve in them at the point they connected with the cam. This was as complicated as it sounds and required much experimentation. Bert's understanding of high-performance cams was that they needed to open the valves with a real wallop and to then allow the valve to dwell in the open position, long enough to achieve the desired period of valve overlap, before closing in a more gradual manner. The initial wallop provided by his hand-filed cams was so severe that he had to make up very heavy valve springs to prevent valve float. It kept happening, however, and Bert appreciated full well that after the valves had been given such an almighty punch by his cams it was to be expected they would not stay in contact with the cam, but would instead try to throw themselves out of the engine.

The opposite end of valve float is valve bounce, and this too Bert had to struggle to avoid. The heavy valve springs were causing the valves to snap shut so violently that they bounced off their seats. Both behaviours killed performance stone dead. It was a perpetual struggle to achieve a compromise that delivered high-performance without either valve float or valve bounce, and all without tearing the heads off the valves.

Johnny Checketts would bring Bert burnt valves from cars and trucks he had repaired at work and Bert would turn them down on the lathe to fit. One afternoon Bert looked up at the familiar sound of Johnny's Douglas approaching, before burying his head again in his work. He had an early 1920s Indian Prince up on the ramp, with another waiting nearby. The Scout was standing in the corner, an old cover thrown carelessly over her tank.

'Afternoon Bert,' said Johnny, 'I brought you some Ford valves. They came out of a puddle-jumper and they're a bit cooked but you should get something out of them.' He parked his machine and placed the handful of valves on the bench, taking another look at the two single-cylinder Princes. 'Gee Bert, they're heavy old bits of kit. Are you sure it's worth the trouble?'

Bert ignored the remark. 'I'll have this head off in a sec. I've got an overhead valve head that might be just the ticket. It's off an AJS 7R!'

Johnny sighed. 'I suppose it might work.'

The truth was, Johnny was puzzled by Bert's enthusiasm for the single-cylinder Indians, which he favoured for grass racing. His faith in them had thus far proven ill-placed. Johnny had watched Bert painfully graft an Aspen rotary valve head onto the other Prince, a transformation that left the Prince more like a lazy frog than anything nobler. God only knew where Bert had found the peculiar Aspen, which had for a while been touted as the answer to poppet valves, as it actuated the valve openings by spinning around instead of pounding up and down. Unsolved problems with sealing and lubrication had sentenced the Aspen to obscurity long before

Bert got hold of one. And the Aspen head had remained a failure in spite of Bert's attentions. Intended to be driven by a shaft and bevel drive, Bert's crude adaptation of the cam to activate the rotary valve had served only to show the pointlessness of further development.

The JAP overhead valve head that followed had been easier to engineer, as it was relatively straightforward to take a chain drive off the cam wheel. But it too proved a dud. The one time Bert raced the bike at Rugby Park it had not been a match for the lighter English machines. It was discarded.

Bert had purchased three of the Indian 350cc singles with his friend Percy Shave, a big, burly fellow who worked for one of Tappers' rivals, motorcycle agents JD Campbell Limited. Percy had owned the very fast OEC that Bert had struggled against on Oreti Beach and a big V-twin special. Both had been powered by 1000cc, overhead-valve JAP engines and Percy had won his share of races on them. For some reason he shared Bert's enthusiasm for the 350cc Indians and they had gone in together on the purchase of the three machines. Their first had cost just £3, the second a still very reasonable £7 10s. The third had been swapped for a little two-stroke Hobart that Percy owned. They had been playing enthusiastically, if pointlessly, with them ever since.

From the outset they'd had to contend with the Prince's design, which was compromised for speed work by the brass cage that held the big-end bearings. This was prone to failure under the kind of loadings that go with racing, and Bert always drained a small amount of oil from the bottom of the crankcase after every race. He would carefully rub the oil between his fingers looking for any glint of brass or feel of grit. All too often he would detect both, signalling the need for a complete strip down and rebuild of the bottom end.

Work on the Scout, on the other hand, had achieved some pleasing results. With higher compression, achieved by removing metal from the bottom of the barrels where they were sandwiched against the crankcase, Bert's fiercely profiled cams and a certain amount of weight reduction, the Indian was already significantly faster.

Above: The Munros about 1915 – a prosperous Southland farming
family. Burt top left.

Below: Back row: June, Burt, Margaret
Front row: Gwen, John.

Top Left: Beryl on the bike with Gwen and Margaret in sidecar, late 1920s.

Top Right: Too tight for comfort – the first hand-beaten aluminium streamliner body.

Mid Right: The heart of the Munro Special in its final form.

Bottom Right: Gravel road racing, 1930s.

Above: Racing on Oreti Beach in the 1930s. Burt nearest camera.

Below: Burt wearing his standard beach racing gear.
Duncan Meikle is leaning against Burt's Vauxhall.

Above: Rollie Free setting a speed record at Bonneville Salt Flats with an average speed of 150.313 miles an hour, 1948.

Below: Burt, Jackie and Marty Dickerson at home in LA.

Unfortunately it had not been enough to keep up with Johnny the weekend before.

On that Saturday afternoon Bert had ridden out with the rest of the crowd bound for Riversdale, which boasted a big grass horseracing track where an all-comers race was to be held the next day. Bert was feeling confident and had warned Johnny he intended taking line honours in the 500cc class. Johnny, who was riding his Triumph, was equally confident, and with good reason. He and the Triumph had already won the Silver Sash, the highest award for grass-track racing in Southland, and most people agreed he looked likely to win again. However, Bert was in high spirits and Johnny had simply accepted the challenge with a grin, as well as the fervent hope that Bert's efforts did not end with a valve head flying off and ruining his meeting. As it happened the Scout held together, but it was not very competitive. Johnny was never troubled for the lead in the 500cc races.

Johnny remained concerned by Bert's lack of significant progress with the Scout. It seemed like he was investing a lot of time trying to make the Princes perform where the Scout had failed. From where Johnny stood the prognosis for the Princes did not look particularly healthy, whereas the Scout was not far off the pace. But there was no point in telling Bert anything. He would come to his own conclusions in his own sweet time.

As Tappers were agents for Triumph they were among the first in New Zealand to receive new products. In 1933 a number of their new parallel twins were unloaded onto the docks at Bluff and then onto the Tappers' truck. Back at the workshop the crates were eagerly broken away to reveal smart-looking motorcycles. Triumph had begun manufacturing motorcycles with parallel twins back in 1913 but the First World War had seen the interesting machine shelved. Standard single-cylinder production resumed after the war, but it was not until the debut of the new model 6/1, drawn up by Triumph's designer Val Page, that the company returned to making twins.

The new bikes were equipped with an overhead-valve 650cc engine featuring a new semi-unit gearbox. Tappers had high hopes for the model in spite of the lingering Depression, but it was a vain hope. The bikes were heavy, underpowered and, worse still, vibrated badly. Combined with a whippy crankshaft that led to too many breakages they gained a consequent reputation for unreliability.

Towards the end of the year Bert bought a cheap Triumph engine from a crashed machine, having already mapped out a radical re-engineering of it in his head, a project that would tax both his ingenuity and resourses to the full. Meanwhile, his full attention was elsewhere and the Triumph engine was unceremoniously stashed under the bench. He would return to it, and the collection of Indian Princes, in due course. Right now the Scout was once more the brightest star in his universe.

Failing to make a splash at the Riversdale races had invigorated his efforts to reduce the machine's weight, drilling holes wherever he felt he could get away with it, and trying different, but always fierce, cam profiles. He had thought long and hard about the way gas swirled around in the combustion chamber as it was compressed prior to being exploded by the spark plug, and had concluded that the plugs were in the wrong position. He moved them by filling in the old holes with bronze, then drilling and tapping new ones. To his delight the change seemed to make an appreciable difference.

Of course, he had no way of measuring horsepower and was reliant on his own instincts. But Bert was now so finely attuned to his machine that he fancied he could tell when something worked. The only absolute measure was to take the bike out to the beach and see if it went any faster. If the beach was not available due to high tides or uneven surface conditions he was not averse to using a well-known, two-lane stretch of road called Ryal Bush Straight, just a few kilometres out of town.

He was now doing well over ninety miles an hour on his fast runs when average traffic was lucky to hit thirty-five. Most motorists had no idea he was coming from behind until a shattering blat from the exhaust pipe woke them up in time to see Bert's backside flash past and disappear up the road. Head on traffic had even less time. A small dot would appear in the distance and by the time they had begun to wonder what it was it had passed them by. Few would have had time to register concern. If there were complaints Bert never heard them.

For some reason Bert resolutely eschewed the easiest modification he might have made to achieve higher power – boring and stroking the engine. Although there was no advantage in terms of the classes in which he raced, he preferred to leave the capacity at 600cc – the way Indian had built it. He had also lengthened the frame by two and a half inches so that he could stretch his body out and present a lower profile to the wind. He fitted rear-set foot pegs and controls, so that his feet ended just forward of the rear wheel axle, and made up a set of handlebars that drooped down, putting the grips at right angles to the ground. These bars had the virtue of providing a much lower hand position while remaining attached at the normal place above the steering head. Even then they were slightly old-fashioned, harking back to the early days of American board-track racing when, with no suspension at all, riders relied on the vertical handgrip to absorb the energy of the bumps they encountered; instead of transmitting the shock directly into their bodies, their hands would simply slip down the grips. Periodically they would shift them back up again.

One way or another Bert's modifications were paying off. The engine was now making at least fifty horsepower, perhaps twice its standard output. He referred to the bike as the Munro Special, figuring there was at least as much Munro in it as there was Indian. In terms of power and speed produced he was clearly correct but he always wore his Indian-emblazoned jumper whenever he raced.

He was wearing it on 23 January 1933, the day the Southland Motorcycle Club held a big meeting on Oreti Beach. The weather was disappointing, with a bitterly cold and blustery southerly blasting in from the Antarctic. Fortunately, the threatening rain had held off and a large crowd had gathered to watch the day's racing.

Beach conditions more than made up for the wind with the surface being the best in years.

The club had decided to change the start from one end of the course to the middle, a popular innovation with the spectators, who could now easily see the start–finish line and both turns. The crowd was kept off the track by heavy ropes strung along posts driven into the sand, although this didn't deter one man from wandering on to the course to fossick for toheroas, the highly prized shellfish that can be dug up at low tide.

The premier event of the day, the Ten Miles Open Championship, had been flagged away just a few minutes before and onlookers watched horrified as the three leading motorcycles bore down on the man who was now bending over with his back to the action, ignoring all the shouted warnings. The lead rider, who was mounted on a very rapid 350cc overhead-valve Velocette, veered to the left, missing the man by centimetres at something like one hundred miles an hour. A split second later the second machine, a big 1000cc Indian, screamed past on the man's right.

Bert, who was thundering along in third place and whose vision was obscured by the two leading bikes, did not see him until the last moment. How he managed to avoid the man, who was now reeling about the beach from the shock of the first two near misses, was something spectators would talk about for some time. He seemed to almost lift the motorcycle sideways and then skate down the beach in a frightening series of full opposite-lock skids, until by some miracle he brought the machine back under control. The toheroa hunter scuttled back to the rope barrier without endangering the rest of the field which was now streaming past. Someone in the crowd gave him an almighty boot in the pants to the cheers of all who witnessed it. They then turned back to the furious action on the beach.

Bert had lost a lot of ground avoiding the stray spectator and, with his brakes being as inadequate as ever, his turn around the marker was characteristically wide. But the Indian was pulling like a train and the second lap saw him close in on the two race leaders. When the big Indian faltered (due to a nut falling off the carburettor, it was later revealed) Bert slipped into second place and held it to the end. He earned £4 4s in prize money, a useful sum.

The second race was the Four Mile Novice Handicap, which of course excluded Bert, but the following Four Mile Open Handicap saw him back on the starting line. He took second place from flag fall, with the 1000cc Indian rocketing away to grab a huge lead of some 350 yards at the end of the first lap. Bert was under pressure from a 500cc JAP-engined Cotton leading a pack of machines including a 500cc Ariel, a brace of overhead-valve Nortons, the 1000cc Harley Davidson, the Velo that had won the first race and a Sunbeam. In spite of his huge sweeping turns around the markers Bert managed to keep his place and slowly whittled down the larger Indian's lead to just twenty yards. It was crowd-pleasing stuff and when he finally crossed the line a split second behind the leader they were cheering him lustily. He happily added the £1 1s prize to his winnings and prepared for the Six Mile Open Handicap.

Just as in the previous race Bert blasted off the line in second place and held it throughout the first couple of laps. The big Indian had established a secure lead and looked like cruising to the finish when it again struck carburettor trouble. Bert pounced and took the lead with the fast 350cc Velocette pressing him hard. On the fourth lap the Velocette managed to get in front and the big Indian, which seemed to have recovered its lost power, also slipped through, opening up a 250 yard gap on Bert as he swooped around the marker. Bert had the bit between his teeth, however, and slowly reduced the gap, passing the 1000cc Indian again in the final lap and opening out his own 100 yard lead over it. Although he continued to press hard, skidding around the markers in a fashion that had the crowd gasping, there was no catching the rider on the Velocette, who went on to win both the race and the prestigious Ariel Cup. Bert was delighted with his second place anyway, and the £2 2s prize money.

The last race of the day, a Twelve Mile Open Handicap was finally won by the Sunbeam with the Velocette in second place and the

Ariel in third. Bert had felt something let go in his engine – a valve head he suspected – as he crossed the line in the previous race. He knew instantly his day was over. He stayed to watch and afterwards had a splendid time reliving events with his mates – a sausage from the barbecue wrapped in white bread and smothered in tomato sauce in one hand and a steaming cup of tea in the other. No one cared that the vicious southerly still blasted the beach, it was a great day and that was that. For Bert the racing had delivered absolute vindication. His tuning work had paid off and he was now firmly established as one of the men to beat. The Munro Special was a force to be reckoned with and so was he.

From this moment on Bert was a starter wherever the Southland Motorcycle Club staged an event, and he was often among the top finishers – when he finished. He continued to refine the Indian, replacing the original Schleber H model carburettor for a Schleber De Lux, as used on the 1924 Indian Chief. He had by now come to the conclusion that two carburettors offered no advantage over one, an opinion he would never change, despite a number of prominent tuners attempting to persuade him he was wrong. He had acquired a good supply of the De Lux carburettors and often boasted that he never paid more than ten shillings for them.

He was constantly trying new cam profiles and experimenting to find the right spring strength to keep the valves behaving without tearing off their heads. It remained a difficult balance to achieve even when he eventually began to wind his own springs, and many races were lost with decapitated valves. He did not care. More than anything else in the world he loved to be in the company of men who loved racing motorcycles. Each setback was just another invitation to lose himself in the wonders of the challenge.

He also returned to the Triumph twin lurking under his bench. He reckoned the excessive vibration of the engine was caused by the fact that its two pistons pounded up and down together. If they followed one another instead, he reasoned, much of the vibration would be cancelled out. It also followed that the resulting, smoother engine would recover lost power, which could then be used for its proper purpose – propelling him around a racetrack at higher speeds.

Bert stripped down the engine and secured the crankshaft in his big vice. He then carefully measured and marked centre points all the way around the edge face of the centre flywheel, finally joining the points with a chalk line before taking up a large hacksaw. After trying the blade with his thumb he began to cut, eyes half-closed in concentration as he guided it with both hands and the utmost care. It took him almost a week of late nights to painstakingly slice the flywheel down the middle and another evening to carefully cut the camshaft in half with a precisely vertical cut. After work the following day, armed with the four pieces, he sought out his friend Irving Hayes.

Irving was one of the large circle of friends who supported Bert's projects one way or another, and he was one of the town's most successful businessmen. In fact, these supporters, who invariably possessed resources Bert lacked, quite often belonged to an elevated stratum of society Bert did not otherwise aspire to. This was true of Irving, whose father Ernest had established a successful engineering company in the middle of the previous century. Located in Oturehua, an isolated rural spot halfway between Alexandra and the east coast highway on the famous pioneering road known as the Pig Route, the complex of factory, farm and domestic buildings had been powered by a large waterwheel and an equally impressive windmill. The company had made its name manufacturing smaller windmills, used mostly to pump water, and a superior fence strainer, which was exported successfully all over Australasia.

Although the old works was still operating, the company's focus had shifted to a large hardware business in Invercargill and an associated light-engineering company. It was the equipment owned by the engineering company, to be found in a big shed behind the Hayes's formidable home, that drew Bert to Irving that day. In particular he wanted to use the big old lathe sitting in a corner, even though he knew its best days had been used up manufacturing munitions during the war. Irving, as always, was pleased to oblige. A gentle and refined man, Irving liked Bert's straightforward practicality and enjoyed his stream of informed and always amusing chatter. It did not hurt that Irving was also mad about racing cars and motorcycles, but he also appreciated the fact that Bert always offered to pay for the use of his machinery, even if he never accepted. In all honesty it probably never occurred to Bert that he would, either, but the offer was made and that was the main thing.

Irving helped Bert set up the crankcase halves in the lathe so he could machine his hacksaw cuts dead flat. Earlier that day Bert had paid a visit to his friends at Johnson Engineering with a piece of axle steel that they had heated in the forge before pounding it flat under their powerful air hammer. This flat disc would become the packer to replace the metal lost in the machining when the time came to weld everything back together.

After completing most of the machining at Irving's factory Bert was able to finish the finer work on his small Myford lathe at home in the shed. He then took all his bits and pieces to yet another engineering business in town and had the two halves of the flywheel and the spacer welded together, with the crank journals now at forty-five degrees to one another. During the process the crank somehow got out of alignment, necessitating a lot of heating and tweaking to make it run true. Finally it did. After welding the two halves of the camshaft together in much the same way Bert welded up the crankshaft. He then modified the magneto cam ring for the new set up and reassembled the engine. It ran sweetly with very little vibration and sounded just like a V-twin, which effectively it had become.

Somewhere he had acquired another engine-less Scout frame, to which he now fitted the Triumph engine and rode out to Ryal Bush Straight. The engine ran with a satisfying smoothness that the original had never possessed and Bert became quite excited about the racing potential of his new machine. Sadly, the flat-out runs on the straight showed that, superior as the engine was in its power delivery, he had not tapped any extra reserves. The experiment had failed, the machine was soon reduced once more to a pile of parts and the Triumph engine quietly disappeared, soon forgotten. On the few occasions the subject did come up Bert would laugh about it as much as he did when discussing his successes. But he was very quickly on to the next project.

After a couple of years' racing it was clear the Scout needed longer legs if he was to win races against the constantly evolving competition. The only way he could envisage achieving that was to convert it to an overhead-valve set up. So far all his tuning efforts had involved a great deal of work with relatively basic machining, but this new goal would take him into the complex and even arcane discipline of metal casting. This represented a step up to a much higher level of effort and commitment in the pursuit of speed that would increasingly dominate his life from now on. In many ways, it marked the true beginning of his life's work.

CHAPTER TEN
THE HOME FRONT

Life in the Munro household was largely a harmonious affair. If Beryl was unhappy as a result of Bert's dalliances she did not let it show, either within her family or to the outside world. At home Bert remained a gentle and supportive husband and there was such genuine affection between the couple that their children were happy and carefree, growing up in a home that they experienced as stable and secure.

Although Bert spent a great deal of time in his shed working on his various motorcycles he made a point of being at home when his presence was most appreciated. Most evenings, as Beryl prepared the family dinner, Bert took his ease in a comfortable old chair next to the warm coal range in the kitchen and read the newspaper from front to back, offering the occasional commentary on the stories that most engaged him. His most frequent comment on political squabbles was to invoke the politicians involved to 'Fight you blighters, fight. We hate peace!'

After dinner was often a magic time, when the girls were allowed to join their father in the shed, most enchanting when Bert had left long curled shavings of metal under the lathe. The longest were carefully picked up and carried back to the house, to be displaced only when a longer piece was found.

His three girls, now aged between six and ten, loved hearing him talk with his customary animation and zeal. He in turn encouraged them to tell him their stories from the day. There was never any smacking in the Munro household, or even raised voices, but neither was there much in the way of indulgence. The children had daily chores and they performed them without complaint. There was wood to chop, vegetables to be harvested from the garden and dishes to be done. The floors, benches, kitchen table, front step and back step had to be regularly scrubbed with sandsoap, and once scrubbed rinsed with clean water until gleaming.

The big quarter-acre vegetable garden was a real family effort. Bert had contrived a rotary hoe of his own design, using an old motorcycle engine of uncertain provenance, and he turned the ground until he had achieved a fine tilth, which he then protected behind a rabbit-proof fence.

He had by then acquired an old Model T Roadster with a dickie seat, which he used about the property as a tractor. It boasted striped velvet seats, the height of luxury as far as the Munro family were concerned. The children helped strip pea sticks from the manuka, which grew in a scrap of regenerating bush on the farm, and loaded the Ford with a great pile of them, tying bundles onto the running boards. Peas were always on the menu during the season and vegetables generally formed a substantial part of their diet.

As soon as his eldest daughter June turned ten, Bert taught her to shoot with his old .22 rifle. She would become the first rabbit hunter among his children and the rest would follow.

There were just two hills in the district, one in town with a water tower on top of it, and the other on the Munro property. A stand of macrocarpa trees grew on its gentle knoll and the girls each chose one as their own. They learned to climb to the very tops, from where they could see the distant water tower, and would contentedly chew on sweet chalmolia, cut from the field where it was grown for stock food. Simple hideaways were constructed in other places – the bottom of a dry irrigation ditch or the top of a hedgerow.

There was a clear creek swarming with koura, the native fresh-water crayfish. The girls would bait a piece of string with rabbit meat and simply pull up the creatures, which refused to let go once they had a hold. All the Munro family prized this delicacy and would happily sit around a pot of boiling water, eating several pounds of delicious tail meat at a sitting.

Often toil and pleasure became one and they were never more excited than the times Bert took them to blow up tree stumps. Nearby Seawood Bush had once been a magnificent stand of huge totara trees but now all that remained were the massive stumps. Bert would take the Model T with a trailer hitched behind, with the girls crammed into the dickie seat as an extra treat. Beside him on the passenger floor were his log gun, hand auger, heavy hammer and tin of blasting powder. They would select a stump and Bert would drill a hole in it with the auger before driving the heavy steel, hollow log gun, which had a pointed end with a hole in it for the blast, into the log. He would pour a charge of powder into the gun and screw in the end piece after arranging the fuse through a hole in the barrel. The girls would be sent to hide behind a carefully chosen log, where Bert would join them after lighting the fuse. The blast would tear the stump to pieces, showering the area with chunks of flying wood. The crew would be kept busy for several hours chopping up the bigger pieces to fit them in the trailer and collecting the scattered chips for the stove.

Grandparents Lilly and William took a lively interest in their grandchildren and could be relied on for small treats. William sold milk in pails directly to the public, dropping the pennies and six-pences he was paid into a little purse he always carried in a waistcoat pocket, opposite the fob watch he would extract by pulling with a flourish on its gold chain. On birthdays his grandchildren would be invited to take a sixpence, often while riding beside him on the horse-drawn mower. The possession of a shining silver sixpence made them feel as rich as the King whose portrait adorned it. Later there would be ginger cake with icing, the most delicious food in the world.

There were entertainments beyond the home. Regular concerts by the local temperance society, the Band Of Hope as it was known, provided surprisingly lively evenings in the local hall, featuring musical and theatrical turns by local talents, some of whom were funny enough to reduce the hall to helpless, hysterical laughter. And there were musical evenings with family, often on Sundays, when the family would visit relations or have them visit. A leg of hogget would be placed in the oven at eight in the morning and the stove would be kept going so it could cook slowly all day.

After dinner Beryl played the piano and as the girls became proficient at their chosen instruments they joined in. June learned the piano, Margaret the steel guitar and Gwen the violin. Lessons were a luxury and they were not wasted. The girls eventually became good enough to lead the extended family singalongs in popular standards such as 'The Black and White Rag', 'Roll Out the Barrel' and 'Lily Marlene'.

In 1935 Beryl gave birth to a son, John. He was a sturdy little fellow and lucky enough to have three doting older sisters the equal of any big brother when it came to introducing him to the adventures country kids find to amuse themselves. It was, in nearly every respect, a happy and well-adjusted family to grow up in. If there were problems between their mother and father the children remained blissfully unaware, for the moment anyway.

Now that he had decided to make his own overhead valve heads for the Scout, Bert determined to learn all he could about casting complex shapes in metal. He spoke to numerous foundry men and became acquainted with the basics of making the patterns and core boxes that he would need to make the heads he had in mind. The design side of the exercise was relatively simple. He had chosen to more or less copy the 350cc AJS cylinder heads from the machines he had so admired in the twenties. Indeed, he had good reason to admire them still, as only months before a 350 AJS of much the same design had beaten him on the beach. He was fortunate to have a friend with a 1924 model which he was able to measure and otherwise familiarise himself afresh with the design. He had already resolved to simplify his task by using AJS rockers, so it was vital that his copy be precise.

One of the beauties of the AJS design was that the aluminium rockers were fully exposed and were located on steel brackets that were simply screwed onto both sides of the heads. He now had to settle on the method by which the AJS heads were held down. The AJS design featured a stirrup that ran from the crankcase, up the cylinder, across the head and back down the other side. The stirrup was tensioned by two long bolts that pulled it down and Bert decided sensibly in favour of the more conventional method of sandwiching the barrels between the head and the crankcase with four studs.

Casting something as complex as a cylinder head was ambitious for a number of reasons but Bert was cheerfully undeterred and forged ahead. First of all the negative image of the head needed to be established in a mould full of sand. This was complicated because a wooden copy, complete with cooling fins poking out at different angles, could not simply be pulled out without destroying the desired impression. In fact, the wooden pattern had to be made in a number of pieces so that each could be extracted without destroying the desired hollow. This hollow would eventually shape the molten cast iron Bert had elected to use for his heads.

Second, the internal shape of the head needed to be established during the pour and this required two cores, one for the inlet tract and one for the exhaust port. These curved shapes were to be made in a core box, using sand held together with a bonding agent, after which they would be carefully positioned in the mould. If nothing moved during the pour a rough casting of the part would result, ready for the months of careful machining he estimated he'd need to finish it.

He further simplified his task by deciding that each head would be identical, the rear head being simply reversed. This would mean that the rear exhaust outlet would face backwards while the front head would have its exhaust outlet to the front. The two inlet ports would then face each other. The only difference between the two would be the attachment points for the rocker brackets, a minor variation that Bert could easily address on the patterns between castings.

Making the patterns and core boxes was a challenge but Bert was always handy with wood. His efforts eventually met with the approval of his foundry friends and the two items were duly produced. Now the real fun began.

Although Bert never hesitated to use someone else's equipment, he knew the machining of the heads would take many months' work. Clearly, the only place to undertake the task was at home in his shed, on a lathe that most would have dismissed as completely inadequate. Again he was completely unfazed. It didn't matter to him how long it would take. It would be finished when it was finished and, until it was, he would devote every bit of time he could to the task.

Johnny Checketts continued to turn up at the shed regularly and offer conversation and encouragement as Bert coaxed the little Myford to do duties it was never intended to perform. Setting up the lathe and the head he was working on, to enable him to machine all the areas he needed to get at, continually taxed his determination and ingenuity.

The work went on throughout 1935, every night after work and throughout the weekends. The motorcycle crowd saw little of Bert through the summer and autumn, and as winter bit he became even more of a stranger. The season was as bleak as usual in those southern latitudes and the shed became as cold as a meat chiller. But Bert beavered on, rubbing and slapping his frozen fingers to restore their circulation whenever they refused to do his bidding.

It was late spring before he was finally finished with the heads and ready to begin making new barrels and pistons for the engine. He elected to use heavy steel tubing for the barrels, machining shallow fins into the outside of the tube for cooling. These would have been entirely inadequate for a petrol engine but Bert had decided to run the machine on methanol, a fuel that burns at relatively low temperatures.

He had also decided to stay with the original bore and stroke, but the new set up also required new pistons. Once more he sought out his foundry mates and mined them for information on aluminium casting. A rumour later made the rounds that he had gone to the beach, lit a fire, melted a few old pistons in a pot and poured the molten metal into holes in the sand. The story surfaced in a number of subsequent press reports and Bert always enjoyed a quiet chuckle about them, doing nothing to dispel the story.

In fact, nothing could have been further from the truth. He made moulds for his pistons that were clever and precise, and the quality of the pistons he produced was exemplary. Johnny brought him a constant supply of old pistons from work and Bert produced new ones more or less continuously from this time on.

At last the day came when his new engine was finished. The old frame had gone through a lot of hard road and race miles and Bert was concerned it might be suffering metal fatigue. When he saw a gorse fire raging on a hill on his way home from work one afternoon he had an idea that made him to rush back to his shed at even greater speed than normal. He grabbed the stripped bike frame and threw in into the Model T's trailer, then raced back to the scene of the fire where he hauled the frame through the gorse until he was as close as he could get to the flames and the choking, yellow smoke. After laying his burden down he staggered away from the intense heat, back to the safety of the road where he climbed into the Model T and drove home.

The following afternoon, once again after work, he retrieved the frame from the now charred hillside, noting with satisfaction that the fire had completely stripped all the oil and paint from it. He had no doubt the heat of the burning gorse had been intense enough to anneal the metal, relieving any stress points that might have developed.

After a quick wash down he brushed the frame with undercoat and black paint, and re-installed the engine. The Scout was again ready to roll and Bert immediately headed for Ryal Bush Straight. Once again he was disappointed. After a year of hard and exacting toil his machine was no faster than it had been. If anything it was just a smidgen slower, a terribly unsatisfactory result.

That evening Johnny called by and found Bert staring at the Indian, which was parked up on the special bench. Bert shook his head. 'The only way it could go any slower would be if I put a reverse gear in it!'

He leaned down and stared hard at the engine. 'I'm trying to imagine I'm a little bit of gas swirling around in there. Trying to think what might make me go bang. Because right now all I'm doing is fizzing a bit.'

He straightened up. 'I'll start by moving the plugs from the sides right up to the top. I reckon they need to be king of the mountain. Then I'll have a look at the cam. I reckon that needs to be a bit steeper on opening and I suppose that'll mean heavier valve springs.'

He grinned and motioned to the little woodstove, which had a healthy blaze in its belly. 'If you want to make yourself useful you can make the tea. I've got to get on with it.'

The next two years were a time of experimentation and gradual improvements. Just as Bert had suspected, moving the plugs again resulted in better combustion and an increase in power. His trials with cam shapes also slowly yielded results as his valve springs evolved. He had become friends with a trucking contractor named Duncan Meikle who knew something about balancing engines and who shared Bert's passion for tuning. Duncan was a sharp-faced individual who wore glasses with lenses so thick his eyes seemed to swim around behind them like oysters. Examining a part for flaws he would screw up his face in total concentration, holding the object within range of his eyesight, a habit that had left his face permanently lined and set in a somewhat sour expression. His sense of humour was also a little on the sour side – but it was robust and he enjoyed Bert's often raucous behaviour, even if his expression seemed to suggest the opposite.

His contracting business was small but profitable; he made a point of recovering every penny he was owed on every job. He loved racing motorcycles almost as much as he enjoyed hotting them up, and being a crusty bachelor his time was his own. He and Bert were made for each other and they quickly became friends.

By 1936 Bert was confident he had made sufficient progress to return to racing and he began to turn up again at Southland Motorcycle Club meetings. The Indian was certainly delivering more power but, as always, he refused to even consider improving his brakes to cope with the increase in speed. He remained adamant that all his efforts be directed at going faster, not slowing down. The net result was that he became a danger to other riders, a danger compounded by his riding style. Although he had phenomenal skill when it came to controlling his machine, he often displayed a lack of judgement. It was as if when racing he suspended all his normal rules of behaviour, becoming so erratic and aggressive that it was inevitable he would cause a huge accident. That accident finally happened at Oreti Beach.

Bert was riding hard, trying to make up for a slow start, but he was having trouble closing on the leading rider, a young local named Hewitt Currie. Hew, as his friends called him, was a rising star and his BSA was more than a match for Bert's Indian. But there was no way Bert was going to concede the win. As they approached the second turn during the opening lap he kept the throttle wide open. Hew's BSA had good brakes and he slowed considerably for the turn. Bert speared straight into him. Even if the Indian had been equipped with a decent front brake instead of its little fifteen-centimetre affair, Bert was so late applying it that everyone agreed the accident was inevitable.

The impact was vicious. Machines and riders were sent cart-wheeling down the beach at high speed. When they came to rest Hew was lying completely motionless on the sand, bleeding profusely from a number of serious wounds, various limbs at unnatural angles. Hew's mother, a formidably stout lady, was assisted into the ambulance as it took off for the accident site, only to faint when it arrived and she saw her badly injured son. Mother and son were loaded onto stretchers, a considerable challenge when it came to poor Mrs Currie, and into the ambulance. The ambulance men then turned their attention to Bert.

They found him on his hands and knees looking for his gold teeth, some of which had been knocked out in the accident. He was not making a great deal of sense and they were concerned to see his crash helmet had been split down the middle, obviously the result of a substantial blow. He was only persuaded to get in the ambulance when his brother Charlie, who had come to watch the racing, took over the search.

Hew Currie took a long time to recover but did not harbour any animosity toward Bert. He later told him that he had found traces of Bert's crash helmet on the sump of his bike. Obviously the tumbling machine had landed on top of Bert's head, splitting his crash helmet and knocking him senseless.

For some reason Bert never saw the accident as being his fault and complained bitterly on a number of occasions about the loss of his teeth, which he had prized greatly. His teeth remained a problem and he finally went to a dentist and had him remove the lot, all without anaesthetic. He had a miserable and agonising few days sitting in his chair by the stove with his gums bleeding profusely, unable to eat and wracked by pain. Hew made a full recovery and continued to race motorcycles, winning the New Zealand Grand Prix in 1936.

The Indian was soon straightened out and Bert, now equipped with a gleaming set of false teeth, was quickly back in the saddle, racing with his usual lack of restraint. There was, however, a certain level of trepidation associated with his appearances. One new rider was warned to watch out for him as he was always either flat out or falling off. The problem, the other rider said, was knowing which of the two Bert was doing at any given moment.

With work and racing to occupy him, life was full, but Bert continued to find the time for family adventures. He liked nothing better than to throw them in the car and motor off to Oreti Beach to hunt for toheroas. But when he decided to sell the Model T, to fund further motorcycle purchases, he had to find other ways of running the family around. He often took his daughters to school, perching two carefully on the tank of the Triumph and one behind, but there was no way it would take six people.

A relative who had a beach house (or crib as they were known locally) at Riverton had offered Bert the use of it. He decided the only way to get the family there was to build a trailer that could be towed behind the bike. He did it and off they went, four little kids sitting in the trailer and Beryl perched on the seat behind Bert. At first all went well. As Bert became used to the trailer he gradually increased speed. Sadly, the inevitable happened. Sweeping around a bend Bert encountered a deep pile of loose gravel. The trailer overturned and all four children spilled out onto the road. They all suffered minor grazes and were understandably upset. But Bert soon cheered them up and they set off once more. Again Bert gradually increased speed and again the trailer overturned, the children suffering another lot of bruises and grazes. This time they took longer to accept their father's reassurances but they were now over half-way to their destination and there was little choice but to carry on.

The rest of the journey passed uneventfully and the family spent a very happy week frolicking in the surf and relaxing. To everyone's relief the return trip was slow but steady with no spillages. In time the children became quite used to the trailer, although it was never popular. Now that Bert knew its limits there were no further accidents.

Yet another relative had a holiday place at Lake Waituna, near Invercargill. The lagoon had a narrow finger connecting it to the sea and it was actually salt water and tidal. A beautiful, wild place, many miles off the beaten track, the only access to the shack was by dinghy, and the dinghy had seen better days. Bert found the hidden oars and dragged the old boat into the water where it promptly began to fill with water. Bailing devices were found for everyone except Bert who, naturally, was going to row.

He did a careful sweep along the shallows to determine if the family could bail the water out faster than it came in. Satisfied they could, he set off. It was a deceptively long way across the lake and it became quite rough in the middle. The children began to tire but Bert kept them at it, and eventually they made it. By now they were all cold and wet but a solid lock thwarted any immediate hopes of shelter, as Bert had no key. In fact, the place was a fairly crude maimai, offering very basic accommodation for duck hunters. Like many such edifices, the chimney was a large corrugated iron structure and Bert decided that this would provide their entrance.

He gathered flax leaves and plaited a serviceable rope, which he then tied around June's waist. Using an old fish-cleaning table he and June clambered onto the roof and made their way along the ridge to the chimney. Once poised over the dark, gaping hole Bert lifted his daughter and gently lowered her down while Margaret wailed in protest from below, convinced she would never see her sister again. But sure enough the door opened to reveal her sibling covered in soot but otherwise no worse for wear, and the family was soon snug and warm in front of a roaring fire. They spent many happy days catching cod before bailing their way across the lake again and heading home.

Bert's spontaneous embrace of anything that might be fun saw the family enjoy many such adventures. If heavy rain had created pools in the paddocks he was the first to encourage his children to swim in them. During a period of high wind he built a cart with a sail and they went scooting around the fields. After a rare and memorable snowfall in 1937, when over 100 millimetres fell throughout the region, Bert whipped together a toboggan. He then took the children for wild rides on it, towing it behind the Triumph after wrapping chains around the rear wheel. Still, no one particularly mourned the passing of the bike trailer when Bert finally bought another car, a sturdy 1929 Dodge Brothers Six. Once again the family was able to travel in style and comfort, with a roof over their heads and doors that held them in securely.

One of the realities of extracting ever-increasing power from an old machine is that previously serviceable parts begin to fail. All Bert could do was fix problems as they came up, strengthening components to ensure their surival. He dealt with endless problems in this way, with varying degrees of success. But he still experienced repeated failures due to his stubborn avoidance of finding lasting solutions for certain problems. One of these was the lubrication system on the Indian.

The Scout had been originally equipped with a 'total loss' oil system that had been perfectly adequate for a relaxed touring machine. Oil was delivered from a tank within the petrol tank by a mechanical oiler that fed a metered amount regularly to splash the bearings, before finally being burned in the cylinder. Many early racers mounted an auxiliary oil pump on top of the tank so they could administer extra squirts when running at higher revs, and the standard oiler could also be modified to deliver a greater flow. Bert did both of these things, but at high revs the flywheels spun the oil away from the big-end bearings where it was needed. In the end, feeding extra oil into the engine simply resulted in the plugs becoming fouled while the bearings were starved of lubrication.

The big-end roller cage with which the engine had been originally fitted broke up regularly until Bert solved that by crowding the rollers without a cage. This did not, however, solve the lubrication problems and the rollers were often burnt blue from the heat, necessitating yet another bottom-end rebuild.

Although Johnny Checketts and Duncan Meikle both pointed out that it would be a relatively simple matter to follow modern practice and make a new mainshaft and crankpin with suitable oil ways, at least compared with making all new overhead valve cylinder heads, Bert would hear none of it. This was curious. On the face of it the task was not that onerous. To drill an oil way through a new mainshaft, have it meet up with another drilled up the flywheel, then to have that meet up with a hole drilled through the crankpin to deliver oil to the point it was needed, seemed relatively simple. Oil could have then been fed in from the end of the line under pressure from a pump, just as it was in most motorcycles at the time. However, for years Bert insisted the task was too difficult and so suffered frequent bottom-end failures.

The Indian's connecting rods were also failing regularly. Their design was peculiar to Indian and Harley Davidson, known as the 'knife and fork' arrangement, and allowed both rods to share the same crankpin, because one was forked at the big-end eye and the other straight one fitted within it. This in turn allowed the two cylinders to be in line rather than offset and reduced vibration caused by the rocking motion of two rods operating on different parts of the crankshaft. But the system had its own problems, primarily a certain inherent weakness with the forked conrod. As with the rest of the engine the system had worked fine on a low revving 1920 tourer, but the forked rods now began to split at the bottom.

Indian had, in fact, produced high-performance rods for racing and after yet another blow-up Duncan Meikle suggested Bert try to obtain a pair from the factory. This only got Bert thinking about making them himself. Johnny Checketts supplied a couple of broken Ford truck axles, which offered suitable high-grade steel but which turned out to be too thin for Bert to cut the profiles he needed. So he took them to his old friends at Checketts, the engineering firm owned by one of Johnny's uncles, where they were heated in the forge and belted to the required thickness and width under the massive steam hammer. Bert then took his two pieces of steel to Melhop Engineering and had his friends there cut them into rough dog-bone shapes. Then it was back to the Myford where he fitted them one at a time into a special jig on the cross slide. Using an end mill on the chuck he could use the power feed to machine away at the rod until he had the required shape. He next fitted a drill bit into the chuck and drilled out guides in the big and little ends before replacing the drill with a boring bar to open them out to the required size. In this way he kept the holes exactly parallel and at right angles to the rod. From the first he always machined the little ends to take twenty-millimetre diameter Ford gudgeon pins, as he believed them to be made of superior steel. They were one of the very few items he ever bought new.

Next he attacked the new rods with files, and bits of files he broke specially for the purpose, to remove all machine marks, finally using up metres of emery ribbon polishing the metal to a gleaming, flawless finish. Finally, he returned to Melhops where he had the rods heat-treated. It was a long, tedious business that would have been significantly reduced had Bert enjoyed the luxury of a decent lathe, a finishing machine and a vertical mill. But rather than waste time complaining about it, he just got on with the job.

He would make many sets of rods in this way, testing each by placing it in his vice, inserting a bar through the little end and giving it a good twist. Occasionally they broke, and his son John never forgot the way his father simply removed the broken end from the vice and dropped the two pieces into the old drum he kept for such rubbish.

'Better in the vice than in the engine, eh John! We'd rather find out it's a dud right now than later on, wouldn't we?' Picking up another blank, he paused for just a moment to contemplate the days and nights of painstaking work that lay ahead, just to return to the point he had been a few moments before. 'Let's hope this one turns out a bit better!'

From the beginning, motorcycle racing in New Zealand had been a dispersed effort by a large number of regional clubs with little cooperation between them. There had never been a national meeting as such, but that changed in 1936 when the first New Zealand Motorcycle Grand Prix was staged on the Cust Circuit in North Canterbury, a few kilometres out of Christchurch. It was an interesting and challenging course with an entirely gravel surface, bound to a degree by fine silt, with a number of steep descents featuring sharp bends. Nine-and-a-half kilometres around, the rectangular circuit also included a number of bridges that were, as a result of successive applications of new gravel, now below the level of the road, giving a bump at the end sufficient to throw motorcycles into the air. The total length of the race was set at a punishing 150 miles and the first event, held at Easter, was an immediate success, with many volunteers turning up to sweep the circuit and spray hundreds of litres of old engine oil to suppress the dust.

Bert knew the Indian was unsuitable for the event, but two years later he had a machine that would work. Although the 500cc MSS Velocette he had bought was a touring machine (the company's KTT machines being their specialised race models), it was still a thoroughly capable and competitive motorcycle.

Velocette was an English company that had produced its first motorcycle in 1905. One of the two founding partners, a German who had changed his name to the very English sounding John Goodman, soon took control of the company and, in association with his two sons, continued to produce advanced and highly innovative motorcycles. The company made four-stroke and two-stroke models at various times and enjoyed competitive success in trials and road racing, winning the Junior TT by ten minutes in 1926. In 1933 the company produced a new overhead-valve, high camshaft 248cc model called the MOV, the beginning of the famous M series.

The 350cc MAC model soon followed and in 1935 the 500cc MSS, the machine Bert now owned. Buying such a prestigious machine when it was just a few years old must have taxed Bert's finances and no doubt was the cause of some added tension at home. But he now had a bike with good power and handling, including modern brakes. He wasted no time in taking the machine to Oreti Beach where he lined up alongside his old friend Percy Shave on a Norton. Bert was supremely confident he would be unbeatable.

Prior to the race Percy and Bert had observed an Otago rider named Lyders arrive on one of the new 500cc Excelsior Manxmen and quietly go about removing his muffler. They decided for some reason that he was no threat. They were quite mistaken. The two friends were flying along together through the final mile of the

race, with Bert slowly edging ahead, when Lyders rode alongside
and flashed them a big smile before engaging top gear and riding
away to win. Bert was appalled by his second place and left the
beach determined to pep up the Velocette, a task made easier since
Tappers were agents for the marque.

By Easter 1938 Bert was ready. He strapped his well-prepared
machine onto the Dodge's passenger-side running board and
headed to Christchurch, more than 500 kilometres north, where a
contact he'd made had offered him lodgings during the grand prix.
Unfortunately he could remember neither the man's street number
nor his name, having met him only briefly at a race meeting down
south, but he was not overly concerned. Finding the right street
Bert simply took the Velocette off the running board, kicked it over
and delivered a few good blasts through the open pipe into the silent
night of the sleeping suburb. The strategy worked and he was soon
comfortably installed in a spare room, completely unconcerned that
he had woken the entire neighbourhood to get there.

The race was held on Easter Monday and from the beginning
the pace was terrific. Bert Rossnan from Dunedin took an early lead
on a Norton International and held it for fifteen laps, averaging 70
miles an hour. When his machine failed, a number of riders held the
lead briefly until the last lap when many front-runners hit trouble.
One ran out of petrol, one had his front forks collapse and another
suffered a broken rocker in his engine. This let Bob Stewart from
Dunedin through to win on his Rudge, with Bert Munro from
Invercargill in a fine second place.

Bert had averaged sixty-three miles an hour for just under two
and a half hours on a twisty, narrow, metal road, a remarkable
achievement. He had also proven himself a capable road racer and
secured a place in the history books. If this surprised some people,
it didn't those who knew him best. They were well aware that Bert
had spent years belting around twisty, narrow, metal roads. They
knew that he always rode like that. He took home £15 in prize
money, about a month's wages.

Bert would return to Cust in 1939, only to retire the Velocette with a blown piston on the first lap, and again in 1940 when he once more experienced piston trouble with his 500cc Tiger 100 Twin. In that year he set a record on the also narrow, twisty, metal road running up to the signal station at Bluff, but it was clear that his path now lay in a different direction. Speed, pure and simple, was his objective. There would still be racing, but more and more it was the adrenalin rush of pushing his machine as fast as it could go that most attracted Bert.

Norman Hayes, Irving's twelve-year-old son, finally met his dad's friend at Oreti Beach when Bert raced against the fastest car at a mixed car–motorcycle meeting. The Bert he met was more than a racer; he was a speed king.

The final event of the afternoon was basically a two-mile dash up and down the beach, and the car, a highly modified 1934 Ford V8, was given a good handicap. Norman watched it all but disappear before Bert was finally flagged off, figuring there was no way the bike would ever catch up. Sure enough, the car was well on the way back before a tiny dot could be seen returning down the beach. Astonishingly, the motorcycle closed the gap and finally streaked across the line at well over 100 miles an hour, a whisker in front of the car.

Bert was given a hero's reception, an admiring crowd gathering around him and his amazing Indian. One small boy, clearly overawed, plucked up the courage to ask a question. 'Mr Munro, what would happen if you opened our mouth when you were going so fast?' Bert considered the question gravely for a moment before giving an answer that reduced the crowd to hooting, roaring laughter. 'Why I suppose it would blow a hole in the back of my trousers.'

Bert continued to develop the Indian. In a quest for greater high-speed stability he changed the front suspension from the leaf-spring set up to a coil spring type from a Prince. On 29 April 1939 he attempted to break the New Zealand land speed record at a trial hosted by the Canterbury Auto Cycle Club. The club had set up a properly surveyed course, with electronic timing equipment, at the Alyesbury Straight, a ruler-straight piece of tarmac road running across the dead flat Canterbury Plains about thirty-eight miles out of Christchurch. Although the straight was a part of the main road linking Canterbury to the West Coast it was quite narrow. Its slight undulations would become quite marked hollows and hillocks at the speeds Bert was hoping to achieve.

It was bitterly cold and the small crowd of riders, helpers and spectators were all stamping their feet and slapping their arms to keep warm. The first bike away was a little 250cc Rudge, which managed a respectable two-way average of 77 miles an hour. Next a 350cc Velocette Mk7 KTT set an average just a shade under 100 miles an hour to set a new class record, before five riders set times over 100 miles an hour in the 500cc class. One of them, a TT Replica OK Supreme established a new record at 115.38 miles an hour, a result that mightily impressed those who gathered around the rider to offer their congratulations.

In the meantime Duncan Meikle, wearing a blue-and-white striped butchers apron, had been carefully checking valve clearances and ignition timing on the spindly red Indian while Bert stood quietly nearby, pensive and withdrawn. When it was time for the open-class attempt Bert was the only contender and a hush fell over the crowd as he fastened his helmet and mounted the machine. Maurice Wear, the man who had earlier set the record on the Velocette, recorded his impressions in a letter to George Begg.

Two strong pushers went into action and at a good pace the engine lit up. The Indian flew past the onlookers at the sides of the road with a flat cackle from its stubby exhausts, a haze of smoke and a smell of God knows what! The crowd surged into the middle of the road and watched Bert's backside and a very narrow tyre recede as he changed into top gear and gave it the lot, disappearing from sight in a matter of moments.

It was quite weird. One moment he was there and the next, with very little noise or drama, he was just a dot in the distance – gone.

We all looked at each other and very little was said until someone remarked, 'Shite, it can get off the mark!'

Alas it was not to be Bert's day. Something let go in the engine and he and Duncan quietly loaded up the machine to drive the 500 kilometres home.

On 27 January 1940 they were back and this time nothing broke in the engine. Bert went through the traps at 126.8 miles an hour on his run up the course and returned at 114.84 miles an hour to set a new national land speed record with an average of 120.8 miles an hour. It was now official. He was the fastest man in the country.

CHAPTER ELEVEN
FREEDOM

With another war in Europe and the rapid advance of the Japanese into the Pacific, New Zealand buckled down to a further long period of austerity. Some racing events, like the speed trials in January 1940, went ahead, but they were more like a final fling for the young men who would soon be shipped off to fight. Johnny Checketts had applied for the air force and after a year's delay he was finally sent off to join the RAF, later to excel as a fighter pilot. By now Bert was forty years old. Not wanted by the armed forces, he continued life much as he always had.

Given the outbreak of hostilities he decided to retrieve his cannon, which was still languishing at the old farm. He found it much as he had left it, apart from its wheels and the solitary shell having gone missing. He soon had a new projectile turned up on the lathe and the whole family gathered one afternoon to watch him fire it. Bert poured in the blasting powder, inserted the shell and a wick and then leaned it up against a fence so that the barrel was almost vertical. With Beryl and the children safely hidden behind a large stump he lit the fuse and joined them. The detonation was satisfyingly loud and the violence of the explosion drove the breech of the barrel some way into the soft ground.

Bert was finally satisfied with the performance of the cannon and the children had been entertained and impressed. But Margaret, who had recently started to take John rabbit shooting with her, often straying onto neighbouring properties in search of prey, soon after came across a recently deceased cow emitting steam from a large hole in its back. Of course, there was no proof that Bert's cannon had been responsible for the unfortunate beast's demise, but there was no other obvious explanation.

Although there was no motorcycle racing, Bert still had the Triumph Speed Twin that Tappers had supplied him, and he was still expected to spend a lot of time on the road. There was just one fly in the ointment – petrol for any purpose had become difficult to buy. With a total allowance of only sixty gallons a month Bert often cut it fine. Early one evening he became anxious about the amount in his tank as he cruised along beside the deep, emerald green Molineux River. He'd been 300 kilometres from home that day, deep in the wilds of Otago at Middlemarch, and he was belting back towards Balclutha on a gravel road to find petrol and the start of the sealed highway home. He eventually got to the gas station at Balclutha at 5.55 p.m., only to find a queue of waiting cars.

'What's going on Bill?' he called out to his friend, the proprietor. The garage man shook his head as he manned the sole pump in the place. 'The Japs have bombed Pearl Harbor! I can't serve anymore petrol after six. New rules.'

Normally Bert would have stayed at the Hotel Clutha for the night, but instead he filled his tank, topped up another can that he carried, and headed back to Invercargill, a 144-kilometre trip in the dark. By midnight he had half-finished building a producer-gas carburettor for the Triumph. Two weeks later he was running on coal.

Bert was already familiar with the technology of producer gas – a by-product of burning char, a partially combusted form of coal that had been stripped of tar and solvents. Char was cheap and supplies in the South Island were plentiful. Each vehicle equipped with a gas producer also had a cyclone, a device designed to strip the larger particles from the gas before it passed through an air cleaner. The air cleaner took care of the finer particles and then the gas flowed through a throttle arrangement on its way to the carburettor. It was a simple enough technology but there were several problems associated with its use.

The first was that producer gas could only supply at best two-thirds of the power an engine would normally deliver running on petrol. With a general open road speed restriction of forty miles an hour, introduced as a war economy measure, this was not such a problem. What was a problem was the fact that gas producers were large, heavy, ugly appendages that bolted onto the side or the front of the vehicle and were awkward and inconvenient to run. Before any journey the firebox had to be lit and coaxed up to operating temperature, after which the driver could expect sixty-five kilometres of motoring at the most, before the clinker formed by the burnt char had to be raked out and new char added.

Bert addressed many of these problems when he designed and built his own gas producer, initially for his car. It was, to begin with, a uniquely compact unit that he was able to mount on the back bumper of the 1939 Ford Deluxe V8 Sedan he now drove. Most gas producers weighed up to 370 kilograms but his weighed just 60. All other components were out of sight, with pipes running under the car and filters located under the bonnet. To obviate the need for frequent de-clinkering stops he engineered a steel poker motivated by a vacuum diaphragm. At the flick of a switch mounted on the steering wheel the poker broke up the clinker while on the move. The system worked well, although the rod would sometimes become caught, its end would melt off and the whole thing would need to be replaced.

Bert made many trips in the car and once took the family to Christchurch, a very special treat, for a total cost of just six shillings but averaging the legal speed limit. He took great pride in the fact that cars fitted with commercially built gas producers needed low gear to get up Balclutha Hill on the way to Port Chalmers whereas he could whoop up in top gear at forty miles an hour.

His first attempt at installation had almost ended in disaster, however, when he accidentally crimped and split a brake line while fitting the main gas pipe under the car. Driving into town he encountered a twelve-tonne tram running up the main street. He later said he had no idea how he missed the thing, but he did, and from that moment on took particular care whenever messing around under a car. He had developed a morbid fear of traffic accidents, though most people who drove with him still preferred not to repeat the experience.

Driving with Bert was uncomfortable at best. Stuck behind slow or stationary traffic he would leave his hand on the horn until the situation was resolved, simply carrying on his conversation at greater volume. On the move he would spend most of the time looking at the person he was talking to, which could be particularly unnerving if they happened to be sitting in the back. All who knew him well agreed that he was as great a menace on the road in a car as he was on a bike on a racetrack.

Yet many people admired his gas producers and he sold them regularly for the not inconsiderable sum of £50, building a lighter and improved version for himself each time. His new design for the Triumph was even more compact. He mounted the gas producer and a supply of char on one side of the back wheel like a pannier bag, with a second opposite it containing the cyclone and filters. To cool the gas he ran a pipe backwards and forwards under the engine. The system worked very well and Bert did many miles, at about fifty-five miles an hour, for very little cost.

Part of the system was a gas valve that regulated the speed. If there was one big disadvantage it was that Bert had to take his hand off the handlebars to slow down or speed up. He was doing just that one afternoon, travelling at his usual fifty-five miles an hour, when he hit a deep drift of gravel, crashed heavily and was knocked unconscious as the Triumph cartwheeled down a bank. Luckily he was seen and help was soon on the way. But he was very badly concussed and so bruised that it was almost a full year before he could resume work. Only later was a brain hemorrhage diagnosed.

When he did get back to work, Tappers made him service manager, recognition of his considerable mechanical and engineering skills, despite having had no formal training. But Bert was not entirely happy with the promotion, feeling he had insufficient knowledge for the job. Alf Tapper, who had been looking for a manager for some time, assured Bert he knew enough for them.

No one in Invercargill at the time could weld aluminium or aluminium alloy, so when a week-long course in Dunedin was announced, Alf sent Bert, who also learned much about welding steel, cast iron and bronze. He would spend three years in charge of the workshop, with eight men working under him. Now recovered from his crash, however, he was itching to get back on the road. Tappers were having trouble finding salesmen and one day Bert took Alf aside to tell him he was sure he could sell a new bike to a bloke he knew out at Merino Downs, about 110 kilometres away.

'I reckon I could get there on a Triumph, sell it to him and be back here within three hours,' he told his boss. Sales were as thin on the ground as salesmen and Alf could not afford to say no. That afternoon Bert achieved his objective and never went back into the workshop. Altogether he covered 38,000 kilometres on his coal-fired Triumph before he finally left Tappers.

But 1945 was not a good year for the Munro family. Not long after the war ended in Europe their house burned to the ground, probably caused by an electrical short in the wiring. All the contents, including Bert's treasured trophies, were consumed. With no insurance there was nothing for it but to start again and build a new house.

Bert resigned from Tappers and began building with his customary single-mindedness, finishing the house in record time. When he announced that he was going to move his motorcycles into the front room, however, the long suffering Beryl decided she had had enough. She decamped for Napier, taking all the children except Margaret, who by that time was romantically attached to someone and elected to stay with her father.

For a time Bert worked on the wharves as a stevedore but in 1946 he was offered a partnership in a fledgling transport company. Mac Tullock, fresh home from the war, was desperate to find some-one who could keep his aging fleet of trucks going and was willing to share his future with anyone who could do the job. From the beginning, alas, it did not go well.

The first argument occurred because Bert did not turn up for work until three months after the agreed starting date. Tullock had been working hard to establish the business but keeping his old trucks on the road without help had been a nightmare. Farmers weren't interested in excuses for livestock not being picked up or fertiliser not being delivered and the business had nearly foundered. Things hardly improved after Bert arrived. His heart was just not in the job. After eighteen months the partnership dissolved in bitter acrimony.

When Margaret married in 1948 Bert was left entirely alone and he took the opportunity to change his life completely. From now on, he announced to all his friends, he would devote himself entirely to the Indian, keeping body and soul together only with occasional work. The farm was running smoothly, with his mother maintain-ing a dairy herd on his part of the land, assisted by her new family of adopted children. There was little need for Bert to be involved.

His old employers the Tappers offered him the chance to race a 350cc Velocette Mk 8, the latest racing machine from the factory. They had high hopes that Bert would enjoy considerable success on their beautiful racer. But when he accepted only on the condition that he be allowed to hot it up, they turned to another rider. One of their new sales reps, an experienced road racer by the name of Dick Lumsden, was happy to ride the machine just as the factory had made it. He promptly won the New Zealand 350cc championship.

If Bert was disappointed he did not show it and immedi-ately began a thorough overhaul of the Indian. The gearbox was badly worn from years of hard riding, with the sliding dog clutch arrangement on its last legs. So far it had been impossible to find a replacement part, the reason Bert had not already done something about it. By good fortune he heard that a cache of old Indian parts was available in Sydney and so took the opportunity to sail over, renew many of his old acquaintances, and secure the bits. In the end he sailed home with two sets of gears, two layshaft clusters and two sliding dogs from the 1916 Powerplus model. The Powerplus had been a more performance-oriented motorcycle than the later Scout, and first and second gears were higher, making for a closer ratio gearbox. This was the very thing Bert wanted. Once home he shortened the clusters by three eighths of an inch to fit the Scout gearbox and then turned his attention to the clutch.

Although he had fitted stronger springs in the 1930s, the clutch was now showing signs of slipping. He therefore fitted even stronger springs and a number of additional plates. With clutch pressure now a massive 590 kilograms it was more than Bert could manage with the hand lever. He fitted an auxiliary foot pedal to enable enough pressure to free the clutch. He also finally made the decision to increase the capacity of the engine for the first time by increasing the bore from the original seventy-millimetre specification to seventy-two. As he retained the original stroke of 77.8 millimetres the capacity went from 600cc to 633cc.

In 1948 the Bluff Hill Climb was reinstated on the Southland Motorcycle calendar, having been shut down for the war. Bert attended in the hope of repeating his 1940 victory. A wet and windy day cleared nicely for the event and Bert attacked his run up the hill with gusto. He was scorching up the course, looking good, when the Indian suddenly slipped away from under him and he crashed heavily, hitting a rocky outcrop with a thump that knocked him out and left huge bruises all over his body. He came to quickly and insisted on staying for the rest of the meeting, watching a new Aerial Red Hunter break his record and take the win.

It was a less than encouraging return to competition, but Bert was never one to brood and his next move was perhaps his most ambitious yet. It had long been accepted that top racing engines were twin overhead cam models, where the cams operated directly on the valves. Pushrods were seen as so much unnecessary reciprocating mass, bendy devices that introduced an element of imprecision into the equation, and ultimately stole horsepower.

Bert was well aware that his pushrod engine was behind the times in race engineering. He decided to construct a double overhead cam engine based on a single-cylinder version of the Scout motor. His intention was to find out what he needed to know with a single-cylinder set up in order to apply the technology to the V-twin engine.

With his usual confidence he started by blanking off the rear cylinder on a spare engine with an oil tank of the right diameter. Next he made a new seventy-five-millimetre piston for the front cylinder that gave a capacity of 350cc with the original stroke. He machined a new cylinder with the correct bore for the new piston and fitted one of his own heads. He then replaced the cams with a sprocket that drove a chain straight up to another sprocket located in a new aluminum casting that replaced the old rocker brackets. The housing contained a train of five gears that took the drive to the overhead cams. These gears were all Scout generator gears mounted on ball races with eccentric spindles so they could be adjusted to ensure correct meshing with one another.

Initially he oiled the system manually while he worked out if the set up was going to work. Because the angle of the cams to the valve stems was such that the stems would be subjected to a great deal of side thrust, he created very large valves with heavy valve stems, which he hoped would take the strain. Unfortunately they couldn't, and his first test run resulted in the valve stems almost immediately bending and jamming in their guides.

He had already decided, if his first plan failed, that he would insert what was called a slipper cam follower between the cams and the valve stems. The slipper was a pivoting item arranged so that the cam operated on its upper side. The slipper then pivoted and the underside operated on the top of the valve stem with a direct push, having absorbed the sideways thrust of the cam. At first he pivoted both the slippers toward the centre of the head so the cam's sideways thrust was towards the pivot on one and away from it on the other. This did not work very well and he changed the set up so that one slipper pivoted toward the centre of the head and the other pivoted away from it. He now added a system whereby the cams were lubricated by lamp wicks that dangled onto them from small pots of oil located overhead. It was crude but it certainly worked well for short bursts, which was all Bert intended the engine to endure.

He fitted the finished engine into an Indian Prince frame and ran it off and on for several years, mostly on the grass track on the farm. On the few occasions he needed to round up sheep he used the double knocker as a farm bike, which must have been one of the first in the world. Later he told friends that it worked well because the sheep soon learned that, unlike a dog, they could not outrun him on the machine.

It was a vicious thing by all accounts, with little low down torque but a brutal, arm-pulling surge from about half-throttle. By 1949 he had decided against investing further time in its development, thinking instead that he would concentrate his efforts on improving the lubrication system on the Scout. And then all work on motor-cycles came to a crashing halt.

William was dead.

In his adult years Bert had drifted away from his father as the two had, on the surface at least, little in common. William simply did not understand how Bert could be interested in anything as frivo-lous as motorcycle racing. Bert was not inclined to bother with his father's objections. But they actually shared many common charac-teristics. Both were incapable of throwing anything away and both were so intensely motivated they allowed nothing to deflect them from their chosen course. They were hard workers and, in the end, somewhat solitary men. There is no doubt that Bert was very fond of his father, and that underneath it all William loved his son.

William's death was a blow but it also led to the additional complication that Lilly now sought to sell the farm. Bert invested his life's savings to buy the twenty-hectare half he lived on and tried to get back to his work in the shed. He was now desperately short of funds, and when a property developer asked him to sell (the city now surrounded the farm), he accepted.

In 1951 he bought a small property at 105 Bainfield Road, north Invercargill, and went to the council for approval to build a new house. At the time the council had a stipulated minimum stud height of eight feet in a domestic dwelling. Bert thought this was ridiculous – it meant heating an extra foot of ceiling that no one ever used. So he asked permission to build with a stud height of seven feet. Furthermore, he requested permission to build with bricks placed with their thin sides in the vertical position, which he calculated would save a lot of bricks.

The council was not inclined to grant his requests. In spite of his conducting an energetic and often aggressive campaign to change their minds, Bert was eventually forced to concede that they had reached an impasse. Rather than admit defeat, he changed tack. He would build a double garage before embarking on the house. It would have a stud height of seven feet and he would use concrete blocks with their thin sides in the vertical position.

Rules for garages were a lot more flexible than for houses and Bert was able to complete the work without council molestation – although they soon noted with concern that he was living in the garage. Inspectors began to call, enquiring when Bert might be expected to begin construction of his proper home. Bert always made a point of showing them a few lines on a piece of paper he had stuck up on the wall. It was the beginning of a preliminary drawing to help him decide exactly what style of dwelling he wanted. The battle would dribble on for twenty-eight years.

Bert had only himself to please and so wasted little time setting up his new garage. A single bed rested across the end wall, under which a couple of old suitcases contained all his clothes. Shelves ran the length of one long wall, while the lathe and a bench were placed against the other. His special ramped motorcycle stand went in the middle of the room and a small wood and coal stove sat just inside the shed with its chimney travelling across the room just under the ceiling and exiting on the other side of the double doors. Guttering fed rainwater into a wooden barrel which in turn supplied water to quench hot castings and for tea, a pot being almost always kept hot on the stove. There was one small window facing north.

He washed his smalls in an old kerosene tin with a little washboard and hung them to dry over his chimney. There was a small outhouse. The shed's exterior received little attention and for most of the time he lived there the grass grew like hay.

Every now and again he would cook a load of sausages in a frying pan, eating a few and chucking the pan back on the stove when he felt hungry again. Visitors were almost always welcome. He would drag a chair out and carefully drape it with a sheet of clean newspaper to keep their clothes from getting grubby. Then he'd serve them a cup of tea, which tasted strongly metallic, with gingerbread biscuits. Neighbouring children quickly discovered they could always score a biscuit from him and he was happy to tell them about what he was doing. Many found his activities interesting and visited regularly.

One new visitor was a strapping young builder called Russell Wright who had recently finished his apprenticeship and, aged just twenty, formed a house building partnership. The immediate post war years were a boom for builders and the enterprise had been immediately successful. Like Bert, Russell had earned early money from rabbit pelts, although he had used a trained ferret for the job rather than a rifle. He'd purchased his first bike with the proceedings, a little James two-stroke, when he was just ten years old.

Also like Bert, Russell's father had disapproved and Russell had ignored him. He had taken up racing at the age of seventeen and he and Bert quickly became friends. Unlike Bert he had never considered riding a bike as a way of just getting around. From the beginning his machines had been dedicated to racing. He started with a Triumph frame into which he inserted a very hot JAP speedway motor, riding it to win the New Zealand Hill-climbing Championship. In 1948 he replaced the special with a brand-new

500cc AJS, taking part in grass-track, beach and speedway racing as well as his favourite hill-climbs. Russell came third that year in the New Zealand Grass Track Championship, scoring a number of other fine results too. He liked nothing better than to talk with Bert about tuning for speed.

Bert had many younger friends, never seeming to bother about age gaps. He treated everyone as an equal; they quickly came to regard him as just another mate. Once or twice a week he scrubbed himself up, stuck on a tie and went to town to have a bath at the tepid pools. Women remained a tremendous enthusiasm and he apparently had the odd liaison, but if he ever went anywhere he went alone. He was entirely self-sufficient and he was happy. It seemed to him he had found the perfect way to live.

Although the war was over, rationing remained and petrol was still in short supply, with periods of even sharper unavailability. One day Bert had a visit from the post master in Invercargill who had heard about Bert's superior gas producers and wanted him to consider supplying the post office. But Bert was not at all interested and the man left with a bit of a flea in his ear. From now on the Indian was the thing.

About this time Duncan Meikle began to court a widow in Christchurch and it soon became clear that his intentions were honorable. Bert was dumfounded and did his best to dissuade him from marriage. 'Why buy the book,' he asked, 'when you can join the library?'

His objections fell on deaf ears and Duncan did marry, finding lasting happiness in the process, and in the end the marriage made no difference to his relationship with Bert. The two happily continued to explore the complex and demanding art of motorcycle tuning. They often went testing, sometimes on the beach and sometimes on the road, but always illicitly. In late 1950 Bert made a run on Ryal Bush Straight with a tail wind blowing and saw the equivalent of 150 miles an hour on the tachometer. Duncan was incredulous but Bert was adamant he had seen what he saw. Whatever the truth, the Indian was certainly flying. When he turned up in early December for a race meeting at Oreti Beach he was determined to do well.

There was no doubting the power of the Indian and all who saw it were in awe of its acceleration. George Begg was there riding his new 650cc BSA A10 Twin and admitted later that he took little notice of the old Indian, which was parked before the race among a collection of impressive new machinery. To his surprise he found himself engaged in a ding-dong battle with Bert in the six-lap scratch event as the old Indian caught him on the straights and blasted past him at such a rate of knots he felt as if his bike had stopped. As they approached the turns, however, the Indian would rocket past the marker to describe a huge arc in the sand way up the beach as Bert slowly came about. Once lined up he would unleash yet another mad surge of acceleration, closing and passing George only to repeat the process at the other end.

Riders who dueled with Bert in this manner were often scared witless if he happened to change gear while going past. The gear lever had no positive stop, being located only by the indents in a piece of spring steel pressed against the lever. When Bert changed gear he often looked down to see that he had the lever in the right place as a false neutral could easily send the revs soaring, wreaking havoc with the engine. The bike would weave alarmingly all over the beach until the gear was properly engaged, then take off again, spitting sand back at the following rider as Bert surged away.

On this occasion Bert's little brakes were fully cooked, but he completed the race and was congratulated by one and all for actually finishing for the first time in ten years. He elected not to compete in the twenty-mile race, as he knew the Indian would not make the distance, but stayed to watch Norman Hayes take a convincing win on his very fast new Triumph, with George Begg in third place.

George approached Bert at the post-race function, held at Irving Hayes's house, and offered the advice that if the Indian motor was put in a decent frame with a four-speed, foot-operated gearbox and a decent set of brakes it would be very competitive. He was somewhat puzzled by Bert's response that he really only had time for old bikes.

If George needed further proof of the Indian's potency and its riders hardy disposition, he got it at a subsequent race meeting on the beach. Bert, who normally managed exemplary starts, overdid it on the throttle and had the bike flip straight over backwards on top of him, only to scramble out from underneath and quickly check it for damage before re-launching. George was both impressed and disturbed to later observe Bert riding flat out through the S-bend in the middle of the straight with one hand on the bars while he fiddled with the carburettor.

By 1951 the engine was delivering strong performances but remained as unreliable as ever. Everything came together, though, at a speed trial in Timaru, over 400 kilometres north of Invercargill, when Bert and the Indian were timed at a quite remarkable 133.33 miles per hour. Many people thought Bert had finally stretched the Indian to breaking point – and indeed he had. But he also had a plan to stretch that breaking point ever further. He was determined to go a hell of a lot faster.

It was at about this time that he finally laid his old canon to rest. The barrel had rested under the shed ever since its second and final firing. When the police announced an arms amnesty, mainly to ferret out weapons brought home by returning soldiers as souvenirs, Bert dutifully called them up and told them about his artillery. He fully expected to be told he could keep it, but he was a stickler for obeying all laws save those directly concerned with road speed limits. The police had no idea what to do about it but they were certainly not going to let Bert keep it. Someone then had the bright idea of burying it in the concrete foundations about to be poured for a new hotel. To Bert's eternal annoyance they turned up and lugged it away. From that time on his opinion of the police, or at least 'the interfering bloody coppers who thieved my canon', took a sharp dive.

If he was to get to the next speed level with the Scout, Bert needed reliable and effective lubrication in the engine's bottom end, a vital improvement he had resisted attempting for over fifteen years. Finally, after dozens of bottom-end failures, he was ready to tackle the job. He began in his usual manner, by scrounging a short length of 127-millimetre diameter axle steel, which he cut in half and took to Johnson Engineering where the two pieces were heated and flattened under the air hammer. He then approached Irving Hayes once again for use of his old lathe to roughly machine the discs to the point where only minor finishing work was required. When he returned home to the Myford he found that the new flywheels would not swing in the chuck, when offset to bore out the crankpin holes. Undeterred, he cut thirty-one millimetres out of the gap in the bed of the lathe, no doubt weakening it, though not to the point it couldn't perform its function.

By now the little lathe was seriously worn out, but one way or another Bert kept it going. He successfully completed the new crankshaft with an oil way running through it to keep the bearings properly lubricated. He did this by drilling though the mainshaft on the timing side to the point where it fitted into the flywheel. Next he drilled an oil way through the flywheel to the point where the crankpin fitted into it. Rather than making a new crankpin, he took one which already had an oil way from a 1928 Scout and machined it down to almost twenty millimetres, before fitting a hardened steel sleeve to achieve the larger diameter needed for the roller track. This meant he now had to make conrods with larger big-end eyes and use smaller rollers. But he was able to use the genuine Indian rollers, which he preferred as they had rounded ends rather than sharply machined faces, which he believed made them easier to keep oiled.

He now turned out a couple of new conrods to suit the longer stroke he intended using to increase the capacity to 738cc, while still retaining the standard bore. A new 750cc class had been established in New Zealand and he had decided to make that his first target. This time he made the rods from used Caterpillar track and from then on he invariably used this material, which he proclaimed to be superior to any other steel for the purpose. The finished rods naturally incorporated the larger big-end eyes needed.

He took the gleaming new rods straight to Melhop Engineering where he could harden them in the company's cyanide salt heat-treatment bath, the only one in Invercargill. The men at Melhops were used to Bert and took little notice of him. The workshop manager, Roger Cowley, had warned Bert on a number of occasions against ever putting parts with water on them into the bath. Like the rest of the workers, he presumed Bert now knew what he was doing. He was wrong.

Everything went well enough at first. Bert preheated the rods and then immersed them in the bath to gradually raise their temperature. When they were hot enough he removed them and quenched them in oil, the same procedure he had followed many times in the past. This time, however, he wanted to further temper them by placing them back in the bath for another session. Before doing so, he decided to further cool them by running tap water over them. At that point he should have heated them once more to drive off any suggestion of water. But he was in a hurry as usual and simply thrust them back into the hot salts.

The bath immediately exploded, showering Bert with super-hot cyanide salts. With his hair and the old overcoat he wore on fire, Bert raced for the bathroom where he attempted to extinguish the blaze with water from the tap. Fortunately one of the company's employees saw him and he was quickly put out, but not before he had suffered extensive, agonising burns.

Only after he was satisfied that his conrods had not been damaged in the explosion did he allow Roger to take him to the hospital. Hours later he reappeared at the factory with his head and his hands wrapped in bandages, badly charred and obviously the worse for wear. Dismissing all enquiries about his health with a curt assurance that he was fine, he collected his conrods, thanked Roger for the use of the bath, and set off for home to continue work on the engine. The story soon did the rounds of the city, the general reaction being that it just went to show what a tough old bird Bert was.

It was now time to make new cylinders. During his travels he had discovered a dump of old iron gas pipe that the city had replaced due to pitting. The heavy gas pipe had originally been spun cast to ensure sufficient density to prevent gas leaks, making it ideal material for cylinders. A careful examination showed that there were sufficient lengths of non-corroded material to provide the short pieces he needed. He was able to bore the pipe to the right size and it was thick enough to turn down on the outside to create a flange at its base where it would join the crankcase. To finish the job a pile of aluminium pistons were poured into a mould to make a finned muff, which he then bored so that it just slipped over the barrel when heated. Once cooled it shrank to form a snug fit.

Up until now he had always formed his pistons by sand casting but now decided to make a steel, die-cast mould. In time this would evolve into a highly sophisticated tool to make high-quality pistons. His method was quite simple and he could turn out substantial numbers quickly. He would start by heating up the mould, simultaneously melting a pot full of assorted pistons with his blowlamp. For a while he stuck with the English Ford items he had long preferred, because of the high silicon alloy they were made from, but in time he came to prefer diesel pistons, figuring that as they had to withstand greater pressures they must be superior.

Once the mould was cherry hot he would pour in the molten aluminium before screwing out the centre wedge of the die that formed the void inside the piston. When that was removed he could knock out the other two parts of the die, and the job was done. If he was too slow the alloy would cool before he could extract the die, but it was no big problem as he simply melted the alloy out and started again. If all went well he would wait until the new piston was cool and then give it a tap with a hammer. If he was rewarded with a clear ring he added it to his supply; if not it went back in the pot.

His final job before refitting the engine in the frame was to sort out a method to push the oil around in the engine. To do this he used two original Scout oil pumps, which pushed oil into the hole through the mainshaft and on through the system. A 1933 Indian pump scavenged the oil from the crankcase and returned it to the feeder pumps to complete the circuit. Unfortunately, the system worked rather too well and the old problem of oiled plugs, caused by an oversupply of the stuff splashing about, resurfaced. Most engineers would have resorted to a larger scavenger pump but Bert was not an engineer. He simply restricted the flow to the two feed pumps and the problem was solved.

Now that his engine boasted nearly 140 extra cubic centimetres it was time to go for a larger carburettor. He elected to retain the single Schleber De Lux he'd fitted back in the 1930s but enlarged the bore diameter by cutting it lengthwise and forcing it open to the desired diameter before braising in a brass strip along the cut. He made a new inlet manifold from 36.8-millimetre steel tubing, once again building up the insides of the right angle turns with bronze that he carefully profiled to improve gas flow.

His routine was now settled and he consistently worked sixteen hours a day, knocking off late at night and rising again after just a few hours' sleep. He did not acknowledge weekends and holidays and on Christmas day allowed himself only a half-day off.

However, Bert still welcomed interruptions from people whose company he enjoyed and one day he was pleased to see Russell Wright striding up the narrow path through the long, straggly grass. Russell accepted a cup of tea before broaching the subject of his visit.

'I'm thinking of buying one of the new Vincent Black Lightnings. And I'm thinking I might go after your record on it.'

Bert whistled. 'You must be doing well. What d'ya reckon that'll set you back?'

Russell relaxed. This wasn't going too badly. 'Six hundred quid.'

Bert's braying laughter bounced around the shed as he gestured to the old Indian standing in the corner. 'By crikey you'd want a world record after shelling out all that loot! My one cost one six hundredth of that.'

The next day Russell went to town and made out a large cheque to Rupert Tall Motor Cycles. He was anxious to get his new bike as soon as possible, but there would be inevitable delays, what with agents in Auckland having to place orders with the company in Stevenage, England. It might be months before Russell got to the front of the queue. But he was determined to have a crack at Bert's record. And he was not the only one.

Bert had now been the fastest man in New Zealand for almost a dozen years. Then, in 1952, Les Lamb, mounted on a 1000cc streamlined Vincent Rapide, broke his record, pushing the speed up to 139 miles an hour.

But Bert was still in the record-business and on 7 March 1953 he took the Indian through the New Zealand Beach Open Capacity Flying Half Mile at 124.138 miles an hour, beating the previous speed by a substantial thirteen miles an hour. Later Bert would explain in a talk he gave to students in America that beach records were the hardest records to break. Beach surfaces, he told them, are fickle, especially when the beach in question has the wild Southern Ocean pounding on it. A storm can howl in and destroy the surface for racing at any time, ruining months of preparation for the run. Or a gentle zephyr might get up, hardly enough to bring a chill to the sunbathers, but enough to push a speeding record breaker off line. Authorisation to use the beach would have to be obtained from various local and national bodies months in advance, after which came the daunting task of bringing together club officials, timing gear technicians, track stewards and all the others needed for such a meeting. On the day, the record-chasing machine would need to be meticulously prepared to complete two gruelling runs – last minute hiccups allowing. Finally, the rider needed to be in peak physical and mental condition, skills honed to a fine edge, ready to accept a challenge that could easily end in injury or worse. Breaking a beach record was a huge challenge and it was no accident when it all came together for Bert that day.

Bert's enthusiasm for motor sport was by no means confined to motorcycles. He had always been interested in any endeavor involving mechanical devices. When Charles Kingsford Smith, the famous Australian aviator, flew over the farm in the early 1930s on one of his pioneering flights from Australia, Bert knew exactly when to expect him and had all the children lined up in a paddock to wave the brave man on his way. He also followed four-wheeled competition and record-breaking attempts around the world. When the first New Zealand Grand Prix was announced he immediately decided to attend. It was no problem finding a ride north with other enthusiasts. On 9 January he joined the 70,000 New Zealanders who had braved enormous traffic jams to attend the meeting at Ardmore Airport, on the southern outskirts of Auckland.

Bert headed straight for the pits and was soon talking to the BRM mechanics, who had come out with driver Ken Wharton to contest the race. Bert was overawed by the tiny, supercharged 1.5-litre, sixteen-cylinder engine, scarcely able to believe it could develop 450 horsepower. He finally got to talk to Wharton himself, who told him of his difficulties getting it off the line. With peak power up to a stratospheric 12,000 revs it would stall if take-off was attempted at less than 8000 revs and sit wheel-spinning if the revs climbed to 9000.

He also met Peter Whitehead, whose two-litre, supercharged V12 Ferrari was regarded as having a better chance, and ran into George Begg, who was racing at the meeting with his friend Doug Johnson. George mentioned that he and Doug were going to attend a motorcycle race meeting at Taumarunui, a rural rail stop in the middle of the North Island, the following weekend. He also mentioned in passing the name of the private hotel they would be staying at, in case Bert was able to make it.

The grand prix turned out to be a wonderfully dramatic race. Australian Ken Jones was awarded the win with his Maybach Special, although many believed with good reason that there had been a lap keeping error and that Wharton had won it in the screaming BRM.

The next weekend Begg and Johnson were soundly asleep in their double room in Taumarunui when the light came on and Bert loudly exclaimed he had been looking all over for them. When Doug refused to bunk in with George to free up a bed, Bert disappeared back into the night. At breakfast a highly embarrassed George learned that Bert had worked his way through the entire place, opening every door and turning on the light to enquire loudly if George was in the room. It was a salutary lesson: never extend an invitation to Bert unless you were absolutely prepared to deal with the consequences.

Back in the workshop Bert continued on his mission to overhaul the Scout. Although the primary gear drive had survived a triple increase in the power it was originally designed to cope with – yet another compliment to the original work of Charles B Franklin – Bert decided to ditch the cogs in favour of a chain primary drive. He reasoned that the gears were eating up perhaps three per cent of the available power, whereas a chain drive would consume just half that. He made and tested four systems before finally settling on one that utlised a model 741 Army Indian triple-chain sprocket. He fitted the twenty-two-tooth sprocket to the drive side of the Scout's mainshaft, a relatively simple task as Indian had not changed the mainshaft over the years. He then ground off the helical teeth surrounding the clutch drum and embarked on a marathon of hacksawing and filing to create forty-six teeth to drive the triple chain teeth in their place. He ran the completed assembly in light oil and had no trouble, although a Reynolds chain expert would later tell Bert that the system could not work reliably. It had by then done ten years good service and would do many more.

Early in 1955 Bert attended the annual grass-track race meeting held at the Invercargill Showgrounds. He had decided to have a final go with his double knocker Indian around the quarter-mile track and for a while he went very well. Russell Wright, who was still waiting for his Vincent to arrive, competed on his AJS while Norman Hayes turned up on his Triumph. Both noted Bert's continuing determination to slide his bike, speedway-style, and kept well out of his way. Others were not so aware of the hazard and several were almost forced into the fence as Bert slewed this way and that. Finally the fuel tank fell off and he coasted to a halt, much to everybody's relief.

It was probably just as well that the meeting marked the end of his grass-track racing days. It was also the end of the double knocker as far as Bert was concerned. He sold it to a mechanic who worked at the local fire station and when the man complained that it was too complicated to maintain Bert converted it back to a push-rod operation for him. It was also the end of any further plans to develop double overhead camshaft heads for the Scout. Pushrods, he decided, were more than good enough for his purposes.

In the middle of the year Bert was having a quiet practice session on the beach when Russell Wright turned up on his brand new Vincent Black Lightning. It had taken twelve months for the bike to arrive but it was well worth the wait. The beautiful, big V-twin impressed Bert tremendously. It combined all the traditional virtues with the latest advances in engine design. Although the bike was an absolutely standard Lightning, it was the very model the company had used to display at the Earls Court Show in London. All the steel parts that were normally cadmium-plated were finished in chromium, and the lustrous black paintwork had been applied with extra care. It was gorgeous.

Naturally Bert wanted to know what she was capable of and Russell, being equally keen to find out, set off up the beach to try it out. At 100 miles an hour he discovered something Vincent owners the world over were beginning to find out – they had a strange and unpredictable habit of suddenly getting out of control. Afterwards, Russell could not remember if he hit a small bump or a soft patch of sand, but he vividly remembered the violent 'tank slapper' that nearly threw him off the bike. It was only with great difficulty that he hung on and slowed without crashing. He and Bert had a long hard look over the bike but could find no obvious explanation for the its errant behaviour. In the end the only advice Bert could offer was typically idiosyncratic: 'It might go away at higher speed. Next time try opening the throttle instead of closing it.'

Six months later Russell took the Vincent to a speed trial held on Tram Road, another arrow-straight Canterbury byway, chosen by the local club for their event after the Alyesbury Straight was declared too busy for closure. Using the Vincent Owners Handbook as a guide to tuning and running on a petrol-methanol mixture, he averaged 140 miles an hour on his two runs and took the New Zealand motorcycle speed record. There was no sign of the wayward handling that had almost made him crash on the beach.

He also met Bob Burns, a very talented precision engineer from Christchurch, who broke the New Zealand sidecar record on a streamlined Vincent Rapide outfit at the same meeting. It was not necessary to carry a passenger in the sidecar and the machine had been beautifully faired for good aerodynamics. Although the streamliner was built over the standard motorcycle, and was therefore quite high, Burns had followed the efforts of the German NSU record-breaking team very closely and had modelled his bodywork on the shapes they had evolved. He was methodical and meticulous, carefully considering issues of down force and stability before building an aluminium shell over a light plywood structure. He had clearly got his sums right as the outfit tracked absolutely true on his two runs down the very narrow country road.

When Burns saw Russell's new machine he realised that a combination of the streamliner body and the new, higher specification Vincent could set world records for both sidecar and solo machines. He proposed a partnership, which Russell promptly accepted. They would attempt the two records, splitting any prize money down the middle. Both the solo record and the sidecar record were then held by NSU, the former at 180 miles an hour and the latter at 154. It was an ambitious undertaking. NSU had achieved their prodigious speeds with the all resources available to a factory that was at that time the largest manufacturer of motorcycles in the world.

Burns, who was twenty-one years older than Wright, was a big, beefy Scotsman with a reputation for extreme bluntness and a somewhat violent temper. He had few friends and his arrogance toward those he considered his inferiors – by most accounts nearly everyone – had made him many enemies. However, the two men recognised in each other that quality of character that would keep the throttle screwed open until the end. Burns and the young builder from Invercargill rubbed along well from the moment they met. Russell left the bike with his new partner to prepare for the record attempt. It was a wise decision.

Burns got to work straight away with encouragement from Phil Vincent, who was impressed with the local records already set. The company sent over a pair of Big Port racing cylinder heads and the huge thirty-six millimetre Amal carburettors that went with them, parts that had been developed for the factory's Grey Flash entries in the 1950 TT.

In December Bob raised the world sidecar record to 157 miles an hour, which was also a new overall speed record in New Zealand. Russell had his turn in February 1955 but failed to reach the speed they had anticipated, due to the factory having mistakenly fitted a twenty-one-tooth gearbox sprocket instead of the standard twenty-two-tooth. The bike was therefore too low geared to get near the required speed and Burns rang Vincent in England to deliver a stinging earful of abuse. Fortunately this did not result in the works withdrawing support. With the correct sprocket Russell had another go on 2 July.

Bob had painted a white mark on the rev counter showing 180 miles an hour in top and Russell noted the needle was comfortably over it as he whistled through the timing trap. He found the faired machine reassuringly easy to keep on the centre line of the six-metre-wide road. The return run went equally smoothly until he flashed past a hole in a hedge and caught a whiff of crosswind. By then travelling at 185 miles an hour, it took all his concentrated nerve to stay on the road. Somehow he finished the run, but his face was ashen as he stepped out of the shell, having learned just how devastating even a light crosswind could be on a streamliner. There and then he swore he would never attempt another record on such a course. But he had done the job and the record was his at 185.15 miles an hour. Within hours he had a congratulatory telegram from William Herz, the NSU rider whose record he had just broken.

When, after his triumphal return home, Russell called around to see Bert he found him working away as usual on the Scout. Bert was delighted with Russell's achievement and offered warm congratulations before asking him to make some tea while he finished what he was doing. As the two sat enjoying a hot cuppa he listened as Russell recounted his adventure. Bert was particularly interested in his young friend's account of how the crosswind had almost run him off the road, which would undoubtedly have cost him his life.

He passed the tin of gingernuts and watched as Russell dunked one in his cup. They both sat in comfortable silence for a moment before Bert spoke again. 'So, are you going to have another go?'

Russell hesitated. 'I might as well. Bob's keen and Phil Vincent says he'll help. But not here. It's too bloody dangerous.'

'Utah then,' suggested Bert.

Russell nodded. 'Yep, the salt's the place for that kind of thing.'

Bert drained his tea. 'Well, if you do go would you mind if I tagged along? I'm thinking of taking my old girl over some time and I'd like to check it out. I'll pay my own way and I'd make myself useful.'

Russell looked up in surprise. His eyes swept around the shed, registering afresh the old lathe, the crowded workbench and the faded, battle-scarred Indian.

'You can come if you like,' he said, smiling. 'But you'll have to make the tea.'

CHAPTER TWELVE
SALT 2

As Russell would not be going to Bonneville, Utah, until the following year Bert began to consider a preliminary trip to the Mecca of motorcycle racing. The Indian's engine development was essentially finished for the moment, the next big job looming on the horizon being the construction of a streamliner body. Bert knew he could only achieve further record-breaking speeds with a streamlined motorcycle and that such speeds could not safely be attempted in New Zealand. He decided not to begin that task until he had been to Bonneville to learn all he could, which meant he had some time up his sleeve. The most romantic and the most deadly race in the motorcycle calendar was still the TT on the Isle of Man. Going there would fulfill one of his most fervent wishes, but he would be going strictly for pleasure, as a spectator. He had been working long hours, day in and day out, for years. He needed a real break. In the end he just asked himself if he'd ever regret going. It was an easy decision.

As he was finishing packing he heard his neighbour sing out to him. 'I hear you're going on a trip, Bert. How about mowing the lawn before you go? It's a bloody disgrace. I'll lend you a slasher and you can use my mower to finish it off. There's even a can of petrol to fill it up.'

Bert looked at the waist-high grass. His neighbour had a point. Later that day he walked next door and inspected the slasher, the lawn mower and the can of petrol. He wet his finger and held it in the air to confirm there was a gentle breeze blowing toward the road. Then he picked up the can of petrol.

By the time the fire brigade arrived the long grass in front of Bert's shed was reduced to smoking stubble. Bert was most apologetic – he had no idea the fire would be so spectacular and promised not to do it again. As the tenders left Bainfield Street with a couple of final toots on their claxons Bert surveyed his handiwork with satisfaction. He could leave now with a clear conscience.

The men running the competition department at AJS in Wolverhampton were perplexed. They had been quietly going about their business when a fellow strolled in to their inner sanctum, introduced himself as Bert Munro from New Zealand and started rabbiting on about carburettors. He explained that he was on his way to watch the TT, and simply wanted to chat. Had he called the previous year they would undoubtedly have sent him packing. But that was then, when the works had been campaigning a race team with two of the most advanced grand prix motorcycles ever made, the E95 Porcupine 500cc twin and the 1954 Triple Knocker three-valve 350cc single. Since the factory's withdrawal from racing at the end of that season it had existed in an atmosphere of uncertainty. Perhaps that was why they listened long enough to this genial stranger, who had to be in his mid-fifties, to become intrigued by his theories.

He had somehow arrived at the conclusion that one carburettor was better than two, an opinion the competition department knew to a man to be nonsense. They knew that each cylinder needed its own carburettor and manifold to chuck in as much mixture as possible while the piston was rising on the compression stroke. Of course, they had never tried a single carburettor so they could not empirically prove this was the case, but it made sense. For some reason their visitor refused to see it, his contrary opinion being based entirely on the behaviour of an old 1920 Indian he had apparently tuned. Finally one of the company's top tuning gurus felt obliged to set him straight.

'Look here, old chap,' he said, 'You may well be right when it comes to riding a vintage motorcycle. One carburettor or two, it probably makes little difference at the speeds you run at. But we are dealing with machines that can make 150 miles an hour. It's an entirely different matter, don't you see.'

Bert took his time before answering. When he did it was clear he was deluded. He told them that he had unofficially achieved 150 miles an hour himself on a road near his home and that he had a national New Zealand record at just under 125 miles an hour – on a beach! Delusional, or merely prone to gross exaggeration, he had at least provided some entertainment. When he had left there had been some laughter. That was until someone thought to call a journalist at the *Motor Cycle* to see if they'd ever heard of the fellow. He had not, but the magazine was doing a story on two New Zealanders who had broken the solo and sidecar records and he agreed to make a few enquiries. A couple of days later he called back to say it was true. A fellow called Bert Munro had set a national beach record in New Zealand on a 1920 Indian Scout at 124.138 miles an hour. He'd also apparently recorded a speed of over 130 miles an hour on a road somewhere in the South Island. The competition department at AJS was amazed and delighted. He'd been such a likeable fellow. The top tuning guru went around for days muttering about carburettors. Could just a single carburettor possibly be superior on a twin-cylinder engine? After all, they had never tried it.

Bert, by now soaking up the electrifying atmosphere at the TT, remained staunchly convinced that one carburettor was all that was needed. But then, he'd never tried two.

Bert's trip through Europe was one of the best times of his life. He quickly hooked up with the tight-knit Australasian contingent competing at the TT, a tradition going back to the earliest days of the contest, relishing the easy camaraderie of the group. There were some among them aware of his achievements, which lent him a bona fide standing among the larger community of racers. He was invited to the official TT dinner dance and met all the stars of the day, exchanging notes with such luminaries as Geoff Duke. Duke was then at the height of his career, a six-time TT winner with his victory in the Senior that year. His brilliant win on his streamlined, four-cylinder Gilera, along with his first place at the previous grand prix in France, indicated that he was well set to take his sixth world grand prix championship.

The smiling Lancastrian had been pleased to share his tips for riding flat out with Bert, who had been equally pleased to reciprocate. Duke had recently taken up one piece racing leathers and Bert was intrigued by the outfits. Duke assured him he would never race in anything else and Bert had made him roar with laughter when he told him he entirely understood. 'I have an old pair of sandshoes back home,' he said, 'that I always wear for record attempts.'

He also met the veteran German racer Hermann Muller, who had come third in the 250 class on an NSU Sportmax. Known as Happy to one and all, the affable German had raced one of the immensely challenging mid-engine grand prix Auto Union cars before the war. Now, aged forty-six, he was going all out on his semi works bike to win his first and, with his decision to retire afterwards already made, final world championship. More than any other machine, Bert loved the NSU. With its streamlined aluminium shell the bike was capable of 124 miles an hour, the single cylinder spinning safely to 9500 revs per minute. Bert spent hours watching the team working on it and came to know them all well, despite their English being almost as non-existent as his German.

At the end of the three-week event Bert threw his old suitcase into the back of a van belonging to a couple of his new Australian friends, just as they were about to leave for the ferry. He climbed into the front seat, shoving the passenger into the middle and onto the engine cover, switched off the radio and announced he was going with them. They were on their way to Nürburgring for the German Grand Prix after which they were to travel on to the Belgian GP at Spa-Francorschamp and the Dutch GP at Assen. Bert had decided they had more than enough room for him. They did not object and the radio stayed off for the rest of the trip.

Bert enjoyed music but he preferred conversation, especially his own, and would always turn off a radio or television when he entered a room or vehicle. He particularly disliked televisions, and the first time he ever saw one he told its proud owners that they should throw it out or they would forget how to talk to one another and lose all their friends. He would not stay in a room if someone objected to it being turned off, preferring the silence of his own company.

He was also free with his opinions on such subjects as sunglasses, women in trousers, shampoo, short haircuts in men and women, alcohol and smoking – being dead set against all of them. Sunglasses, and even most ordinary glasses, he condemned as eye crutches that would weaken the wearer's vision. Women in trousers were simply a disappointment. He thought washing hair scrubbed out all the natural oils that provided lustre and health, believing it should simply be brushed vigorously; short haircuts relieved the hair roots of work, making them lazy and promoting baldness.

He avoided people who drank more than he thought they should and imbibed only tiny amounts himself. He reserved his most adamant condemnation, however, for smoking. No one ever smoked while he was around without being told in the most direct fashion that they were ruining the only pair of lungs they had and would die an early and horrible death. In spite of his forthrightness he seldom caused great offence.

During the trip Bert visited many factories connected with motor-cycle manufacture. In Belgium he acquired a supply of wheel spokes from one and a couple of alloy wheel rims from another. When the chance came up to cadge a lift with a French team to Paris after the Dutch GP he waved goodbye to his Australian friends. He stayed in a little central hotel and flirted with the two young women who ran the desk, boasting later that he taught them many English words they had not heard before.

Finally he made his way back to London. He visited the Tower and saw the Crown jewels and waited with the crowd for a procession of the Royal Horse Guards escorting the Queen in her carriage, cheering as loudly as anyone. The year before he'd made the trip to Bluff, along with 40,000 other Southlanders, to see the monarch when she left New Zealand by ship after her triumphant first tour and he was a fervent fan. Later he made his way back to Wolverhampton, where he renewed his acquaintance with the competition department at the AJS factory.

They were delighted to see him again and made quite a fuss of him, introducing him to the man who ran the machine that threaded the spokes for their wheels, who gladly ran more thread onto the spokes Bert had brought from Belgium, as they were too long for the rims he had bought. Someone gave him a bit of alloy that he turned into a pair of wheel hubs on a handy lathe and he was just completing the assembly of the two wheels, all the while regaling everyone with tales from his trip, when the legendary sales manager for AJS, Jock West, walked in. West was too polite to openly object to Bert's presence, but he took rather a dim view of any diversion from the serious business of volume motorcycle production. Everyone quickly got back to work. Bert took the hint and left, running in to George Begg on the way out.

By coincidence George was at the factory to take delivery of a new AJS 7R, which he intended to race in an upcoming amateur event on the Isle of Man, and spotted Bert first. Ducking back around a corner he tried to figure out what might happen if he revealed himself. It was not that he did not want to see Bert, but he knew that meeting his old friend 12,000 miles from home could easily lead to unforeseeable complications. His affection quickly overcame his fears and stepped out to greet him. He was very relieved to find Bert was catching the boat home the next day. Later, Jock West told George of the strange visitor and expressed the fervent hope that AJS would not have more New Zealanders like him dropping by.

George was able to assure the Englishman that it was unlikely.

Bert arrived back in New Zealand in October after being away for six months. Not long after settling back into his shed he had a visit from his old mate Percy Shave. Percy was very excited, as he had just heard a rumor about two old Velocettes lying in a disused henhouse in Nightcaps, an old coal-mining town in western Southland. The two friends smelled a bargain and wasted no time getting to the sleepy little town where a few enquiries led them to an irate landlady. She had been saddled with the remains of the machines by a shearer who'd shot through owing several months rent. To Bert and Percy's delight they turned out to be 500cc MSS Velocettes, one a 1936 model identical to the bike Bert had come second on in the New Zealand Grand Prix years before. The other was a 1938 model and, although both had been substantially disassembled, all the parts seemed to be there. The wheel rims had rotted through from standing in highly corrosive chicken droppings, but otherwise both bikes were quite restorable. Bert put on a good show of having misgivings about taking on two wrecks that were clearly little better than scrap, and whittled the landlady down to £10 for the pair. A toss of a coin saw Bert take ownership of the 1936 model, which suited him just fine, and they strapped them on to the trailer behind Percy's car for the trip home.

It was the beginning of a new love affair for Bert, who would come to feel as strongly for the Velocette as he did for the Scout. Perhaps there was something in his make-up that only allowed him to feel real affection for old, unloved machines – he had happily quit his first, identical Velocette when it was still quite new. Whatever the reason, the new old Velocette was given a place in the shed where it remained, alongside the Indian, for the rest of Bert's motorcycling days.

He embarked on a quick tuning programme to be ready in time for a race meeting of cars and bikes scheduled for a new, enormously fast triangular course at Ryal Bush. He fitted a huge carburettor of uncertain provenance, which he referred to ever after as 'the Wadonga', after enlarging and polishing the inlet port and fitting a larger inlet valve. Next he got stuck into the cams, reshaping them in his usual manner with a vicious profile that immediately bent the valve stems and jammed them in their guides. He would later overcome the problem, but he'd missed the race and there was no time to fix it. There was a boat to America to catch. He was off to the salt.

From the beginning it was clear the trip was not going to be easy. Russell and Bob had been roundly feted in England after their successful record breaking and had attracted generous sponsorship for another effort at Bonneville, including money from the New Zealand government. However, there was a great deal of uncertainty about the Federation Internationale de Motocyclism's (FIM) willingness to accept the Bonneville time-keeping system, or even that the Kiwi pair would have a run on the salt flats. They had no idea what garaging facilities might be available and had not managed to arrange accommodation. To make matters worse for Bob, a BMW outfit driven by German Wilhelm Noll had smashed his sidecar record by twelve miles an hour on the Munich-Ingoldstat autobahn on 4 October 1955. The day had been a spree for the German, who broke no less than eighteen records.

Although Bob believed he could retake the record, and Russell was keen to be the first to break the magic 200 mile an hour mark, both knew that NSU had the salt flats booked for two weeks and that they were turning up with a huge team and a large number of FIM officials in early August.

The famous English record breaker George Eyston had also booked the salt flats as manager of an MG and Austin Healy team that was going after records for their parent company BMC. Eyston had expressed a willingness to help but was unsure of what he could offer until he got there. The New Zealanders were also nervous about their fuel choice. They had elected to run with a petrol and nitromethane mixture, this being the easiest way they could see to increase power. They had experimented with this new fuel before leaving home but knew little about it. Its use was still in its infancy and they feared the higher altitude at Bonneville might complicate things.

The atmosphere on the boat over was not helped by the immediate and scathing dislike Bob Burns took to Bert, who he dismissed as a know-nothing idiot. Bert was used to people not taking him seriously and did his best to shrug off the criticism. But at one point matters were so bad Russell had to intervene, telling Bob that Bert was a valued friend and asking him to back off. The Scotsman took little notice. When the boat arrived in Honolulu and Bert discovered the NSU team had brought their plans forward by a week, he left, catching a plane to Los Angeles.

Travelling by bus he made his way to Wendover, a small town on the edge of the salt flats, found cheap accommodation and was immediately at home. There were big professional outfits like NSU, which arrived with various machines and a party of thirty, including timing technicians, mechanics, team managers and riders, but most teams were amateurs operating on a shoestring. These folks were exactly Bert's kind of people and he soon began to make friends.

From the moment he saw them Bert loved the salt flats. Under the fierce sun they glittered a pure, almost incandescent white, stretching away as flat as poured concrete to the low purple hills on the horizon. During the day the mirage of an island shimmered in the middle distance and sometimes a phantom lake formed. Sunsets were spectacular, seeming to set the flats alight against a fiery red and gold sky. It was a place made for magic.

The 30,000 acres of salt flats had slowly formed when an ancient lake began to dry up about 15,000 years before. Every winter, a shallow aquifer, with help from a number of violent seasonal rainstorms, flooded the flats, erasing any scars left by the racers. The shallow lake then dried out under the punishing sun during spring and when the last moisture had evaporated in the broiling summer heat, the salt flats were ready for the next season: pristine once more, firm and dead flat.

The area used for record breaking had a salt crust at least fifteen centimetres deep and was about twenty-four kilometres long and sixteen wide. A huge plane of thinner salt surrounded it with thick mud trapped below the surface. In places the crust was only four millimetres deep, obviously a danger to any vehicle that strayed off course.

Humans had historically avoided the area, which offered nothing in the way of flora or fauna. Native Americans had found no use for it and even Captain BLE Bonneville, the US Army officer who explored the area and gave it its name, had given the place a wide berth. Early wagon trains of settlers had learned the hard way how risky crossing the thin salt could be, and several had very nearly perished. In 1896 a cyclist named Bill Rishel won a competition staged by newspaper mogul and self-publicist William Randolph Hearst to pedal across the wasteland.

Rishel later became the president of the Utah Automobile Association and it was he who first thought of racing cars on the salt. He and two Salt Lake businessmen took a Pierce Arrow onto the flats in 1907 and found the surface satisfactory for driving. Encouraged, they convinced American racer Teddy Tezlaff to run his famous Blitzen Benz on the salt where he easily eclipsed speeds set on the beach at Daytona. When the automotive community refused to recognise his records the indefatigable Rishel continued to promote the salt flats as the place to go fast and, in 1927, after a cross country highway that ran through the area was completed, the celebrated record breaker Ab Jenkins won an 125-mile race against a train full of celebrities between Salt Lake City and Wendover.

Jenkins returned to the salt to race from then on and in 1932 set an unofficial record over twenty-four hours with an average of 112.94 miles an hour, establishing it as a place for long distance record attempts as well as all-out speed records. Many automobile industry leaders criticised Jenkins for taking wild rides in the middle of nowhere, but the ideal nature of the salt flats for speed record attempts had been clearly demonstrated, particularly to those inter-ested in breaking the absolute land speed record.

For a time the European record breakers had used beaches like the vast Pendine Sands in Wales, while the Americans had favoured Daytona Beach. As speeds rose such venues became increasingly inadequate and there had been a number of tragic deaths due to poor track conditions. A new venue was desperately needed.

One of the first to try for the land speed record at Bonneville had been Sir Malcolm Campbell, who had arrived from England in 1937 with his Rolls Royce aero-engined streamliner. Campbell was there by special invitation of the State of Utah, which had suggested their salt flats were superior to Daytona's beach. This proved to be true. Bluebird, as Campbell christened all his record cars, had bellowed across the salt flats to break the 300-mile-an-hour mark for the first time. From then on all land speed records had been set there.

Following Campbell's record British drivers George Eyston and John Cobb arrived with their cars to go for the fastest mile, setting new records in 1938 within a month of each other. Ab Jenkins was back on the salt too, and he and the two British drivers battled to break each other's twelve and twenty-four hour records. The Second World War put an end to racing, but Cobb returned in 1947 and achieved 394.2 miles per hour, a record that remained unbroken. By then a new invasion was under way. Speed-crazed hot rodders finally discovered the salt flats.

Californian hot rodders had started racing their tuned Model T and Model A Fords on dry lake-beds in the Mohave Desert in the 1930s. The movement became widely popular and in 1937 they set up the Southern California Timing Association (SCTA) to control events. After the war the cars become a great deal faster. When they started running out of room on the smaller Mohave flats the association started Bonneville Speed Week in 1947.

One of the first to race there was a returned soldier named Bill Burke, who turned up with a device that eptomised the free-thinking of the time, a cigar-shaped special made by inserting a flat head Ford V8 into the aluminium belly tank normally found dangling under a P-38 fighter plane. He had paid $35 for it ex-air force and after cutting out a cockpit and fitting minimal seating and controls he managed 158 miles per hour. Belly tank specials, and all manner of vehicles, ranging from the mad to the sublime, had been turning up at speed week ever since.

CHAPTER THIRTEEN
NEW FRIENDS

The NSU team was cordoned off but it was possible to get close enough to watch them preparing their machines. The two Germans chosen to drive the record breakers were the tall and elegant Wilhelm Herz and the stocky, irrepressible Happy Muller. Bert was thrilled to see Happy again and was soon on first name terms with others in the team. He watched enthralled as the team took out others' records with a streamlined 350cc supercharged twin. Delphin 111, as it was called, was a perfect teardrop shape with a long tail. The rider was completely enclosed and peered out through a curved Plexiglas screen set into the nose. A second machine for smaller engines was even more radical, with the driver lying back in a hammock within the low streamlined bodywork, the engine sitting behind him. The tiny projectile also featured spring-loaded flaps that the rider could thrust his feet through as landing gear. It was variously run with an un-blown 250cc engine, a 125cc motor and a tiny 49cc unit.

Fitted with the 250cc engine the small machine provided the first dramatic incident. With Herz lying on his back inside, it was hit by a side gust at over 200 miles an hour and rolled. Incredibly, Herz survived with only a few bruises.

Rain delayed events for a few days but as soon as the salt dried the Germans were at it again. Herz went out in the beautiful Delphin 111 streamliner and hit a patch of still damp salt at very high speed. He veered off course, demolishing a timing light stand, but was again unhurt. After further delays he set various records on 2 August but the big one, the outright speed record for motorcycles, did not fall until the 4th, when he achieved a two-way average of 210.64 miles an hour.

Bert was right on the spot when he did it. He had left the starting area to jog, in forty-degree heat, four kilometres to the area where the timing officials were gathered. Fortunately a safety marshal had seen the lone figure on the salt and gone to find out what the hell was going on. Bert persuaded the marshal to give him a lift and before long was happily ensconced with the officials.

One of the them was Roscoe Turner, a senior employee of Bell Auto Parts and a founding member of the SCTA. Roscoe (not to be confused with the record breaking Southern aviator whose name he shared) and Bert hit it off right away, in part because they were both simple men from country backgrounds who'd worked hard with the talents God gave them to make a modest living – that, and the fact that they were both complete speed freaks. Elbert Roscoe Turner had migrated to California to escape a dirt-poor existence in Texas in the 1930s, hidden in a railroad boxcar. After being violently evicted by railway security goons in the town of Bell he'd met George White, proprietor of Bell Auto Parts. They got on well, perhaps because they shared a railway connection. George always said he'd been born in a railroad caboose somewhere in Arizona.

Roscoe was a born mechanic. As White had just acquired the assets of the Cragar Company, manufacturers of overhead valve heads for Model T and Model A Fords, he needed help. Roscoe had been with the company ever since. Over the years it had expanded to make a large range of speed equipment, including cylinder heads, manifolds, steering wheels, a huge selection of alloy wheels and safety apparel – in particular the famous Bell helmets. Naturally the company's interests and his own passion for speed made it almost inevitable he would gravitate to the salt flats and eventually to this meeting with a talkative New Zealander who entertained him enormously as they observed the Germans make history.

Later that day the two new friends watched as Happy Muller established a raft of records for 100cc motorcycles with incredible runs of just under 140 miles an hour in the smaller machine, a startling tribute to Gustav Baumm, the design genius who had developed the 'Flying Hammock' before being killed testing one at the Nürburgring. Several days later Muller averaged 151 miles an hour with a 125cc engine and 119 miles an hour with the tiny 49cc powerplant, to establish two new outright speed records. Herz then made another run with the 240cc engine, averaging 152 miles an hour. This was obviously well below the machine's potential when compared with his first run, but it was enough to set a new class record. By the time it was over the Germans had broken fifty-four international records, records Bert would always acknowledge as the most impressive achievements he had ever witnessed.

By now Bob Burns and Russell Wright had arrived to discover that they did indeed have problems with their fuel. At the 1220-metre altitude of Bonneville, and in the extremely dry atmosphere, the Vincent's settings were way out. The first time Bob went for a test run with the sidecar he burned holes in both pistons in less than three kilometres. This occasioned an exhausting all-night rebuild followed by a lot of messing around to retune the bike to run properly. The pair endured days of frustration waiting for a chance to run the bike. Eventually George Eyston was able to slot them into his own programme and give them a little of the time allocated to the BMC team. The frustration must have put Bob in a fouler temper than usual for he managed to aggravate nearly everyone he came into contact with. It was later said that the only person in the history of motorcycle racing on the salt who ever had to pay for a push start was Bob Burns. When they finally did get a run Bob immediately set a new sidecar mark that should have been a record, while Russell was able to achieve a highly credible 198 mile an hour average, unfortunately a long way short of the new NSU record.

After a lot of dithering the FIM decided not to accept Bob's new sidecar record on the grounds that the timekeepers and the clocks on the site had not been sanctioned by them. It was a heartbreaking outcome for Bob as he and Russell had agreed that there would be no more record attempts. The bike had already been sold to an eager American.

Bert, who was now extremely wary of Bob Burns, kept well clear and instead spent his time with Turner or Eyston. The latter was exactly his kind of man and about the same vintage. In England he lived his life among the aristocracy; he had introduced one Phillip Mountbatten to his future wife Elizabeth, the woman who would become Queen of England.

Their respective social positions made no difference to either George or Bert, who liked to share stories of races and crashes. Bert particularly enjoyed hearing about how George had survived while setting records in an MG during the 1930s at the banked oval circuit at Montlery in France. His car had caught fire at the very end of an attempt to cover 100 miles in an hour. He'd flicked the gear lever into neutral to coast as far as he could, not knowing he had already passed the 100-mile mark. As the flames licked back into the cockpit he was forced to scramble onto the back of the car, leaning forward to steer. When the flames really took hold and the car had slowed down to about fifty miles an hour the big man bailed out.

'It was a rude shock,' he told Bert. 'The mere fifty miles an hour had seemed nothing after droning along at the ton for so long, but when I decanted myself the impact was quite startling!' Half-dazed, he ended up on the verge, with his overalls alight and his boots and socks burned away.

Once mended he travelled to Pendine Sands in Wales to set more records, this time wearing a fireproof, asbestos suit. The gathered press photographers insisted on seeing the suit tested while George wore it so he obliged by having mechanics hose it with blowlamps. His good-humoured approach to life appealed to Bert, who was equally impressed by his quite incredible motor-racing career, which included hill climbs, beach races, road races, grand prix, and breaking records.

Of all his exploits the ones that most intrigued Bert were his land speed record attempts in the car Thunderbolt. Possibly the most intimidating vehicle ever devised, this six-wheel behemoth was powered by a pair of V12 Rolls Royce aero engines with a combined capacity of 73,000cc, making collectively about 4700 horse power. Eyston had taken the record in it three times before the Second World War, with a top speed of 357.53 miles an hour. After the last attempt the car had been shipped to New Zealand to tour on public display, and the outbreak of war had stranded it there.

'I thought it would be safe,' George complained to Bert, 'way down there, miles from German bombs and whatnot. But some beggar burned down the barn you fellows had it stored in. As if that wasn't enough it was flung into the Wellington rubbish dump and covered with hundreds of tons of muck! The poor old thing is still there. It really was a rather uncivilised way to treat a perfectly good motorcar.'

George had ended his record-breaking only the year before when he had driven a streamlined Austin Healy on the salt as part of a twenty-four-hour record attempt. It finished when the car went into a 275-metre skid at 140 miles an hour, tearing a wheel off as it went, when conditions on the salt deteriorated. Somehow he had controlled the Healy but it seemed like a good time to retire from active record driving. He was at pains, however, not to discourage Bert from pursuing his record dreams, insisting he had accepted retirement only because he realised there was nothing left that he wanted to achieve. Eyston was a director of Wakefield Oil, manufacturers of Castrol R, and before he left Bonneville he promised Bert that his company would supply free racing oil as long as the New Zealander continued to chase records. Their parting was tinged with genuine regret. Eyston patted Bert on the shoulder and quietly told him to keep going, 'to show these young fellows just what we Victorians are made of!'

Bert was now determined to stay on for the National Speed Trials, or Speed Week as it was popularly known. A conversation with a visiting Australian alerted Bert to the possibility that he might have to extend his visa. He would need a letter from someone who knew him attesting to his character and the unlikelihood of him becoming a burden on the state. Bert asked Russell, who was by now packing up, if he would oblige but Russell pointed out that Bob Burns, as the nominal boss of the team, should be the one to do it. Bob turned him down flat. Bert was never one to carry a grudge or waste time feeling resentful, but from then on Burns enjoyed the distinction of being the only man Bert ever truly loathed.

He elected to forget the visa extension and stay anyway – a decision he would never regret. It led to him meeting a number of fellow worshippers at the altar of the God of Speed who would become lifelong friends and invaluable allies.

One was a short, powerfully built fellow wearing a T-shirt with the Vincent logo emblazoned across the front. He had introduced himself to Russell Wright and somehow Bert came to know that he was Marty Dickerson, a man celebrated for setting a number of records on Vincent motorcycles. Marty had turned up to watch the NSU team in action and like Bert stayed for Speed Week. The year before he had ridden a supercharged Vincent Lightning across the salt at a blazing 177 miles an hour to take the record for fastest non-streamlined bike from BMW.

Bert's open and friendly manner combined with his tales of impossible speeds on an old Indian Scout soon intrigued the Californian. Of course, Russell Wright was still around and Marty soon confirmed that Bert's stories were true. He really had built a Scout and ridden it at over 130 miles an hour.

Marty was at the salt flats with his partner Jackie. Bert wasted no time laying on the charm for her. Before long the three of them were hanging out together. Marty heard about racing motorcycles in Invercargill and Bert heard Marty's accounts of his early days gaining a reputation in street drags. Jackie mostly listened.

Marty told Bert about growing up on a family ranch on land that now formed part of a runway at Los Angeles Airport, and of the time he bought his first machine, a derelict 1929 Harley Davidson, for $65 while still at school. It was wartime and the Harley had good tyres, an important consideration when they were virtually irreplaceable. He had managed to coax the moribund machine back into life, falling off on his first ride. The tumble did nothing to diminish his passion and he hammered the old Harley all over the landscape.

After graduating he worked for Northrop Aircraft, where his first job was fabricating parts for the top-secret B 35 Flying Wing. The exacting standards of the aeronautic industry meant he picked up many of the technical and mechanical skills that would later prove invaluable for motorcycle racing.

His first sporting motorcycle was a Triumph Tiger 100, which he bought new and hotted up until it would run at a shade under 100 miles an hour, a very good speed for these 500cc twins. He raced on dry lake-beds and around the streets, taking particular delight in besting the bored and stroked Harley Davidsons that many street racers preferred. But it was when he saw his first Vincent that everything changed.

It was not love at first sight. His first impression of the big British V-twin, which he had tracked down at the agent's dealership in Burbank, was disappointing and he considered the sand-cast finish of the engine cases particularly ugly. But in time he grew accustomed to it and began to pester the agent to take his Triumph as a part exchange. Finally a deal was worked out and Marty had his Vincent B Rapide. When the repayments stretched his finances the dealer, Mickey Martin, suggested he tour the bike around the country, street racing it to ramp up some interest and hopefully a few sales. The interest was certainly there and Marty raced many of the hottest local rods and bikes in towns all across the west, though few sales resulted. When it was clear there was no real future in what he was doing, he decided to set up his own shop. In 1951, with Mickey Martin's help and encouragement, he opened his own Vincent dealership in his hometown of Hawthorne.

The previous year he had ridden his Rapide out to Bonneville to help a Vincent-mounted record breaker named Rollie Free. The trip home on the Vincent would turn out to be the last time it was ridden on the road, at least while Marty owned it. He now wanted to go record breaking. The next year, after fitting Lightning cams and pipes, he attained 129 miles an hour, a disappointing speed compared with his expectations, but enough to take a class C record. An Aerial Square Four soon broke that, but the following year Marty returned, having fitted larger carburettors supplied by Phil Vincent, and having altered the gearing. Class C stipulated that machines had to run on regular pump petrol and retain the equipment supplied with the standard machine, including items such as the kick-start, lights and fenders. Still, he found a loophole in the rules allowing him to replace the seat with a low pad over the rear wheel. After turning the handlebars upside down he was able to hunker right down in the machine to significantly reduce drag. Thus equipped he smashed the Class C record with an average speed of 147 miles an hour, a record he still held.

He was still racing the Vincent in Southern Californian road races, in addition to a stove-hot 250cc two-stroke Jawa on which he'd won his class in the prestigious offroad Catalina Grand Prix in 1953. As with many gifted motorcyclists it did not matter if he was racing on the track, salt, street or dirt; as long as he had two wheels underneath him he was at home.

One morning Marty introduced Bert to Bill Bagnall, a journalist who wrote for the *Motorcyclist*, one of the biggest bike magazines in the US. Bagnall was absolutely flabbergasted that Bert could have achieved over 130 miles an hour on a 1920 Indian Scout and interviewed Bert at length, organising photographs to go with the story. He asked Bert to stay in touch and let him know if he set any further records. Bert agreed and also promised to send over a few pictures of the Indian, quietly delighted that the magazine would be interested in his activities on the other side of the world. Bagnall checked a few final details before they parted, including how to spell Invercargill. Bert told him, then added, 'Sometimes I only spell it with one L, to save ink.'

At the end of Speed Week, when all the bikes, hot rods and belly-tank specials had done their thing until the next year, Bert asked Marty if he could catch a ride with him back to Los Angeles. He was short of cash after flying in and keen to stretch out what little money he had left. Roscoe Turner had already left after inviting Bert to stay if he ever went through Bell, which Bert intended to do at some stage. Marty was happy to help but he only had a pickup and had already agreed to take another passenger. With three in the cab the only place Bert could ride would be on the back.

Bert's face lit up at the suggestion, even if Marty had meant it more as an apology, and assured him that such an arrangement would be perfect. Marty explained that he would be driving straight through, a distance of about 1200 kilometres, stopping only for food and gas. This just made Bert beam even brighter. There was no point in dawdling; a straight run was just the ticket! There seemed little left to discuss and Marty helped Bert clear a space on the tray out of the wind. As they left Wendover and headed on to the highway Marty looked in the rear view mirror to check on Bert and he saw him leaning back in the corner of the deck, hair ruffled gently by the breeze as he gazed at the landscape sliding by. For a moment he thought Bert was shouting at something. Then he heard the faint strain of an old song above the noise of the wind. Bert was singing.

He sang all the way back to Hawthorne, where Marty found him a cheap hotel. Bert was glad of the chance to look around the Los Angeles area. He paid for five nights at the hotel and caught a bus to Bell to see his friend Roscoe, who showed him around the plant and gave him a good lunch, before catching the bus back to Hawthorne.

On a visit to the San Dana Drag Strip the bus dropped him off eight kilometres short. Having spent hours getting that far he decided to hitchhike but no one would stop. Finally, he waved a dollar bill at a guy on a Harley who gave him a ride. Blasting through traffic at ninety miles an hour, Bert yelled in the rider's ear to take it easy; he never did extend the same rights of passage on the road as he presumed for himself.

After two weeks he found he was missing $100 – a serious matter. As American money is all the same size and colour he wondered if he'd mistakenly given his landlady the big bill in the gloom of the hall. He knocked on her door in a state of some trepidation. She was hostile at first, but Bert explained he was just eliminating the possibility. When she reluctantly checked her purse, sure enough, there was a $100 bill. She was so mortified she offered Bert the reduced rate of $10 a week whenever he wished to stay. He would often take her up on the offer in years to come.

Marty took Bert to meet his very good friend Rolland Free, who lived in Hollywood. Bert soon discovered that Rollie, as he was known, knew a great deal about Indians, having raced them and been a dealer for the company for many years. He also knew a lot about breaking records, having set a number on Vincent motorcycles.

Rollie was nearer Bert's age than Marty's, not quite as tall as Bert, with a sharp-featured, friendly face topped with a glistening bald pate. He had been a highly successful motorcycle racer in the twenties and thirties after acquiring his first motorcycle, an NSU, at the age of twelve. As soon as he was old enough he had became a salesman, selling Ace motorcycles in Kansas City. He was soon racing and setting records on them, changing to Indians when he joined an Indian dealership.

He earned a reputation as the fastest street racer in the city, taking special pleasure, as Marty would later on his Triumph, in thrashing Harley Davidsons. In 1923 he had his first race on a board track, a 100-mile event in which he finished out of the money. From then on, however, he was a frequent winner and earned such a reputation in the long distance events held in Jacksonville, Florida, and Savannah, Georgia, that he was offered a drive in the 1930 Indianapolis 500. His engine blew after 172 miles and a second shot the next year also ended in mechanical failure.

But he now got into motorcycle record breaking and in the late thirties set several AMA class records riding an Indian on Daytona

Beach. During the war he joined the air force and ended up in Utah, when he had his first look at the salt flats. After the war he was approached by a Hollywood sportsman called John Edgar, who had sponsorship from Shell Oil for a speed record attempt on a Vincent Black Shadow. Rollie agreed to ride it and in 1949 he averaged 148.6 miles an hour across the salt on his first two runs.

In earlier days he'd watched another record breaker, Ed Kretz, riding in a pair of swimming trunks and decided to try the same thing, hoping the reduced drag might help him to crack the 150 mile an hour mark. A photographer with a long lens travelling in a car on a parallel course captured an image of Rollie lying stretched out on the bike with his feet trailing behind, clad only in his trunks and an old pair of sneakers. Unable to lift his head, Rollie simply stared down at the black stripe on the salt and kept the throttle open until he had covered the distance. At the end of the two runs he'd broken the previous eleven-year record with an average speed of 150.313 miles an hour. The photograph became one of the most iconographic images in motorcycle history.

Rollie acknowledged his mentor with a typically modest comment to reporters: 'I stole the swimming trunks idea from Ed Kretz, who used to do the same on Southern California dry lakes. Incidentally, Ed looks much nicer in a swimsuit than I do.'

He returned in 1950 with a streamlined egg fitted over a Vincent Black Lightning, which went out of control at 144 miles an hour, flipped on to one side and then the other, sliding over 300 metres before it finally came to rest. Rollie was unhurt and after stripping off the shell he pushed the bike to 156.77 miles an hour, breaking his old record by a handsome margin.

Rollie was tremendously impressed by Bert's efforts on the Scout. When he learned Bert was considering shipping it over to run on the salt he immediately warmed to the idea, promising Bert all the assistance he could give. For Bert the day was a confirmation of all the qualities he now attributed to Americans in general. They were encouraging and inclusive, naturally inclined to help a man achieve his best, rather than hold him back with petty resentments.

There were further trips with friends of both Rollie and Marty. The word got out that Bert was a good fellow and a very willing travel companion. Bert even hitched a ride with someone heading in the general direction of Indianapolis, hoping to visit the famous racetrack on the way. To his immense disappointment they had already overshot the track by 300 kilometres by the time they stopped for gas and directions, and he never did get back to it. But the trip showed him more of the country and he couldn't get enough of it, in heaven just watching America rolling past the car window.

All too soon it was time to go home. Marty and Rollie drove him to Long Beach to catch his ship for the long voyage back to New Zealand. They both urged him to return and he promised he would. Little did they know he'd make a habit of it, making fourteen visits in all.

CHAPTER FOURTEEN
FISH

Home once more, and well rested after a pleasant sea voyage, Bert resumed the gruelling schedule of work on his two bikes. His circle of friends was constantly expanding but there was a core group who went out of their way to keep a kindly eye on him, generous souls who would visit armed with a great pile of steaming fish and chips wrapped in newspaper; people such as Irving Hayes and his son Norman, who entertained Bert, or were more often entertained by Bert, every Wednesday night when he turned up to share a roast meal cooked by Irving's wife Kitty. Who had, meanwhile, ensured that Wednesday was her night to be out playing bridge, the better to avoid Bert's endless stories of motorcycle adventures and misadventures which she found beyond tedium. She always greeted him affectionately, listened to his complaint that she was always going out, and made her escape. Irving and Norman, of course, were more than happy to talk about racing cars and bikes all evening.

Irving had started racing immediately before the war in a bored out 1939 Dodge D11 Deluxe Sedan equipped with triple Tilottson carburettors and a shaved head; a big, elegant hot rod that he threw sideways at every opportunity. After racing motorcycles Norman had also started racing cars, and he and Irving had built a supercharged Morris Minor for Norman and one for his sister. Irving in the meantime had moved from the Dodge to a Triumph Vanguard and then eventually up to a Jaguar XK120. Racing was very much at the centre of their lives. The care and warmth they gave to Bert were a backstop that gave his world a richness and depth he might otherwise have missed out on.

Bert also met a young man at one of the engineering concerns he haunted who would become a close and lifelong friend. Ashley Bell had been a motorcyclist from the moment he took over his brother's Malvern Star, a lightweight Australian moped he used to get to school. When Ashley left and became an apprentice at the engineering shop H E Melhops (where Bert set himself on fire), his father bought him a Francis Barnett from Tappers to replace the inadequate moped. Ashley rode this until he could afford an old 1930s Triumph 250cc single. He raced it a little on grass tracks and then rapidly moved through a succession of British singles including a proper JAP speedway bike. Along the way he became great friends with the eldest son of the widow who Duncan Meikle had by now married. John, or Jack as most people called him, shared his stepfather's love of motorcycle racing.

Inevitably Ashley became one of Bert's inner circle and was soon dropping by regularly at 105 Bainfield Road, sometimes to help and sometimes to simply share a yarn and a cup of tea. Duncan had by then bought an older model girder-forked MSS Velocette and he and Bert were always bouncing ideas off each other in their common quest for more power.

Sometimes the collaboration could lead to terrible arguments, usually when Duncan was exasperated with Bert, who inevitably compounded the situation by being unapologetic about whatever he had said or done. One thing that really annoyed Duncan was Bert's habit of accelerating immediately his bike started, a habit that left Duncan, who was inevitably pushing, stretched out full length and face down on the ground. No matter how many times he yelled and swore at Bert for doing it, and no matter how many times Bert promised not to do it again, he always did. The quarrels never lasted long – they had too much in common, including extreme frugality.

Whenever motorcycles gathered for racing, a representative for the famous racing oil Castrol R was usually around giving away free samples. Bert and Duncan always drained it from their machines after racing. Ashley would quite often find them gently simmering a brew in one of Bert's aluminium cooking pots on the little stove so they could scoop the scum off the top and use it again. They were always busy doing something, and sometimes in such a hurry that things could go seriously awry.

One such incident occurred when Ashley arrived and found them about to start the Velocette. Bert suspected his back wheel was buckled and wanted to check it, so he mounted the machine on a block of wood that left the back wheel free to spin a few centimetres off the floor. Duncan was kneeling behind the machine about to start it by pulling the underside of the rear wheel towards him while the machine was in second gear. The bike fired up and Bert slipped it into top, all the better to detect a wobble should the wheel prove buckled. But when he revved the engine hard the machine jumped off the block, bellowing away and spinning its wheel on the floor. The handlebars were barely big enough for each hand so Bert's grip on the bucking machine was marginal, but he had at least managed to grab the front brake.

As the shed began to fill with tyre smoke, Ashley, who had been standing beside the bike and now felt helpless to intervene, backed up against the bench to get as far away as possible while he awaited developments. They were not long in coming. Bert made the mistake of shutting the throttle. The tyre slowed, of course, but also suddenly found traction on the aging linoleum, rocketing the bike forward on an arced course around Bert, who somehow kept a grip but was eventually dragged under the cluttered, all-purpose table. There was a tremendous crash and suddenly pots and pans were showering down while the engine kept booming away and the back wheel kept spinning, still gripping occasionally and throwing everything back in the air. Finally, Duncan managed to reach in and switch off the bike. He and Ashley dragged it from the wreckage to free Bert, who was unhurt. The bike too had sustained little damage. The three men looked at each other blankly for a few seconds and then laughed. Bert recovered his breath enough to ask Duncan if the wheel was in fact buckled.

Duncan shrugged. 'Hell man, d'ya seriously expect me to notice with all that going on?'

Bert snorted. 'Well of course I do. You could see I was busy!'

Ashley never knew Bert to be egotistical but he could sometimes stretch a friend's tolerance. He could seem rude. 'Those eye crutches will wreck your vision,' he once admonished Ashley for wearing sunglasses. 'I never wore them and I can look at the sun.' Other times his parsimony could become plain meanness, as Ashley discovered when he asked for a small end of thick aluminium plate Bert had picked up somewhere. He wanted to build a set of engine mounts and thought Bert might sell him a scrag end. He was wrong. Bert had paid £10 for it and Ashley would have to buy the lot, minus the small amount Bert had used. Ashley handed over the money reluctantly. About a month later Bert approached him and asked if he still had the plate. Ashley had only used a small bit, so Bert said he would be around after work to cut a bit off for his own use. Ashley laughed. 'Oh no you don't. You made me buy it all and now you can flaming well buy it back. Less the money for the little bit I used, of course.'

Bert was outraged. 'You can't do that to a pensioner, Ash! It's just not done.'

Bert eventually found the plate he needed, but it was not from Ashley.

Meanwhile, back at 105 Bainfield Road, work was under way to substantially alter the frames of both the Velocette and the Indian. Bert had thought long and hard about streamlining and had come to the conclusion that rather than fitting a high teardrop to a standard frame as most record breakers had up until that point, it would be more sensible to make the bike as low as possible. This would reduce frontal drag and also, he hoped, reduce the machines vulnerability to crosswinds.

He now knew, from his time on the salt flats, that the breezes there could come from any direction; it was not unusual for a record breaker to encounter several puffs from different angles. He realised it would also be necessary to lengthen the machine to achieve the high-speed stability he was after and to carry the long, low, streamlined body he wanted to build.

Walking through the botanical gardens in Invercargill one fine afternoon he stopped to enjoy a moment in the sun by the big ornamental goldfish pond, idly watching the fish when something startled them. In an instant they flashed from one end of the pond to the other – proof surely that they possessed a superbly slippery shape. The combination of a long, low machine and a goldfish-inspired body, he reasoned, would have to be a winner. He sent a sketch to Rollie Free who wrote back and told him that it looked unusual but sound enough, adding that if God had intended fish to fly it might work. As it happened, Bert had seen thousands of flying fish on his sea voyages, gliding through the air at speed on the high-pressure zone preceding the great ocean swells. He decided to press ahead.

Bert returned to the park a number of times to properly study and sketch the fish. This was unusual behaviour for Bert. Normally he made parts, and often quite complex parts, without ever putting a line on paper. He could also complete quite complicated mathematical equations in his head, a tribute to the thoroughness of his rote learning. But he was eager to replicate the goldfish shape as nearly as possible, and detailed sketches were the only way to achieve that.

With customary zeal he set about hacking and altering the frame of the Indian to make it 60 inches longer and as low as possible. He cut the single top tube out of the frame and replaced it with two square-section steel tubes that flowed around a flat, oblong fuel tank, located as snug to the top end of the motor as he could get it. He then did the same thing with the Velocette before lightening both machines. Frame gussets were drilled full of holes as were all cogs in the driveline. Anything that could be shaved was shaved. Everything that could be junked was junked. The oil tanks were discarded and a length of lightweight aluminium pipe, clipped to the frame's front down tube with a Tia Maria cork as a filler cap, was substituted. By the time he'd finished, the bikes had lost about half their weight. The Velocette, for example, had shrunk from 350 pounds to just 187. Norman was astonished to see that the accelerator cable on the Velocette ran straight through the head to get to the carburettor. He asked Bert if he had done it to eliminate material or because his cable wasn't quite long enough to go around the long way. Bert was adamant. He had done it to save weight.

For some reason Bert did not tell Duncan of his plans to stream-line the machine. He kept his intentions very much to himself, at least in New Zealand. Why he did that is hard to say, but it was unlikely to have been false modesty. Whatever the reason he and Duncan were soon back in the business of breaking records for unfaired bikes. On 9 February 1957, they took the Indian to Oreti Beach where Bert raised his New Zealand beach record to 131.38 miles an hour. A couple of months later, on 13 April, they took the Indian to the Pioneer Motorcycle Club speed trials to have a crack at the New Zealand record for the 750cc class.

They had decided to take Ashley and at five in the morning, still cold and dark, Bert stood outside the house and bellowed for him to get a wriggle on, waking Ashley's family and half the street. Cringing with embarrassment, and with his mother's shouted admonition to tell the old fool with the fake American accent to pull his head in, Ashley climbed into the cramped cab of Duncan's pickup and they were off.

The adventure was almost over before it started. They submit-ted the bike for scrutineering and Bert was told that he could not possibly run.

Up until the fifties Bert had used beaded wheels – vintage tyres suited to old crocks but manifestly unsuitable for high-speed runs. Bert always argued that the bead at least held the wheel securely in the rim by hooking into it, although there was no wire in the bead to provide real strength. He believed the greatest danger lay in the treads flying off at speed, so he simply cut them off and made the tyre smooth with a file and sandpaper. This left only a thin rubber covering on the tyre's carcass, but Bert achieved well over a hundred miles an hour on such tyres before switching to old road racing models. He had probably been more than a little lucky to get away with it for so long. After his record run in 1940, Norman Hayes had examined the Indian and found the front tyre had expanded so much during the run that it had rubbed all the paint off the inside of the mudguard.

The road racing tyres Bert switched to were still far from ideal for the speeds he was now achieving, speeds that demanded proper, high-speed race tyres. But these were beyond his budget. He could use old road racing tyres because, of course, the first thing he did was remove the tread and smooth them off. Sometimes he went a little far, which was easy to do, and exposed the canvas. The scrutineer pointed at just such a patch and told Bert he could not run.

Bert was quick to respond. He fixed the scrutineer with a look of cold determination.

'If I'm game to run on them, what's your damn problem?'

The hapless official looked at the patch of canvas and then back at Bert. He was clearly conflicted but in the end he relented. As he said later to a fellow scrutineer, 'The old bugger's been riding on tyres like that for years. Who was I to tell him he had to change his ways?'

With the mission back on track the little team fueled up the bike and waited for Bert to get a run. It was worth it. With little fuss he set a new record at a remarkable 143.58 miles an hour. This was a stunning achievement and one that many might have considered a fitting climax to thirty-seven years' dedicated racing. However, they were not Bert.

Duncan and Bert often took their Velocettes to hill climbs and beach races, usually on the back of Duncan's light pickup. They would fiddle about with the timing and carburettor settings, bickering away like the crusty old boys they were, generally having the best time. Their efforts were paying off and both bikes, but particularly Bert's, were becoming genuinely fast, even against much younger opposition. It did not always work out that way, but their failures were often as fascinating as their successes.

Ashley sometimes tested their bikes and on one occasion took Bert's for a blast up the beach after the engine had been carefully balanced in accordance with several pages of calculations Duncan had made. Once under way Ashley found the vibration disturbingly odd. It was not exactly unpleasant but it made the handlebar grips feel as if they were growing thicker and his vision began to blur. He returned to the two men waiting on the beach and switched off.

'How was it?' asked Duncan. 'Good?'

'Not bad so far as the overall smoothness went, I suppose. There's just one problem. I seem to be going blind. Everything is going white. Bloody hell! Now I can't see a damn thing!'

'Bugger!' exclaimed Duncan. 'I'll have to start again.'

'What about my eyes?' asked Ashley. 'I'm completely blind.'

Bert's voice boomed out of the white mist. 'Hold your horses Ashley. Can't you see Duncan is thinking?'

It was only a temporary condition, and not all of Ashley's test runs ended so strangely. On another day he had the Velocette absolutely tapped out on Ryal Bush Straight, travelling at a tremendous speed with trees and fences and telegraph poles flicking past in a grey-green blur, as he lay flat on the tank with the machine pounding beneath him. Trouble was, the rev counter didn't seem to be working.

When Ashley returned, Bert asked, 'Was she pulling all the revs she had, do you reckon? It sounded like she was to me.'

Ashley told him the bike had been singing and he doubted it had anything left to give.

'Well then,' said Bert, 'I reckon you must have been doing close to 140 miles an hour.'

There was plenty of racing on the beach and the little team seldom missed a meet. Mostly the distance between turning pegs was a mile or two miles, with no markers in between. At one meeting Bert had the idea that a flag should be planted at the halfway point to tell riders how far they had to go before turning. Perhaps bearing in mind Bert's past form while turning, and with the hope that he'd manage it better with more warning, everyone agreed and a flag was shoved into the sand at the halfway mark. Bert was doing pretty well in the race, riding as always in his T-shirt, crash helmet, jeans and sandshoes, when he managed to clip the flag stanchion at about 120 miles an hour, breaking a couple of toes. The accident finished his race. In considerable agony he complained all the way home to Ashley and Duncan about the stupidity of sticking a flag in the middle of the course, refusing to hear any reference to his part in putting it there.

The bikes were finally performing reliably and well enough for Bert and Duncan to take them to Cust for the New Zealand Grand Prix. It had been 17 years since Bert had come second and he and Duncan elected to run in a support race, the Rangiora Handicap. On the way there Bert decided to have a last run on his bike. They unloaded it and ran it along a dead straight Canterbury Plains road. They then leaned the carburettor out a bit and Bert had another run, promptly burning a hole in a piston. They drove on to Christchurch to a garage they knew, where they stripped the engine.

Bert found an aluminium rivet that fitted the hole and, peening it over to ensure a tight fit, the quick fix might well have worked had they not forgotten to change the carburettor setting, which remained over-lean. As soon as Bert started the race he burned another hole in the piston. Duncan did not fare a great deal better and so they drove home again.

There was another speed trial coming up in Canterbury and Bert was eager to have a crack on the Velocette. One Sunday, with a week to go, he and Ashley were out testing on Ryal Bush Straight. The bike was running well but Bert had replaced a piston with one he had accidentally manufactured a little undersize. Instead of melting it down he'd decided to micro peen it, a process that expands pistons and was commonly used with cars. The piston worked fine for a while but when it gave up and flew apart Bert was accelerating hard at over 100 miles an hour. As always he pulled the clutch in with lightning quick reactions, but the damage was done and the engine was wrecked.

He had spares on hand for everything except the conrod so on Monday he went hunting for a bulldozer axle and began the long process of making a new one. Ashley dropped by to see him from time to time. Bert was working eighteen hours a day to finish in time to travel on Friday. He was ready at five o'clock on Thursday afternoon, only to learn that the event had been cancelled due to high fire danger in the Canterbury forests.

'Fire danger,' he scoffed. 'They should be banning idiots from wandering around with cancer sticks hanging out of their mouths. That's the fire danger!'

Bert was now busy on his streamliner shell. He built a light frame that attached to the bike and formed the shell by gently hammering the aluminium sheet over a small bag of sand to achieve the compound curves he wanted. As each section was finished he welded it to the growing body, making slow but steady progress. If he intended hiding this activity from his friend he was not successful for long.

When Duncan discovered what Bert was up to he was livid about not being told, and hurt that Bert would keep such a major development from him. He stalked off with badly bruised feelings. Later, when Ashley asked Bert why he had not seen Duncan around, Bert simply replied, 'Duncan was not playing speaks at the moment.'

Like most people closest to Bert, Ashley sometimes needed a break from his loud chatter and often challenging way of dealing with the world. He and his father regularly went angling for trout or salmon in the clear rivers that rushed out of the mountains and curled across the flat coastal plains to the sea. The would share quiet conversations and comfortable silences against the soft music of the river.

After one such trip they were relaxing over lunch at Oamaru's Grosvenor restaurant, about halfway between Christchurch and Invercargill. Ashley had been there before with Bert and Duncan, and witnessed Bert's habit of shouting for service and generally embarrassing those around him. The contrast of sitting with his father was so striking that Ashley remarked on it. No sooner had he mentioned it than his father, looking suddenly flabbergasted, said, 'Don't look now, but Bert is on his way in.'

Sure enough there he was, large as life and noisy as ever. 'Hi Ash. Hi Pops!' Bert sat down and bellowed at the waitress, 'Hey, Missus, can a starving man get something to eat around here?'

Ashley and his father smiled apologetically, but they need not have bothered. In moments Bert was chatting away to the waitress, ladling on the compliments and generally charming her. When she had gone Bert explained that he was on his way home after blowing the Indian up at about 135 miles an hour at a speed trial in Timaru. The conrod had invaded the gearbox, demolishing the bottom half of the crankcase, mangling the gearbox, bending the mainshaft and generally causing havoc. He was on his own as Duncan was still apparently not playing speaks.

While he was talking a motorcyclist pulled up outside the restaurant. Bert paused to watch him before telling the Bells that the rider was obviously inexperienced. 'You can tell,' he said, 'by the way he sits on his bike.'

Ashley's father laughed. 'Well, I'd hate to hear what you'd have to say about me if I ever rode a bike.'

Bert looked astonished. 'You mean you never have?' he exclaimed. 'By golly, you might as well be dead!'

Any embarrassment Ashley might have felt was balanced by Bert's sheer likability. Most people recounting a tale of demolition such as this latest misadventure on the Indian would expect sympathy, but Bert never did. The fact that he would go home and start again without complaint meant that ultimately he was a positive person to be around – even if he had just accused his father of wasting his time on earth.

By mid-year Bert was back in America, looking around the car yards of Los Angeles for a suitable old bomb to drive. He finally arrived at Marty's in a 1950 Plymouth Coupe, for which he paid $28. One of America's greatest pleasures for a wily old Southlander of Scottish decent was the quality of its junk. The car was a good investment, and after a catch up with Marty and Rollie he headed for the salt.

Back at Wendover, safely installed once more in the State Line Motel, he almost immediately encountered his friend George Eyston. Eyston had returned to the salt to supervise an MG record attempt and introduced Bert to his drivers, Stirling Moss and David Ash. Bert would follow the team's fortunes closely. Eyston was going through a worrying time. Unseasonable rains had made the surface on the flats soggy, hardly conducive to high speeds. Fortunately it dried out enough for Moss to power the pretty saucer-shaped streamliner, with its little 1506cc supercharged, mid-mounted engine, to a highly creditable 246.6 miles an hour and five Class F records, including a twelve-hour record.

Both the drivers and Eyston were delighted with the result and Bert joined them to celebrate with a memorable dinner at the small State Line Casino. On the eight-kilometre trip back across the salt flats to the road the team's high spirits led to an all out drag-race. Bert joined in with the Plymouth but afterwards was disturbed to hear a slight knock that he diagnosed as worn piston. The old heap continued to get him around, and he decided it would hang together as long as he did not push it and kept an eye on the oil level.

The MG team left just before Speed Week, when Marty and Rollie turned up along with all the other speed-mad amateurs who made the event such a colourful blast of organised mayhem. Bert wandered about boldly introducing himself to anyone associated with anything he found interesting. He met Californian John Vesco who was there with a 1932 Ford Model B-powered streamliner of delicate beauty. The Ford had started racing on the salt in 1953 as a belly tanker, but had flipped with Vesco's friend and race partner Jimmy Dinkins in it. Dinkins's helmet was worn away as he slid upside down along the track at 175 miles an hour. Fortunately he stopped before the highly abrasive surface reached the top of his head, but it was a close thing.

After examining the hole in Jimmy's skid-lid, Vesco decided to build something slippery and safe. He constructed the thinnest, safest, most aerodynamic car yet seen on the salt, using an aircraft-quality, alloy-steel tube space-frame incorporating the first full roll cage compartment for the driver. Clad in a sleek, voluptuous body, and with a Riley overhead valve head on the old Ford engine, the Vesco Family Streamliner No. 444 had topped out at a disappointing 168 miles an hour after experiencing teething problems. But it was a hit with the crowd and it would be back. So too would John's quiet sixteen-year-old son, Don, who had raced on the salt for the first time on a hotted-up Triumph T100 motorcycle.

Another beautiful racer at the salt that year was the CT Streamliner. Known in previous years as the Shadoff Special, the shapely machine had been re-powered with a big 7600cc Chrysler. It had been loaned to a friend by its owner in the hope that he could take advantage of the presence of the MG team, which ensured the timing system was officially approved, to set an international record. When that plan went west with the rain, the driver left the car with mechanic Don Clark who hated the thought of going to all that trouble for nothing. An absolute novice at speed driving he gradually worked himself and the car up to set an SCTA Class D record at 248.281 miles an hour.

A club of friends called the Roadrunners were there with a Chrysler powered Henry J, having the time of their lives and running in the high 170s. They topped off their week by thrashing the team station-wagon down the strip at 120 miles an hour.

There were also, as always, a number of crashes. Fred Larson, an original Californian hot rodder, who had constructed his first car in 1938, was on the salt for the first time. He had bought a rear-engined roadster off another drag-racer, Ak Miller. Miller's Missile, as the car was known, needed a makeover and got it from Larson in the form of a big block Chrysler. When travelling at speed

something let go and the car slowly spun until it was going backwards when it flew into the air, flipping upside down and landing
about sixty metres later, still upside down and still going backwards.
For an agonisingly long time the machine slid along the salt. At
some point the magneto tore off the engine and smashed Larson
on the head, ripping his helmet off so that his head was rubbing on
the salt. By some miracle he survived, although it took 180 stitches
to patch his head and face together.

And, of course, there were the bikes. Big ones, tiddlers, blown
ones, mean ones, strange ones, streamlined and naked ones, all going for glory and nothing else.

What was not there was a radical Triumph Thunderbird 650cc
powered streamliner called the Texas Cee-gar. First seen in 1955,
when it ran as the *Devil's Arrow*, the low, mid-engined machine
had rider Johnny Allen lying down with his feet forward, steering
by way of a remote linkage to the front wheel. Allen was separated
from the engine compartment by a bulkhead at his back and had
set an absolute world record for motorcycles with a speed of 193.3
miles an hour (which fell the following year to NSU). Just days later
he had returned and smashed that record, raising it to 214.17 miles
an hour, only to have the FIM refuse to ratify it, as none of their
observers were present. This was of no concern to the ad-men at
Triumph who were quick to name their brilliant new sports bike the
Bonneville in honour of Allen's achievements, creating a machine
that would become as famous as the salt flats themselves. In time,
and due mostly to NSU's insistence that they had been beaten fair
and square, Allen's record was ratified.

The Texas Cee-gar, with a red Texas rose proudly adorning it's
low, thrusting nose, clearly showed the way of the future. Traditional
machines, with riders astride them, were becoming a thing of the
past – other than for setting speed records for unfaired bikes. This
would not have worried Bert. His old bike was so wedded to the
past it belonged in a special, as yet undefined category, and the good
folk who turned up for Speed Week seemed to fully understand that
this was so.

These were Bert's people now, his favourite folk in the world, and by the time he left he had become, more than ever, one of them. A large number had now heard about his Indian and Bert was encouraged to bring it over. The reason so many knew him was that Bill Bagnall's story had been published in the *Motorcyclist*, along with a photograph. Throughout the article his name had been misspelled 'Burt', a mistake that left its owner feeling quietly chuffed. Burt was a uniquely American name and the more he saw it the more he liked it. In the end he decided to stick with it, as a kind of tribute to his adopted country. Bert Munro never came home from that trip to America in 1957, but Burt Munro did.

The boat back to New Zealand did not sail for three months. Burt took advantage of the time to traverse the Rockies and the Midwest on his way to the Great Lakes. He took every opportunity en route to attend all manner of motor sport events, including road racing, oval-circuit racing, dirt-track racing and drag-racing. He made friends at racetracks, friends in diners, friends in gas stations and friends at every other place you could make them on the road.

His happy progress came to an abrupt end at a three-day motor-cycle rally in Dodge City, Kansas, when he developed a headache that became increasingly serious. He had known an Invercargill lawyer who had suffered a brain tumour, and after several days of almost going out of his mind with pain he began to believe that was what he had too. Confiding his problem in a gas-station operator who allowed him to park his car in the forecourt after each day's events, he was advised to drop in at the famous Halstead Clinic on the way to Kansas City, Burt's next destination. After waiting six hours to see a specialist he learned that he was suffering from 'Midwest sinus', a common condition arising from the extreme dryness of the air. He was given pills and a spray, and to his relief the condition cleared up quickly.

He carried on through Kansas City, Chicago, Detroit and Cleveland, taking a detour to see the Niagara Falls, which to his disgust stank of sewage. He made his way back to Euclid, a satellite city of Cleveland, where he parked up for the night outside a huge yard full of the heavy dump trucks bearing the town's name. He awoke at three in the morning convinced he was dying. His bedding was soaked with sweat but he was icy cold and it took all his energy just to dress. He managed to drive to an all-night gas station but could not memorise the attendant's directions to a nearby hospital. Finally a taxi was called and Burt followed it to the hospital. He somehow managed to find the ninety-five cents owed to the taxi driver and staggered into the building where he was immediately put to bed. His temperature continued to drop while he oozed perspiration. When it went below fifteen degrees Celsius the doctors were sure Burt was not long for the world, but he gradually began to recover. By morning he was feeling a little better and was told that he would have to stay in hospital for at least a week while doctors monitored his progress. The cost of such care, he was told, would be $40 a day. This was way out of Burt's budget. He immediately rose and dressed. 'I'd pay forty cents a day for a bed at home. I'd rather die in my car than pay that much money!'

His exit was so abrupt no one thought to ask him to pay for the night he had already spent. He hit the road for Springfield, Massachusetts – home of the Indian motorcycle – feeling better and hoping things would stay that way.

The Indian Motocycle Company had been largely mismanaged since the departure of the founding partners before the twenties, but it had still thrived due to the popularity of their slowly evolving products. A reputation for excellence had reached every corner of the globe, including Japan, where a young Sochiro Honda rode his 1920 Scout for many years. The old company's survival through the Depression owed much to a new boss, E Paul duPont, who took over in 1930. DuPont discovered a staggering culture of corruption among senior management and purged them with Stalinist zeal, just staving off bankruptcy. In 1927 Indian had acquired the Ace Company, manufacturers of a grand four-cylinder in-line motorcycle that its new owners continued to produce under

Above: The Munro Special on the trailer Burt made from an Indian side-car chassis, 1962.

Below: Burt and Rollie Free before Burt's first run, 1962.

Burt with money collected for him by well-wishers, 1962.

Above: Burt displaying characteristic gratitude to the women who collected money for him (note the one looking for an escape route).

Below: Bill Johnson and the Triumph streamliner he rode to 224 miles an hour in 1962.

Above: Outside Marty Dickerson's house with the bike in the Pontiac after the trailer collapsed.

Below: Burt talking to Rollie Free before his first run, 1962.

Above: Marty and Earl Flanders, 1963. The streamliner now has a single tail.

Below: Team Indian pushes Burt off, 1966.

Above: Burt's great friend Art Arfons with his jet car, the Green Monster, 1966.

Below: Burt and Team Indian. Rollie on left, Burt third from left.

Burt farewells Jackie in typical Munro fashion before sailing for New Zealand.

Above: Glory days: the Munro Special, Bonneville, 1962.

Below: Living legend: Burt at home in Invercargill with his first love, 1978.

their own badge. It completed a great lineup of popular machines; including the impressive and much-admired Sport Scout, introduced in 1935.

Although the Second World War brought orders for thousands of motorcycles for the military, the company cut profitability to the bone and, unlike their rivals Harley Davidson, emerged cash-strapped and desperate. Work on a promising new shaft-drive V-twin, with its engine mounted across the frame like a Moto Guzzi, was abandoned in favour of a range of hastily engineered singles and parallel twins, built to compete with the English bikes that GI's were bringing home in their thousands. AMC, British owners of Norton, Royal Enfield, Matchless and Velocette, eventually bought half the ailing company and in 1953 the last real Indian, an 1300cc Blackhawk Chief, rolled out of the factory. A British built 700cc Royal Enfield parallel twin with fat tyres, wide handlebars and the word Indian painted on the tank had kept the candle flickering. But by the time Burt arrived the factory, which the company had moved into from across town in 1947, was largely empty. Yet it was not entirely moribund as Burt discovered.

Wandering around the vast brick structures he came across a collection of cars parked near an open roller door. From the door he saw a number of men working under the beams of massive overhead floodlights, in an area dominated by racks of shelving that stretched away into the gloom. He hailed them, his voice echoing in the huge space, and one walked briskly over to investigate. Burt explained who he was in his usual forthright manner and was invited inside. To his astonishment he found the shelves sagging under the weight of hundreds of tonnes of Indian spare parts. The spare parts department was the one area of the massive complex with a pulse, and the men who worked there were kept busy supplying orders. Pistons, crankshafts, bodywork (including the deeply valanced fenders Indians had become so deeply identified with), brake shoes and headlights – the list went on and on.

It was not long before everyone had gathered to hear Burt's story, which he willingly told. He had no money to spare, but when he finally left hours later he had a new crankpin and enough bearing rollers in his pocket to keep him going for years. He had also made a number of friends who would from that day follow his achievements with a renewed sense of pride, friends he would make a point of keeping in touch with. Indian might be down but while people like Burt were about it could never be dead.

Burt then suffered a second attack of whatever it was that had nearly finished him in Euclid. He had parked his car across the road from the works but before he could get to it he felt the same terrible chill. There was a small fire station next to the Indian factory and a number of firemen were lounging around in easy chairs waiting for action. Burt managed to stagger up to them and was given permission to sit down, sweat pouring out of him. Two of the firemen helped him to a nearby surgery where the doctor was as puzzled as they had been in Euclid. Burt asked if he might be suffering side effects from the pills he had been taking for Midwest sinus. The doctor agreed it was possible and booked him into a motel, where the manager apparently knew to call directly if Burt rang a special bell from a button installed next to the bed. But he had a good night's sleep and woke up ready to hit the road again. He threw the suspect pills away and never suffered another attack of the cold sweats.

His travels now took him to New York where he dropped by at the apartment of the legendary actress Mae West, insisting to an unimpressed doorman that her famous invitation to 'come up and see me sometime when you've got nothing on' had somehow been directed to him personally. He left a disappointed man.

But he got to see the Empire State Building and the Statue of Liberty and set out to find Idlewild International Airport. Trying to navigate through the vastness of New York in his old Coupe was a challenge and at one point Burt became convinced he had just completed a big circle. A magnificent vintage tourer drove alongside him and Burt attracted the driver's attention with one of his stentorian barks. 'Hey Mister, am on the right track for Idlewild?' The immaculately attired driver of the gleaming barge, seeing only an old Plymouth with an elderly man driving, minded his own business. Realising he was being snubbed Burt upped the volume. 'Hey, you in the Isotta Fraschini!'

This time the other driver heard him loud and clear. There were precious few people in the world that could identify his car, and those who knew it were of interest to him. He yelled back and asked what Burt wanted.

'I want to go to Idlewild. I'm from New Zealand and I'm lost.'

The man in the Isotta Fraschini waved his arm like a cavalry officer and shouted across the lanes, 'Follow me!' He led the way for miles, resuming his own journey only after Burt was actually on the road to the airport. As ever, Burt's reliance on the kindness of strangers had not let him down.

After New York he made his way to Washington, where he was refused entry to the White House. Like Mae West, the president apparently had more pressing business than receiving Burt Munro from New Zealand.

He decided to travel all the way down the east coast to Cape Canaveral to watch a rocket launch, but not far out of Washington he heard a strange noise under the bonnet. He lifted the hood to find steam spurting from a crack that extended right across the cylinder head. He pushed on to a garage where, it being a Sunday, the owner was unable to recommend an available welder. Burt noticed an identical model Plymouth in the yard next to the garage, its snout pressed against the wire mesh fence. The owner of the yard lived several miles out of town so Burt walked through the heat, only to be informed by the man's wife that he had gone fishing. After walking back to the garage Burt accepted the owner's recommendation that he try a forty-cent shot of powdered radiator additive. To his surprise the leak stopped. He pressed on again as far as Vicksburg, Mississippi, where a careful examination of his finances revealed it would be prudent to turn west. He crossed the Mississippi into Louisiana on his way to Texas. It was here that the main bearings on the Plymouth began to knock so loudly he knew they would not last the distance. Once more he pulled into a gas station and asked the man running it if he could use his workship as he was in big trouble. The man agreed, eventually supplying a new piston at cost, and Burt continued on to Texas, crossing into Mexico at El Paso.

Burt enjoyed the Mexican people, especially the pretty senoritas, very much. The language barrier proved only a minimal impediment to communication. But when he arrived in Chihuahua, he was again feeling poorly. By the time he found a clinic he had a raging fever and his condition again grew steadily critical. He was given a vaccination for something but by then he was too far gone to really understand what was happening. Later he came to believe he had had malaria, but the vaccination seemed to have brought on a bout of smallpox. He broke out in suppurating sores that covered his back and surrounded his eyes, but again his flinty constitution allowed a full recovery, and he was able to drive back into the United States and continue his journey. When he finally pulled into Marty's driveway he had completed over 17,000 kilometres in a car that most people would have hesitated to drive to the shops.

CHAPTER FIFTEEN
SKIN

Marty and Rollie had seen Burt off at the docks and again they noticed how Burt always arrived with a suitcase weighing practically nothing and left with one that challenged the strength of both men to unload from the car. In fact, Burt was laden with booty.

On his visit to Roscoe Turner he had been presented with a brand new Bell helmet in a special case, his new pride and joy. Someone else had given him the head of an air-cooled Lycoming aero engine, which he thought looked right for the Velocette. He later hacksawed off the attached barrel in the engine room of the ship, casually tossing it overboard. It had been a good voyage, with a large female choir also on board, travelling to New Zealand to perform. Burt was kept busy entertaining a number of them.

Duncan had recovered from his pique over the streamliner plans and was again dropping by at 105 Bainfield Road while Burt tapped away at the fishy body when he was not busy filing and hacking the Lycoming head to fit the Velocette. When he did, it looked, as Ashley said, like the duck's nuts. With the huge 'Wadonga' in place and an oversize spark plug, which had once apparently served on a Catalina flying boat, the engine oozed horsepower – or at least seemed to while sitting on the bench.

The reality was different. After trying all the usual tricks Burt was forced to admit that the engine made less power than it had with its original head. With a small sigh he found a space for the Lycoming head on the shelves among all the other offerings to the God of Speed.

Work refining the Indian and the Velocette continued but Burt still managed to devote many hours every day to the streamliner body. He had been running on the local beaches for so many years that he knew when and where conditions were perfect for testing. Whenever the opportunity presented, he and Duncan would head for the coast with their machines on the back of Duncan's little pickup truck. Burt had bought himself a 1956 Vauxhall Velox and had devised a system whereby the front wheel could be removed from the bike to hook it up to the back of the car. In this way, if Duncan was not available, Burt could still get to the beach to go testing.

By the time the New Zealand Grand Prix rolled around again the Velocette was going very well indeed. Burt and Duncan decided to make an all out assault on the Rangiora Handicap. Duncan insisted Burt buy a new race spark plug for the occasion and although Burt grumbled he finally gave way and did so. The race started splendidly with Burt well to the fore and he was able to run in the top three or four places, lap after lap. As the end of the race approached it looked like Burt would manage a podium finish at the very least, but all such hopes were dashed when the Velocette suddenly gave up and coasted to a halt.

Once the dead bike had been retrieved Duncan set about performing his usual post mortem back at the pits. The first thing he found was that an old spark plug had been fitted. Seething with silent rage he replaced it with the new one and the bike ran faultlessly. He switched the machine off and turned to Burt, who suddenly remembered he had urgent business elsewhere. He had not gone five paces before he found Duncan barring the way, eyes flashing with genuine anger.

All over the pits, riders, mechanics, wives, girlfriends and assorted rubberneckers stopped to hear Duncan Meikle tell Burt Munro exactly what he thought of his stupid, idiotic, thick-headed, time-wasting, plain bloody perverse, mean as sin attitude, and to learn just what Burt Munro could, in Duncan's opinion, do with it. This seemed to involve inserting a motorcycle inside himself, after first wrapping it in barbed wire and dunking it in battery acid.

Having made his point Duncan stormed off, leaving Burt to find his own way home. His old friend had once again stopped playing speaks. This went on for some months, by which time Burt was ready to catch a ship back to America. The day before he was due to leave, Duncan turned up and had a cup of tea and a gingernut as if nothing had happened. He wished Burt a good trip and quietly left. Burt was much relieved. It was bad enough when Duncan went off his head, but it was worse when he just went off.

Back in America he followed his usual pattern and bought a 1949 Chev before making his way to see Marty and Jackie. Like all the vehicles Burt purchased in America the car was old enough to be almost valueless but not so old that it didn't have plenty of life left in it. He also caught up with Rollie while he overhauled the car for some serious travel. He wanted to return to Mexico, as his previous visit had whetted his appetite for its exotic charms. Within days he was on his way, heading through Colorado and Arizona and finally to the border at El Paso.

Once across the border he drove all the way south to Mexico City before running southeast to Acapulco. He maintained his normal pattern, stopping whenever he saw anything interesting, talking eagerly to anyone who seemed inclined to chat and cheerfully refusing to acknowledge a language barrier, especially where the senoritas were concerned.

He then retraced his steps to Mexico City and drove north to Monterrey where he fell foul of the law. A local policeman who pulled him over for some minor traffic infringement became agitated when he saw that Burt's passport contained no visa for Mexico. It had never occurred to Burt that he might need one and no one had asked him for it on his way into the country. Had he been an American, the policeman explained, in very broken English, it would not matter. But he was not, he was something else entirely!

Burt had heard tales of foreigners going into Mexican prisons and never coming out again. He began to suspect he was in real trouble. Mustering all his powers of persuasion he tried to convince the suspicious policemen that New Zealand was in fact part of the United States of America. Whether or not the policeman accepted this wasn't clear, but when Burt promised he was driving straight back to the nearest border crossing at Laredo the man relented. A very relieved Burt drove off with the policeman's warning against ever showing his face around Monterrey again ringing in his ear.

Once safely back in America, Burt meandered his way west until he was only 160 kilometres north of Los Angeles, driving along beside the razor wire surrounding Edwards Air Force Base. His attraction to the place was almost magnetic for it was the home of the X15 aircraft, the latest stage of the programme that had begun in 1947 with the creation of the Bell X1 – the aircraft that broke the sound barrier for the first time.

Located at the confluence of two dry lake-beds in the Mohave Desert, which together formed the biggest runway in the world, the base had long been the centre for advanced and secret military aircraft testing. There were more hush-hush projects going on there than at almost any other place in the United States. The X15 project was a joint programme run by NASA, the air force and North American, the company chosen to make the rocket-powered aircraft. Its existence and mission were not secret and most air buffs around the world knew the plane, which like its predecessor the X1 would be dropped from beneath a bomber to begin its mission, was intended to fly higher and faster than any other aircraft by huge margins. In fact, it was estimated it should fly at over Mach 5 and reach an altitude of over ninety-five kilometres, qualifying the plane as a spacecraft. While the existence and purpose of the aircraft might have been publicly known the craft itself was not. Much of the technology, including the metallurgy of the three aircraft to be built, was highly classified, as might be expected of one of the most advanced and ambitious aeronautical projects ever undertaken.

Eventually Burt found an open gate with a large sign saying 'Welcome to Edwards Airforce Base'. This was all the encouragement he needed. In the absence of a guard to report to he motored on in, ignoring the finer print on the sign warning unauthorised personnel of the likelihood of being fired upon and subsequently being locked up for good in the unlikely event they survived.

He had gone some way toward the still distant airbase buildings, and had actually stopped his car to take photographs, when a jeep carrying two heavily armed soldiers came screaming across the barren landscape. Telling them he was Burt Munro from New Zealand did not seem to impress them, and he was soon on his way to the administration building with a military Colt pointing at him.

After passing through a number of security gates he finally found himself in a small office inside a foreboding concrete building, facing an officer who clearly had no idea what to do with Burt, other than pass him up the chain of command. The next in charge was equally perplexed, and in this way Burt finally found himself on the carpet in front of a Colonel Thomas, who demanded to know who Burt was and why he was taking photographs in a prohibited military area.

Burt was soon in full flight, telling the colonel about the Indian and his hopes to take it to Bonneville, along with his enthusiasm for projects like the X15, when the officer suddenly snapped his fingers. 'Now I know who you are!' he exclaimed. 'I read about you in a motorcycle magazine. You have that old Indian running pretty fast as I recollect.'

It seemed the colonel was a motorcycle enthusiast. In no time he was listening rapt as Burt told him of his adventures setting records and his plans to go even faster. At one point Thomas interrupted Burt long enough to buzz for coffee for two; a sergeant smartly brought it in. Half an hour later, with Burt still going, his host suddenly sat forward. 'You came all this way to eyeball the X15,' he said, 'and I think it would be a damn shame if you went away without doing just that.'

Before long Burt was sitting beside the colonel in another Jeep as it whizzed between huge hangars, finally driving through a set of enormous open doors and stopping before the long, needle-like snout of a black X15. It was one of the few times in Burt's life when he was lost for words. When he was asked if he'd like to sit in the plane, they came back fast enough.

After Burt had been helped in and out of the cramped little cockpit a technician walked him around the aircraft, pointing out where the lower ventral fin would be blown away to provide ground clearance as the plane landed on its nose wheel and rear skids. He answered most of Burt's questions and complimented him on his grasp of the issues involved in building such an aircraft, before Burt was whizzed off to see the modified B52 that would carry the X15 up to 45,000 feet before letting it go. This was almost as fantastic as the rocket plane. Burt stood in silence beside the colonel as he tried to take in the scale of the bomber.

'I see 'em every day but these big birds still knock my socks off,' said Thomas.

They walked quietly around the massive aircraft, examining where the bomber had been chopped to accommodate the piggy backed record plane. 'There's not enough clearance to wheel the X15 under the B52,' he explained, 'so we are going to put the X15 in a pit and then drive the bomber over it. Once everything is in place we can winch up the X15 so its tail is inside the B52 and everything is clear for take off.' Thomas looked at his watch. 'Say, we're test firing one of the rocket engines in five minutes. You want to see that?'

Later Burt would tell an incredulous Marty and Rollie about standing sixty metres from the rocket engine as it was fired up had been like standing inside a tunnel within centimetres of a speeding train. He had never experienced such raw, earth-trembling power. When it was time to accept a lift back to his old Chev he scarcely knew how to thank the colonel. The American just grinned and told Burt not to sweat it. 'We love what we do here Burt,' he said. 'It's a pleasure to share some of it with a kindred spirit.'

Back on the road Burt headed for San Francisco, then ran north to Sacramento in time to catch a round of the AMA Grand National Championship being held on the dirt track there. He had fond memories of his speedway days in Australia and was curious to see how the sport had evolved in a country where they still ran big bikes, almost exclusively Harley Davidsons, on the super-fast ovals. He watched the young Texan Carroll Resweber slide his factory Harley through the turns at over eighty miles an hour, controlling the huge power slides around each end of the course with his foot down, just as Burt had tried to do on the grass tracks back home. Resweber won in masterly fashion and Burt left convinced he had seen true genius in action. The Texan had won the championship for the first time the year before and Burt left Sacramento convinced he'd win it again, barring accidents. The man really was outstanding.

Back at Wendover Burt settled into his pre-booked room and headed out to the salt to see what was going on. As usual he was early but this time his friend George Eyston was absent. He had been there the year before, along with grand prix driver Phil Hill, who raised the record set by the MG streamliner in 1957, in the same car, with an average speed just a few miles an hour faster. Burt missed George but the arrival of Marty, Jackie and Rollie soon had him in his usual high spirits.

There were all sorts of new cars to look at, but the one that grabbed Burt's attention was an elegant, electric blue streamliner belonging to an ebullient young Californian drag-racer named Mickey Thompson.

Thompson had been on his way to a national drag meeting the year before when he decided to stop off at the salt and have a run. He'd built his streamlined, aluminium-bodied dragster single-handed for only $8000 but he was confident it could run with the best. With two Chrysler Hemi engines powering his machine he set a new land speed record in his class at 294 miles an hour on his first try. Inspired by the experience, he decided to go all out the following year with a new car featuring four Pontiac V8s, with which he hoped to achieve a staggering four hundred miles an hour and the land speed record.

Burt and Mickey warmed to each other almost immediately. Burt admired Mickey's dedicated approach to the task at hand and the electrifying energy he seemed able to summon to shift obstacles in his way. He told Burt that his biggest problem had been to find tyres capable of handling the speeds he intended running. He had gone to every tyre company that would see him, all of whom turned him down flat. His luck finally changed with Goodyear, which happened to be developing a radically new commercial tyre. They were so impressed by Thompson they decided to make the tyres he needed, thus also tackling the problems they needed to solve before applying their new technology to a range of production tyres.

As the two men grew to know each other they shared their stories. Burt confessed he'd been born Herbert and Mickey owned up to Marian.

'My old man was a construction boss on the Pacoima Dam back in 1928,' he explained. 'When I was born he came to see me in the hospital for the first time with this big Irish worker who was with him for some reason. Anyway, the guy looks at my flaming red hair and says I was a Mick if ever he saw one. It stuck and I've been Mickey ever since!'

Mickey had started racing at fifteen when he drove a friend's hot Model A Ford on El Mirage Lake and got it up to seventy-nine miles an hour, only a whisker off a class record. As a teenager at school he made a point of having the fastest car and anyone who wanted to argue the point was welcome to a drag – which he always won. Burt particularly admired the fact that Mickey could do almost anything required to build a radical record car from scratch – that and the fact he had the guts to push it to the outer limit. Mickey admired exactly the same qualities in Burt. They were destined to be good mates.

When the time came for Mickey to put the pedal to the metal

he was disappointed not to manage a better two-way average than 367.48, although it was easily enough to set new world records in his class. Characteristically, he immediately decided to return the next year with superchargers fitted to each engine.

'It's just a matter of horsepower,' he told Burt before he left. 'Four big blowers should at least double the power. That oughta push the sucker past 400!'

Also back that year, after a two-year absence, was Fred Larson. He'd made a great recovery from his injuries and in the meantime built up a 1927 Ford Model T Roadster on a 1932 Model A chassis, with a supercharged 7300cc Chrysler shoe-horned between the rails. It was a wonderfully executed, traditional hot rod and would soon feature on hot rod magazine covers all over the world. It would also set the first of many class records.

Burt enjoyed watching all the machines run, but the motorcycles disappointed him. He could not help thinking that had he finished the Indian, and had it delivered a good run, he could have been the fastest thing with two wheels on the salt in 1959. He wanted to run and he wanted to do it soon.

Burt's sea voyages usually terminated in Auckland where he would spend some time with his family (except for Margaret who was now married and living in Invercargill). Beryl had moved them to Waiheke Island, a little water-borne suburb in Auckland Harbour. He would give everybody presents from abroad, then head south on the train.

On this return his old suitcase was burdened with the rear head off a Vincent and he also carried a curious round case – actually two alloy wheel rims for the Velocette, which he had taped together with round cardboard ends to contain all the baggage he carried in it. A rope running around the outside had been artfully tied to furnish a handle. Burt did not believe in wasting anything, including space.

The Vincent head had been sitting in Marty's workshop and Burt had been intensely interested in it. He believed he could adapt it to the Velocette and to his surprise and delight Marty gave it to him, saying he had plenty of rear heads. Marty almost immediately regretted his gift as Burt set to with a hacksaw, chopping away chunks of the head. He told a protesting Marty not to worry – he didn't need this bit or that bit and the sooner he carved them off the better. Fitting the Vincent head to the Velocette was hard enough, but getting the new set up to make better power than the old one was a lot harder. As always, he persevered and eventually had it going at least as well as with the hot Velocette head. He was happy with the progress, convinced that although the Velocette head couldn't be improved the Vincent had yet more potential. Various standing quarter miles sprints confirmed that the Velocette was indeed a machine to contend with. Burt's launch technique was ideally suited to sprint meetings, as he seemed to get the bike off the line with minimum fuss and maximum efficiency. His departures might have been understated but at the end of the day, barring blow-ups, he would inevitably have set the fastest time, with many of his standing quarter miles in the mid-thirteen second area. At that time, the most powerful sports cars on the road could not have come within three seconds of his mark.

Perhaps the success he was having with the Velocette made him a little cockier than usual, or perhaps it was simply that accidents will always happen. But Burt was heading for a particularly nasty fall.

It happened when he and Duncan were at Invercargill's Teretonga Racetrack with their two Velocettes, practising quarter mile sprints down the main straight. At the same time, two young local road racers were putting in practice laps; Ossie Bulman was riding his 350cc Norton Manx while his mate Trevor Emerson was astride his 350cc AJS 7R. During a break, when the four men had gathered for a trackside chat, Burt issued a challenge. Ossie and Trevor could come around the fifty mile an hour sweeper leading on to the long pit straight. As they drew level with him Burt would take off. He told them confidently he would beat them across the start–finish line, about 400 metres away, a bet they were more than willing to make. With their fifty mile an hour advantage they could scarcely see how they could lose.

As the two 350s approached the finish line they were all out at about 90 miles an hour and it must have seemed victory was theirs. Then, in the last few yards, Burt swept by, going at least twenty miles an hour faster. At this point everything went horribly wrong for Burt.

The start–finish line consisted of a narrow strip of concrete running across the track. Over the years it had become slightly proud of the asphalt, which had slumped about half a centimetre on either side. For some reason this was enough to send the Velocette into a horrendous tank-slapper from which there was no possible recovery. With the bike bucking and kicking toward the infield like a bronco with a burr under its saddle, Burt decided it was time to step off and roll into a ball. He was wearing his usual attire: sneakers, light T-shirt, battered ex-army trousers topped off with his ancient pudding-basin helmet – hardly the best rig for the occasion.

The first impact was so terrific Burt was sure it had killed him. It drove the wind out of his body and caused his vision to grey out. He felt he was hanging in the air a long time before he hit the deck again with another tremendous thump, tearing more chunks of flesh off his frame. One massive crack on the head knocked him out completely but his flailing body carried on, losing more flesh every time it ricocheted off the hard track, one impact breaking an arm, another splitting his helmet and grinding his watch face flat while his light clothing was reduced to strips of rag. In the meantime the bike tore off into the rough ground and launched itself nine metres in the air before smashing back to earth and dismantling itself as it cartwheeled into the infield. When finally it came to rest it had shed the back wheel and much of its body, leaving parts all along its violent course.

Burt finally flopped to a halt, covered in blood with his arm at a strange angle, lying horribly still. Ossie and Trevor were at his side immediately, both terrifed that Old Burt, as everyone called him by now, had finally cashed in his chips. To their tremendous relief he was still breathing and soon came to.

'I beat you young buggers then,' he said as Ossie and Trevor swam into focus. They confirmed that he had and he tried to sit up, gasping as his moved his arm. 'Gee, that hurts,' he said, before asking anxiously where his bike was.

Ossie gave him the direct answer. 'It's scattered all over Teretonga Park, Burt.'

Burt rested for a moment as he considered the situation. 'Right. You two can pick up all the bits and put them on your truck and I'll get them back when I can.' His eyes flicked to Duncan who was now kneeling at his side. 'And you can take me to the bloody hospital.'

That evening Ollie and Trevor went to see Burt. A nurse showed them through the ward to a figure swathed in so many bandages he resembled an Egyptian mummy. But his first words concerned the safety of his bike.

Ossie grinned. 'It's fine Burt. As a matter of fact we rode it here tonight.'

Burt laughed. 'Cheeky young bugger! You just make sure it's safe where no beggar can knick it.'

Ossie nodded. 'It's safe where it is, but I doubt anyone except you would consider it worth a second look, let alone want to steal it.'

Burt raised his good arm and waggled his index finger. 'I'll have that bike back to normal inside a week when I get out. And the first two fellas who'll want to steal it will be you two. To stop me whipping you again!'

The morning after the crash Duncan Meikle went around to give news of the accident to Burt's eighty-year-old mother. He told her that her son had been badly barked and was suffering a broken arm but was otherwise all right. She received the news calmly then shook her head sadly at her son's enthusiasm for bikes. 'When will that foolish boy give them up?' she asked, overlooking for the moment Duncan's complicity in Burt's deadly pursuit. 'Really, it's gone on long enough.'

Ashley Bell was sitting with Burt when his mother arrived at the ward later that morning and was most amused when the old woman paused dramatically at the door and waved her cane at her sixty-year-old son. 'Herbert,' she addressed him, 'you are not to get on that wretched motorcycle again!'

Burt winked at Ashley and told him not to take any notice, confiding that his mother 'Got a bit excited from time to time but eventually she gets over it.'

Burt's half-brother John Munro, the Labour member of parliament for Invercargill, also dropped by and there was a surprisingly merry family get together. But Burt's many abrasions and contusions were painful and it was seven weeks before he left hospital. By then he was recovered to the point of being dangerous, both to himself and the nursing sisters, who soon learned to keep a wary eye on him. One even told a doctor that Burt suffered from 'desert disease' – its most obvious symptom being wandering palms. For all that he was popular with the women who looked after him, described by one as a 'dirty old man but nice with it'.

He was soon looking to relieve the tedium. Asked by one nurse to describe how he had rolled off his bike he set about re-enacting the scene for her. He asked her to procure a gurney and proposed she give him a good fast shove down the wide hall. Once up to speed, he told her, he would roll off it, demonstrating the dismounting technique that had brought him to hospital. It was an endearing but completely mad idea and she had to enlist her superiors to dissuade Burt from his plans. Burt made it home without adding to his injuries.

Ollie and Trevor brought the mangled Velocette back to the shed. True to his word Burt soon had it back together and running as fast as ever. At a speed trial in Canterbury he was lucky to avoid another spectacular smash when the front down tube on the Velocette frame broke at 120 miles an hour. The bike swerved off the narrow road on to the rough grass verge where it plunged and reared over the ruts and bumps so violently that Burt's ancient helmet flew off. Somehow he hung on and managed to ride the wounded machine to a halt without being tossed off, slammed into a tree or shredded in the wire fence that kept the farmer's sheep off the road. It was a remarkable display of skill and determination that left spectators and competitors alike in awe. As Burt and Duncan loaded the Velocette onto the back of the truck for the drive home, someone remarked on Burt's calm demeanour after what might easily have been a fatal crash. Burt considered his escape for a moment, then laughed nervously. 'Don't think for a moment I wasn't bloody terrified. I was sure I was on my way to join the choir eternal. I'm buggered if I know how I managed to hang on. Sheer bloody fear I reckon!'

As always the Velocette was soon mended. The reason it had broken in the first place was most likely a result of Burt's obsessive weight-reduction programme. He had sanded all the frame pipes on the Velocette and the Indian until he'd removed what he considered a useful amount of material and weight – a matter of guesswork. He had clearly overdone it on the down tube, but it did not occur to him that the rest of the frame might now be in a similarly parlous state. He simply set about repairing the damage.

He went about it in typically unorthodox fashion, making up a length of rod with an eye in one end that he then secured at the steering head with a bolt through the down tube. Having threaded the other end of the rod, where it protruded from the bottom of the down tube he now tightened a nut with a washer, thereby drawing the two broken halves of the down tube together. He welded the down tube back together, removed the bolt through the steering head, welded up that hole and slid the rod out.

He had had plenty of time to think about his earlier crash and had come to the conclusion that the Velocette's girder suspension did not allow enough castor action on the wheel. So he made a new set of top links for the girder, providing greater trail and, he hoped, an end to such shenanigans. It seemed to work.

With the Velocette back in action Burt wasted no time. On 16 December he set a new national beach record with a speed of 129.078 miles an hour for the Flying Half Mile in the under 750cc class. To show this was no fluke he celebrated his sixty-first birthday by winning a standing quarter mile sprint event at Timaru in 13.1 seconds.

Both results were outstanding and illustrated just how effective his tuning programme had been. He continued to test at Ryal Bush Straight and on one occasion swore he managed over 140 miles an hour, just as he had suspected Ashley had during his previous test run there. Burt's highest recorded speed on the Velocette was a shade under that, at 138 miles an hour, almost certainly the fastest speed ever attained by a Velocette of any description, anywhere.

Burt also raced it on the beach whenever he could. On the eve of one such meeting Ashley finally managed to relieve Burt of his gnarly old pudding-bowl helmet. Now a scrutineer for the club, among Ashley's responsibilities was ensuring that riders' gear was up to scratch. Burt's relic had seen better days, obviously held together by a number of dodgy repairs. Ashley knew that Burt was saving his brand new Bell helmet in its special case for Bonneville and no threats of disqualification would force him to give up his old one. A financial inducement, however, might succeed.

He casually mentioned that it was unfortunate but undeniable that Burt might die of old age or kill himself on a motorcycle at any moment. Given this regrettable reality, Ashley wondered if he could have a souvenir to remember him by. He was quite willing to pay good money for something suitable. His eyes wandered around the shed, finally alighting on the old pudding basin. He mentioned a sum of money and sat back with his cup of tea to let Burt mull it over.

Burt was torn. If he sold the old helmet he'd have to use his new one. On the other hand no one else was silly enough to give him anything for his old lid. The deal was quickly done. A relieved Ashley left with Burt's battered helmet tucked reverentially under his arm. 'I'm so pleased I got hold of this before you really wrecked it, Burt,' he told his friend. 'I'll treasure it for ever.'

When Burt turned up at Oreti Beach the following day his gleaming new white helmet attracted much attention and he enjoyed the envious glances as they lined up to race. It was a handicap event and Burt's old nemesis Bob Burns was in the second row on a very fast competition Norton 500. Burt was at the back of the grid. As the riders waited for the starter his voice carried clearly to the front. 'Hey Burns – aren't you a bit ashamed to be way up there in the front on your fancy Norton while I'm way back here on my crappy old Velocette?'

There was a roar of laughter. Bob had made no secret of his contempt for Burt, adding to his own unpopularity in a community that almost universally liked and respected Burt. To add injury to insult, Burt swept past Bob and into the lead in the first lap. Even if the old Velocette did not last he'd made his point. Burt Munro was not the fool Bob Burns said he was.

Back at the shed Burt's days were filled mainly with working on the streamliner body, finishing it in time for the 1960 Canterbury speed trials. Once more he and Duncan made the voyage north with the now streamlined Indian on a special trailer Burt had constructed out of an old Indian sidecar. Although the body had been hand beaten, the tiny and consistent hammer marks in the aluminium gave it a pleasingly crafted appearance, rather like antique pewter. It had three little tails, the outer two on stubby outriggers, and a pair of small wheels he could deploy as 'landing gear' by pulling a lever.

However, his first attempted run revealed a terrible error. Burt had been so concerned to reduce frontal area, and to copy as precisely as possible the goldfish shape, that he had made the body too narrow. Crouching inside the shell in the workshop all had seemed fine, but it was a different matter on the road, where the cramped cockpit prevented him from weight-shifting to control the bike. In fact, it was so tight he could hardly get his hand down to the gear lever.

He made a run anyway and somehow got the bike up to 161.75 miles an hour. It was a frightening experience. The machine became airborne whenever it hit a bump. On the return run, at something approaching 150 miles an hour, the mainshaft broke on the drive side of the engine, locking the motor. Burt always had lightning fast reflexes on the clutch lever when something broke, an ability he often said had kept him alive. This time he almost lost it and the bike skidded straight down the road for 150 metres. How he kept it on two wheels, given the way he was stuffed rigidly into the cockpit, was something he could not explain. He did know that this had been his most terrifying escape yet. He was badly shaken by the experience, openly admitting to the horror he had felt as the bike seemed to slide forever. He made only a couple of extra test runs before concluding the shell was useless and, worse, dangerous. After countless hours of work over five long years he would have to make a new one.

At this point Burt hit upon the idea of using the aluminium shell as a mould with which to make a fibreglass replacement, thus saving his efforts so far. He reasoned that fibreglass would be a more forgiving material that would allow him to make changes should they be needed.

Normally, a mould, into which the fibreglass would be laid, would be taken from the object to be replicated. This seemed overly time-consuming to Burt, especially as he wanted the second body to be larger than the first. He therefore smothered the body in releasing agent, to allow him to detach the fibreglass from the aluminium once it had set, and began laying cloth over it one layer at a time as he brushed on the two-pack epoxy resin. Someone had told him the fibreglass should ideally cure at twenty-one degrees Celsius; a dubious piece of advice, as the resin would cure quite happily at most temperatures, the only difference being the time it took. Nevertheless, Burt stoked up the potbelly and soon the shed was swelteringly hot, an uncomfortable arrangement he kept up until he had finished the work.

When Ashley visited he was almost knocked over by the heat and fumes from the curing fibreglass. Burt yelled at him to shut the door and he decided to beat a swift retreat. A few seconds was all he could handle; it felt as if a migraine was coming on for hours afterwards. How Burt handled such hellish conditions day after day was something he would never understand.

The new shell was finally glassed up, with additional length and width added, so Burt smothered the rough surface in fairing compound and started sanding. Finally it was done and it looked good, if a little rough. Ashley came by to see the finished product in a car he had recently repainted. Burt was much taken with the colour.

'By crikey, I could never find it in any of the charts and there it is. Indian Red!'

Ashley told him it was actually Carnation Red, but Burt was having none of it. 'Carnation Red? So that's what they call Indian Red.'

Burt bought a tin of Carnation Red but his application was less than perfect, being put on with a large, lumpy old house-painting brush. It satisfied Burt, though, and when Norman Hayes objected to the crudity of the finish, the artist just shrugged and observed that the paint job would not alter its top speed.

The road usually used for speed trials in Canterbury had been shut down for such activities but Burt had already decided against another run in New Zealand. He needed space, lots and lots of space. He had no ambitions to break records or win fame. He knew that even if he did break records he would not win fortune. He wanted to go to the salt for one very simple reason: he had put all his effort into building the machine and now he wanted to find out just how fast it could go. He asked for nothing more than one good run, just one time when the God of Speed would smile down upon him and grant him the luck to run down the salt track and back without anything going wrong.

The God of Speed never did have a more faithful servant than Burt Munro. But fealty was of no account to this cruelly indifferent deity, who demanded everything and gave only a shot at fleeting glory in return. Burt would never have his perfect run. Against the odds, however, he would survive. And he would achieve more than anyone could possibly have expected of him. More than that, he would stand before his uncaring god and look him straight in the eye, demanding respect. That much would be granted.

CHAPTER SIXTEEN
WEST

It was typical of Burt's close friends that rather than pointing out the burden of both his age and the Indian's they encouraged him whole-heartedly to go. He wrote to his friend Bill Bagnall at *Motorcyclist* magazine and received back an assurance that the way was paved. 'They will never even notice your old bike,' he assured Burt, 'and you will get a run.'

His words would not prove prophetic, but it was all the encouragement Burt needed. He booked freight on the *Cap Ortega* out of Bluff, and set about making a crate for the bike and the trailer, which he would pick up in San Francisco in time for the 1000-kilometre trip to Bonneville. Burt would travel by passenger ship from Auckland, arriving in Los Angeles in time to buy an old car. It was a good plan; there was no way of knowing at the time that it would go dreadfully awry.

Norman now insisted that the streamliner be painted properly, pointing out to Burt that he would effectively be representing his country. Norman's appeal to patriotism still could not overcome Burt's perfunctory objection that a good paint job would not make the bike go any faster. So Norman changed tack and suggested that a shabbily presented machine might discourage the Bonneville officials from granting Burt a run. This did the trick and the machine was painted. Jim Council, another good friend and enthusiastic supporter of Burt's decision to go to the salt, offered his daughter Linda's services as an artist. She very capably painted the Indian logo, a brave wearing a feather war headdress, on the streamliner's flank, and a tasteful black stripe with a yellow border that ran the length of the body on both sides and flared around the nose to form a smart prow. Even Burt was pleased and had to be restrained from expressing his gratitude to Linda with a bear hug and a kiss on the lips, his preferred method of thanking women.

There was time for a final run out at Ryal Bush Road. Burt towed his long red fish there on its new trailer behind the Vauxhall with Ashley and Duncan on board. With Burt ensconced in the cockpit, which was snug but not too tight, Duncan and Ashley began to push. The streamliner was naturally geared for a theoretical top speed in excess of two hundred miles an hour, a figure Burt was increasingly attracted to, and the two pushers had to run at a flat-out sprint before Burt judged the engine would turn over fast enough to fire when he would drop the decompression lever.

With Burt's encouraging shouts of 'Faster, faster', they were soon up to speed, hands stretched out on the machine's low rump. Burt dropped the lever, accelerating away as soon as the engine caught. Of course, Duncan and Ashley found themselves at a full sprint, bent forward with nothing to lean on. As they picked themselves off the road Duncan waved his fist at the rapidly diminishing red dot. 'You bloody old bastard. You gave your word you would never do that again!'

In spite of the grand claims made by the shipping agent, the *Pacific Star* was hardly an ocean liner. In fact, it offered only a few small cabins for supercargo, as the handful of passengers were labelled on the ship's manifest. But it was luxury compared with his workshop home. Burt leaned happily on the rail and watched the pale blue coast of New Zealand slowly merge with the low cloud stretching along the horizon. Aotearoa, Maori called it, land of the long white cloud, and now he knew why. He felt the faint trembling of the deck beneath his feet whenever the ship shouldered a small swell on her way east – he was on his way.

For the first few days he enjoyed mooching about, reading all the paperback Westerns that jammed the shelves in the ship's little lounge. By the fourth day he was impatient and beginning to wonder if he should not have found the money for an airfare. The captain's table, where officers and passengers dined, provided Burt with a willing audience for his accounts of high and low adventure in the pursuit of speed. But the sudden absence of work to eat up his days and nights left him restless and the emptiness of his days made him weary.

Some mornings he woke up and felt every day of his sixty-three years. But a walk around the deck in the sea air usually had him right by breakfast time and he knew the enforced rest was doing him good. His usual buoyant spirits were never far away, even when the days seemed to grow longer. As the west coast of America loomed ahead, time seemed to slow to such a desultory pace he feared the ship would never arrive.

When it finally did the captain shook his hand solemnly, wishing him the best in his speed attempts and telling him to take care. Burt smiled at that. You couldn't have it both ways: when you ventured into his realm, the God of Speed might smile on you or he might smite you. All the care in the world would make no difference. Crew and passengers wished him well as he lugged his suitcase down to the dock. And then, after a final cheery wave, he was alone again.

Long Beach was sultry and the sun bouncing off the dock's old metal warehouses was so bright that his eyes hurt. He was sure he would adjust to the harshness of the light. He'd never worn a pair of eye crutches before and he wasn't about to start. Shading his face with his spare hand, he lugged his battered suitcase all the way from the customs shed to the bus stop. Burt Munro did not use taxis; there was no allowance in the budget. After an hour in the heat without shelter, a tired looking bus came grinding along and he was on his way to Los Angeles. He was the only passenger save an old black couple at back, and he settled in the seat opposite the driver, also an elderly black man. The breeze through the open window revived him and he turned to the driver for a chat.

His first attempt was met with a series of wary glances, but when Burt explained he had just stepped off a boat from New Zealand the driver warmed. He had spent leave during the war in Wellington before shipping back to the Pacific war. When Burt told him his plans he became even more enthusiastic. A friend who had ridden Indian motorcycles during the war as a dispatch rider insisted they were the best machines in the world. How fast did Burt hope to go on this particular Indian?

'Two hundred miles an hour.'

'Man, you must be some kind of crazy!'

The old couple at the back, curious to know more, shuffled forward and joined in. Like the driver, it turned out they had once had a friend who rode an Indian. They too expressed amazement at Burt's ambitions. None doubted for a moment, however, that Burt was telling the truth or that he fully intended to go through with his plan.

The road along the coast swung inland through miles of tract housing, emerging onto a busy road with car yards on either side as far as Burt could see. This was the end of the bus trip for him. He picked up his suitcase and got off the bus. Most of the cars were far too modern and expensive. It took another hour of trudging before the lots became visibly seedier and he finally spotted a likely target.

It was a 1940 Nash, a cheaper car by American standards when new, now something of a wreck. Every panel carried at least one major dent and the black paintwork was peeling like sunburnt skin. But the chrome was still shiny enough and the car seemed rust free (not unusual in Los Angeles, where rain was so rare it was rated a driving hazard). Better yet it had a tow ball. The trouble was the asking price of $80. Burt reluctantly turned away, only to find his way blocked by a salesman. He introduced himself as the Pete of Pete's Auto Emporium. He had seen Burt admiring the old beauty and wondered if he might like a closer look.

'They don't make them like that anymore,' he assured Burt, smiling at the old hump-backed heap. 'And Lord knows it is cheap!'

Burt climbed into the driver's seat and Pete pointed out the original radio, which he said actually worked – along with everything else except the gas gauge, which always registered empty, and the interior light, but hell, who needs them, and the windscreen wipers were vacuum-driven so they only worked when the car had up a head of steam. Burt fiddled with the key, found the starter and wound the engine over. After half a minute he was about to give up when to his surprise it suddenly started, obviously running on about four of its six cylinders and blowing a lot of smoke.

Equally surprisingly, it seemed Pete was telling the truth about the windscreen wipers and the radio, both of which functioned in a feeble fashion. Burt left the car running and climbed out to inspect it, at which point the engine coughed and died.

An inner voice was telling him he should leave, but Pete was right behind him talking like a champion and Burt was finding it hard to break away. In desperation he offered the man $50, his budget, sure that he would be turned down. Sure enough, Pete shook his head and looked disappointed. Burt quickly shook hands with the salesman, wished him a good afternoon and headed for the street.

This time Pete did not bother to pursue him, calling after Burt's retreating back that $50 would be fine if that was all he had. Burt reconsidered his offer. 'I'll take it,' he said, 'if you can lend me a tool box for a few minutes.'

Burt took the few tools Pete could find and dived under the hood of the Nash, humming as he worked. Pete stuck around, curious to see what Burt might achieve with such rudimentary equipment. When Burt asked him to hop in and turn the engine over he was suitably surprised to hear the car start on all six cylinders. Burt continued to fiddle and within a few moments the engine had settled to a steady even beat. It had also stopped smoking. Pete was both annoyed and impressed.

'Mister, you really know your way around cars, don't you? I could do with a man like you around here.'

Burt shook his head. 'Sorry Pete, I've got a date at Bonneville.'

Now the less than proud owner of a six-cylinder, flathead Nash, Burt drove up the road to a gas station and filled the car up, grinning when he paid the attendant. Petrol, more precious than whisky as far as Burt was concerned, was so damn cheap here.

Misgivings about the car allayed, he finally allowed himself to rejoice in the pleasure of being back in the country he had come to love. Americans were expansive, friendly people who would open up and talk to you with just the slightest encouragement. It was the home of 'Can do' and 'No trouble at all', the land of cheap gas and cheap cars – real cars, not puffy little English buzz boxes that could hardly pull the skin off a rice pudding. He patted the Nash on its bulbous nose. How bad can you be? he thought. You were made here.

He bought a map of the city and asked the attendant about the best route to Marty Dickerson's home – a considerable distance involving a number of different freeways. Although he had made the journey a number of times, it was easy to get hopelessly lost. He thought of phoning Marty to tell him he had arrived but decided not to. If Marty was not home he would wait. He had nowhere else to go. Out on the busy streets he was instantly swept up in the traffic. Driving in Los Angeles, he thought as he bowled along looking for signs, was a lot like speed record riding. You had to be calm, alert and ready for action.

When he arrived hour and a half later at Marty's modest house he was relieved to see a car in the driveway. His journey across Los Angeles had been taxing and he felt the need of a friendly face. The Nash had done nothing wrong but he was still deeply suspicious of it. The prospect of breaking down on a freeway had made him edgy. He had not budgeted for anything like a tow truck and he knew there was no way he could fiddle with the car for long before a cop came along and had it moved.

His funds allowed him just enough to get by, so long as he dealt with problems himself or with minimal help from the kindred spirits he always seemed to meet when he needed them. Marty was one such spirit. When he opened the door to see Burt climbing out of the car, he grinned delightedly and positively skipped down the front path, pumping Burt's hand and patting his back. 'It's damn fine to see you, Burt. But why the hell didn't you call when you arrived?' His eyes swept over the battered old Nash and he could not suppress a grimace. 'Gee Burt, you sure know how to pick 'em.'

Burt scratched his head. 'Yeah, it's a bit of a worry, but I've always been lucky with my old bombs over here. She should be right.'

Burt's suitcase was carried inside where he enjoyed an affection-ate reunion with Jackie before settling his gear in a cool bedroom at the back of the house. Marty called Rollie to tell him of Burt's arrival and he wasted no time in coming around. The four friends gathered around the Nash while Burt bashed out the worst of the dents.

In the cooler late afternoon Burt enjoyed working the metal with Marty's hammer and dolly, and he made a more than decent job of it. When Marty suggested they buy a tin of black paint Burt shook his head – there was no provision for paint in the budget. Besides, it wouldn't make the Nash go any better, would it.

They all went inside for a cold beer – Burt had a cup of tea – while Marty and Jackie prepared steaks for the barbecue. Inevitably, the conversation turned to setting speed records. They talked about the way things had changed, as they always do, with the passing years.

When Rollie and Marty had first ventured onto the salt flats of Bonneville in the decade after the war, to set American speed records on un-streamlined Vincent motorcycles, Speed Week had been a more relaxed event than the circus it had become. Back then you could lie stretched out on a motorcycle with your legs trailing out behind, wearing nothing but a pair of swimming trunks, and open the throttle. Marty's own successful speed attempts on his blown Vincent had been scarcely more formal, but that was then.

Now you needed flameproof clothing, parachutes, and all man-ner of special equipment. It was a different game, even if these things were not yet mandatory. Burt thought of his ancient, worn sandshoes, the only footwear he ever wore for record attempts, and felt a moment of apprehension. In spite of Bill Bagnall's assurances, he wondered if he really would get a run. At the time Bill's confidence had been inspiring, now Burt was not so sure.

All he wanted, all he had ever wanted, was just one good run – to see how far he had come with his successive modifications since 1920. One good run and he would be satisfied.

Burt shrugged off his doubts and relaxed, glad to be in the company of fellow worshippers of the God of Speed, glad to be back in America, a country that had surely been fashioned for people just like himself, glad to spend another hour sitting in the yard in the warm evening air before hauling his weary old body off to bed. He was here, and right now that was all that mattered.

The next day dawned as bright and sunny as the last, and found Burt tearing the rear seat out of the Nash. Marty had found an old single mattress and Burt had already test fitted it. With the rear seat removed he could slide it in through the trunk and fit it neatly against the back of the front seat. He bought a single sheet of construction plywood (well within the budget) and cut it to fit inside the back of the car, laying the mattress on top. He now had a perfectly comfortable mobile bedroom, ready for the journey to San Francisco to pick up the bike and trailer. Marty and Rollie waved him off. They would next see him when he rolled into Wendover with the Indian behind the Nash.

Burt decided to get as far as he could out of town before stopping at a diner to eat, after which he intended to retire to the car park for a good sleep. Showers and toilets were freely available at many of the gas stations along the way and Burt was confident his journey would be a comfortable, relaxed affair.

He should have known better, for it was almost over before it started. Intent on waving goodbye to his friends, he forgot for a moment that Americans drive on the opposite side of the road to New Zealanders, confidently setting off straight into the oncoming traffic. Rollie and Marty yelled warnings, which Burt mistook for even more enthusiastic farewells. Only at the last moment he realised the car coming straight at him was where it should be while he was not.

He reefed the wheel over and missed the other car by slightly more than a layer of paint. Burt and the two ladies he'd almost killed were so shocked they stopped and got out of their cars. Burt apologised effusively, explaining the reason for his lapse and begging their forgiveness. Marty and Rollie were quick to the scene. After ensuring no harm had been done Burt set out once again, this time on the right side of the road.

Four hours later as the sun was setting he was still driving around in circles in Fresno looking for the freeway north. In his agitation he drove through a stop sign and was pulled over by a highway patrol car. Burt climbed out of the Nash and greeted the patrolman by shaking his hand, introducing himself as Burt Munro from New Zealand and asking politely how he could be of assistance. A little bemused by Burt's greeting, the cop nonetheless reprimanded him for failing to stop, a matter he clearly regarded as being of the utmost seriousness. Burt agreed wholeheartedly, but explained he had been trying to find the sign for the freeway and his lapse was not so much due to carelessness than to diligence. If only, he complained, the directions for the freeway were a little more prominent, then a man would not be distracted from seeing even more important signs. He supposed such a shortcoming would not be so critical to those who lived in the area, but when your home was an entire ocean away it was downright dangerous.

The patrolman conceded that Burt had a point. But there remained the matter of his tail-lights, which were not working. Burt was shocked. Not working? Why, he had checked them himself not half an hour before and they had been just fine. He reached in and fiddled with the switch and was as surprised as the patrolman when they flickered into life. He assured the officer he would have them checked immediately. Imagine driving in a place like America without tail-lights. It didn't bear thinking about. It was about as dangerous, he guessed, as doing two hundred miles an hour on a 1920 Indian motorcycle on the Bonneville salt flats.

The patrolman looked at the elderly tourist in the wreck of a car with fresh interest. Sure enough, after a few questions he was hooked. It was a good twenty minutes before Burt stopped to draw breath. Any thoughts the patrolman had of issuing a citation were forgotten, although Burt was not going to give him a chance to remember it. He turned the conversation back to the whereabouts of the freeway and was given clear directions. Burt shook the man's hand again and climbed back into the Nash, finally able to relax. An expensive ticket for running a stoplight was definitely not in the budget.

Burt hated driving at night and he was soon parked up outside a cosy diner where he enjoyed a hearty meal of steak and fries while flirting outrageously with the mildly amused waitresses. If anyone had suggested that Burt was less than respectful of women he would have been baffled and hurt. But the fact was he did not always know where to draw the line; he could confuse a little encourage-ment for a lot more. Sometimes, too, his old-worldly deference to women could be mistaken for something closer to cunning, while his devilish charm, often appreciated by women of a similar vintage, could put off the younger generation. When he tried to pull one of the passing waitresses into his lap she instantly became stern. Burt knew better than to push his luck but his apology was so artless and patently sincere that the moment was quickly forgotten.

Soon enough he was safely ensconced in the back of the Nash, sleeping soundly as the big rigs pulled in and out through the night. In the morning, after he had showered at the gas station across the road, a new shift of waitresses took his breakfast order. Not long after first light he was on his way again, the old six-cylinder flathead beating strongly as he headed north.

It was mid-afternoon by the time he arrived at the docks in San Francisco, only to learn that his ship had been delayed and would not reach port for another sixteen days. This would mean Burt would not make it to the salt flats in time for Speed Week, which ran from 21–27 August, rendering the whole trip a complete waste of time.

For a moment he almost gave way to despair, but further enquiries revealed a glimmer of hope. The ship would be docking in Seattle before sailing to San Francisco. If he could unload his bike and trailer there he could make it to Bonneville in time. It took Burt all of half a minute to commit to the 1350 kilometre journey to Seattle. By the time he was driving through the northern outskirts of San Francisco he had already decided that the new plan was nothing less than a splendid opportunity to see even more of America.

If Burt was happy to go the extra distance, the Nash was not. About an hour north of San Francisco he stopped at a fruit stall on the side of the two-lane blacktop. When he let the clutch out to set off again, he was greeted with what felt and sounded like a minor explosion in the gearbox. He could see no external sign of damage on the gearbox and to his relief there was no stream of oil spilling on to the ground. He climbed back in and engaged second gear, giving the engine plenty of revs. The car pulled away smoothly and gathered speed slowly before reaching about fifteen miles an hour when it resumed its normal steady rate of acceleration. At twenty-five miles an hour he gingerly put it in top gear, uttering a little prayer to the God of Speed, and was rewarded by more smooth running. Obviously the gearbox had lost a few teeth off first gear but it seemed otherwise sound. He decided to ignore the problem. Early American cars had only been equipped with two gears and they'd managed all right. Three gears was really a luxury, two was enough.

The Nash cruised comfortably on the gently undulating roads of northern California. As the sun dipped below the low hills to the west Burt rolled into another gas station with a diner next to it. As always he found the facilities clean and comfortable and the food in the diner plentiful, tasty and cheap. The loss of first gear had persuaded him to follow the inland road that ran up the

Sacramento valley rather than the hillier coastal road.

He was now within an hour or two of the California–Oregon state line, having driven straight through Sacramento, following the Sacramento River as it skirted the Cascade Mountains through vast conifer forests. After his usual early start he soon found the road climbing into the foothills of the Cascades, but the Nash kept going, only rarely requiring second gear. By the middle of the day the road had dropped back into the flat lands where the forests gave way to arid wastes of desiccated scrub and low dusty hills, the razorback Cascades marching along to the west. Burt drank it all in, marvelling at the scale of the landscape, confident now that the steady beat of the Nash's engine would carry him to Seattle.

His serenity was shattered by the short wail of a police siren and a flashing light wobbling in the loose rearview mirror. Burt pulled over to the shoulder, climbed out of the car and introduced himself.

He encountered two highly suspicious police officers, impassive faces shaded by the brims of their hats, their eyes hidden behind dark aviator glasses. They began to take an interest in the Nash's cracked and misty windscreen. Cutting Burt's chatter short they told him the windshield was a danger and that it would be impossible to see through properly at night. Burt agreed, but insisted he never drove at night because of all the maniacs who failed to dip their lights, a crime that ought to be a jailable offence in his humble opinion. The daytime posed no problems, he claimed – he could read a newspaper through the windshield, no worries!

The officers looked unconvinced and Burt began to fear he would be ordered off the road. One of them was now inside the car, trying all the switches, while the other checked the various lights. To Burt's surprise everything worked.

The officer at the wheel then announced he was going to test the brakes. Burt became even more alarmed. The non-functioning first gear would surely be the final straw. He was hugely relieved when for some reason the officer slipped the floor shift into second gear and got the car rolling. When he jammed on the brakes the car stopped sharp and straight with a satisfying crunch of gravel. The brakes were one of the few things better than average about the Nash.

There was still the windshield, of course, but Burt thought he detected a slight thaw in the policemen. He asked if either had ever been a motorcycle patrolman, and his heart sank when they said no. Burt persisted, asking if they knew anything about Indian motorcycles, which he understood had once been used by various enforcement agencies. Before long he was in full flight, explaining his incredible mission. As he talked the officers slowly thawed until they were chatting away to him like old friends, in thrall to the old codger from New Zealand on an adventure like no other. With a handshake and a friendly wave goodbye, they turned their car around and disappeared back up the highway. Burt mopped his brow and patted the old Nash. It had done okay, all things considered.

Over the Oregon-Washington state line the road began to climb once more into the foothills of the Cascades. The map told him of his greatest challenge yet, crossing the mountain range before dropping down into the conifer forests of southern Washington State. After that it should be an easy drive to Seattle, the port city at the southern end of the massive sounds that breach America's north-west coast.

The next day dawned bright and fair. Any fears he might have held about the mountain crossing were left behind as he breasted the last sharp ridge and began the long decent toward his destination. But the road on this side of the mountain seemed even steeper than the climb he'd just made, and he found the Nash's old drum brakes beginning to fade as they got hotter. There were precipitous drop-offs beyond the metal rails edging the road, and Burt had a few nasty moments when he feared the brakes would fail altogether.

He had read that many people were killed driving out of the Rockies. Some descents were almost thirty-kilometres long, completely cooking a car's brakes by the time they got to the bottom.

But years of driving the equally fearsome mountain passes of the South Island of New Zealand had taught him a trick or two. Opening the driver's door created an effective airbrake, albeit at the cost of startling traffic coming the other way. Burt found that even on the steepest sections the Nash would not roll at more than about 60 miles an hour with the door open. Before long he was safely bowling along on flat ground through a gentle forested landscape.

By mid-afternoon he was standing by the gate to Pier 21 of the Seattle docks. The shipping agents assured him that the boxes containing the bike and trailer, being light, would have been loaded near the top of the cargo in the hold and could be easily retrieved. Cheered by this he made his way to the vehicle licensing authority to obtain an authority to tow his trailer, which would cost $10 to pass through Washington State on a temporary licence. Burt suddenly saw the problem. He would also have to go through Oregon, Idaho, Nevada and Utah. If they all wanted $10 he'd end up paying $50. That was definitely not in the budget.

Burt eventually found a manager who listened to his story and even offered him a cup of coffee. Burt was not much of a coffee drinker but figured it was probably a good idea to accept. The man poured two cups from a glass urn that was kept warm by a special electric hotplate, the likes of which Burt had never seen. He sipped the bitter brew and waited while his host leaned back in a large swivel chair and lit a cigarette, blowing smoke up at the ceiling while he considered the case. Finally he tipped forward, fetching up with his elbows on the desk while his eyes examined Burt carefully. 'Tell you what,' he said, 'why don't you just forget it. Take the chance. It's a misdemeanor at worst and they won't lock you up. Sounds like you won't be back this way for a while, so what the hell.' He smiled. 'I never told you this. Good luck.'

Burt walked back to the Nash and laughed out loud. One place he wasn't going was California, the state where licence plates were black over yellow, the same as in New Zealand. He wondered why he hadn't noticed this before. To any casual observer the New Zealand plates on the trailer would look like Californian plates, which would tie in with the plates on the Nash. It was something to take comfort from.

At the customs department he was told that, as the bike was a record breaking machine, it must be worth a great deal of money. It would not be a problem issuing a permit for it to enter and leave the United States, but a bond of $10,000 cash would be required. Burt was stunned. He walked outside, took a deep breath and then walked back in again. Once more he explained his situation. He was a pensioner from New Zealand. He wasn't a big deal record breaker, he was just a bloke with an old motorcycle who had come to America to see how fast it could go after modifying it for over forty years, because there was nowhere back home long enough to get a decent run.

Burt's case was kicked upstairs to a man named Brewer, who listened intently before consulting the rulebook for himself. What Burt needed, he said, was a lawyer. He handed Burt a list of names, all top men he assured him, and made a phone available in a spare office. The name McPherson leapt out at Burt for no better reason than it was Scottish. Burt rang the number.

McPherson turned out to work in a very big office at the very top of a very tall skyscraper. His receptionist looked like a model out of a fancy fashion magazine and the view from the picture windows gave Burt a momentary attack of vertigo. Like all the officials Burt had already spoken to that day McPherson listened to Burt's story politely. Then, for two hours, he consulted a range of law books, occasionally asking Burt a question. Burt sat as silent as stone, desperately aware that the large gold clock in the reception area was surely ticking away his life's savings. The last thing he wanted to do was to prolong the agony with a single unnecessary question and in doing so extend the fee from the impossible to the unthinkable. By the time McPherson gave a little grunt of satisfaction, Burt was in a cold sweat.

'Mr Munro. I believe I have found the solution to your problem. It would appear that as your machine is essentially American, being manufactured here, there is no reason why it should not come home for as long as it likes with no bond whatsoever being required.'

He snapped the book shut and reached for his phone, instructing his secretary to get hold of Mr Brewer at customs, to whom he promised a note setting out his opinion and the reasons in law supporting it. He added that, as the trailer Burt wished to temporarily import was also apparently of American manufacture, being a modified Indian sidecar, it would be exempt as well. Returning the phone to its cradle he delivered the further good news to Burt that Brewer was prepared to issue the necessary permits without a bond.

Burt was in turmoil. The news was good but the fee he would now have to pay for it was calamitous. He could see no point in de-laying the awful moment so he thanked the lawyer and asked what he owed as calmly as he could. McPherson walked around the desk, guided Burt to the door with a friendly hand on his shoulder, and told him he owed him nothing. He smiled for the first time since Burt had met him and offered his hand. 'It has been a pleasure,' he told Burt. 'I wish you the very best of Scottish luck.'

Burt's next destination was a Harley Davidson dealership owned by a friend of Rollie and Marty's named Otto Drager, who turned out to be very friendly and helpful. The Boeing company was based in Seattle, and Otto was a friend of one of the Boeing family who still had a personal interest in the company and was also a motorcycle racing enthusiast. When Otto had told him about Burt's Indian and his intentions to race the streamliner on the salt he had immediately offered the use of one of the company's wind tunnels. This was a fantastic opportunity. The units were capable of subjecting the object being tested to winds of hundreds of miles an hour. With this and the help of some of the world's best qualified aerodynamics experts, Burt could have easily and safely checked the behaviour of his shell at speed. Not only that, but a comprehensive prescrip-tion to achieve stability through the range of speeds he hoped to run could have been developed, always presuming that he had not already stumbled upon a perfect shape. But Burt could be strangely pig-headed at times. For some reason he rejected the offer, later telling friends that he 'wasn't having that on'.

This was undoubtedly a great pity, as the only way he could now refine the shape of the shell was by trial and error, a process that would always involve extreme personal danger. It also involved a high degree of uncertainty that he could correctly interpret the machine's behaviour and make appropriate modifications.

The bike was finally unloaded, strapped on to the back of Otto's truck and taken straight to the workshop. Burt eagerly tore the crate open. Finding that all seemed well he prevailed upon a couple of willing pushers and they fired the bike up. When he heard her running as sweetly as ever Burt declared that this had to be partly due to her delight at finally returning to her native country – even if she was surrounded by Harley Davidsons, her deadly rivals.

With the bike safely secured on the trailer Burt took off again to tackle the Cascade Mountains. Otto volunteered to follow him in his station-wagon and it was as well that he did. Burt hit the hills with as much speed up as the Nash could manage, hoping to make it over the hump in second gear, but the car stalled fifteen metres from the top. He pulled on the handbrake and climbed out, only to have the car begin to run back down the hill. He ripped the driver's door open and piled in, his right foot punching for the brake. Once he had the car safely stopped he pulled the handbrake on as hard as he could but the car still ran backwards as soon as he released the footbrake. The only thing he could find to use as a chock was a hammer; hardly ideal but he was able to leap out and jam it under the back wheel where it just held the heavy car–trailer combination.

Had the Nash run over the hammer and continued accelerating backwards down the mountain it could have been disastrous. Burt could hardly avoid the conclusion that his actions had been foolish in the extreme. Why he had not simply sat in the car with his foot on the brake until Otto arrived he could not fathom. There was little point in berating himself about it now, but he made a solemn pledge to keep a cooler head in future.

By the time Otto caught up Burt had a plan to deal with the

steep slope. He had already wheeled the bike off the trailer, which allowed them to easily manoeuvre the light trailer on to the back of the station-wagon. They then manhandled the bike back uphill on to the trailer and Otto towed it over the top of the range, parking in a flat lookout area.

In the meantime, Burt had jammed the old Nash into first gear and forced it up the last slope, the broken gearbox crashing and banging like a concrete mixer full of anvils. Somehow it made it up and Burt was able to take up the tow again. He said goodbye to Otto, who looked extremely concerned at the idea of turning Burt loose in such a wreck of a car.

The next crisis occurred only 160 kilometres later, when the bolts holding the coupling to the trailer's drawbar fell out. Suddenly the trailer and bike were swinging around on the safety chain. The first inkling Burt had was when the Nash began to sway all over the road. He managed to stop without hitting anything and made temporary repairs with a pair of vice grips. This got him to the next gas station where both customers and proprietor were so taken with the visitor and his streamliner that the latter refused payment for the nuts and bolts Burt needed.

He managed another 150-odd kilometres before the hood suddenly flew open, completely obscuring his view of the road. Again he managed to stop without incident, wiring the hood shut before continuing. Unfortunately he had to top up the engine with a gallon of oil every 150 kilometres and so now had the additional inconvenience of unravelling the wire to do it. Because the device that normally held the hood up had been destroyed when it flew open he used the dipstick to hold it while he poured the oil. In the middle of what was now a scorching hot day he forgot about this and slammed the hood down. The dipstick, being made of spring steel, bent like a bow and then fired itself with unerring accuracy through the radiator. Burt suddenly found hot water cascading over his shoe. After prising the old hood open again he found he had a gusher to contain. He removed the offending dipstick from the radiator and once more propped the bonnet open with it, berating it loudly. 'You bastard! You could have hit the air cleaner, or the firewall, or the engine, or the genny, or the bloody inner guards or any bloody thing and you managed to avoid all of them just to bugger me about!'

The highway disappeared in both directions in a sweltering, shimmering haze. As far as he could see the flat landscape consisted of stunted, spiny bushes and the odd desiccated tree. 'Crikey,' he muttered to himself, 'I didn't think Idaho would be like this. You couldn't grow a spud here, that's for sure.'

He began to cast about the roadside until he found a suitable stick. Sitting in the shade of the Nash he quickly whittled it to shape with his fruit paring knife, creating a plug that he then wrapped in cloth and jammed into the hole in the radiator. This slowed the flow to the point Burt could manage ten kilometre runs between top ups. Fortunately Burt always carried plenty of spare water.

In this way he made it to a small town called Mountain Home where he pulled up outside a diner. The car was steaming and Burt was too, perspiring like a man with a fever. In spite of driving with all the windows down the temperature in the car had been close to unbearable and he was dizzy with the heat. A large thermometer fastened to the diner wall read 110 degrees Fahrenheit. A sign underneath it read 'It's cooler inside'.

Burt drained a long, cold Coke before engaging the locals in his usual, forthright fashion. They were as helpful as he had come to expect and directed him to a radiator repair man just out of town at the end of a lonely side road. The man said little but went about plugging the ruptured core tubes as Burt told him all about his plans. When he had finished, the man warned him that the old radiator would no longer be as effective as it had been. 'Real hot days like today will overtax it unless you take it easy.'

Burt thanked him and asked nervously how much it would cost. The man wanted only $4, the cost of the materials. 'I enjoyed listening to you,' he told Burt, 'and I believe in paying for my entertainment. I hope you go real well at Bonneville.'

Burt was now behind schedule and in spite of his reluctance to drive at night he decided to press on. His high beam failed some time around midnight but he drove on in the gloomy pool of light he still had on dip. The night was impossibly hot and he still had to top up the radiator regularly. At some point he stopped to read a sign that informed him he had just passed into Utah. This heartened him somewhat, although about thirty kilometres from Wendover a passing car kicked up a rock, smashing one headlight altogether and reducing visibility to the point he could only just make out the white line on the road. His already slow progress was reduced to little better than a crawl by the time he finally pulled into Wendover at three in the morning.

His room in the State Line Motel was air-conditioned and the crisp sheets on his bed so inviting he decided to skip the luxury of a shower till morning. He might be all in now, he thought, before drifting into a deep sleep. But he had arrived, and in the morning he would be just fine.

CHAPTER SEVENTEEN
SALT 3

Wendover was a delightfully schizoid little town, as the Utah-Nevada border ran right through the middle of it. The ultra-conservative, fundamentalist Christians who had settled Utah governed one side, while the free-wheeling casino crime families for which Nevada was so famous more or less governed the other. Moving between those worlds was sometimes just a case of crossing a room.

Originally established as a railway maintenance town, its population had swelled during the war when a bustling airbase was built on the outskirts; the discreet home of the B29 crews chosen to drop the two atom bombs on Japan. The base was a universally unpopular posting, known as Siberia by disgruntled military personnel who had to travel 150 kilometres to get to Salt Lake City, which offered little in the way of action anyway.

Most went west 100 kilometres into Nevada, to the little town of Wells. A dedicated community of working girls soon settled to ease the suffering of the isolated flyboys and their ground crews, and the little town had maintained something of that character ever since. Burt was a frequent visitor, although he resolutely refused to pay for somthing he could still occasionally win with the same charm that had thawed a few glacial hearts on the West Coast of

New Zealand forty-five years earlier.

Wendover's only real entertainment was provided by the State Line Hotel and Casino, a small two-storey brick building built on the Nevada side of the border in the 1930s. Prior to 1951 a generous porch across the entrance had been the gathering place for those attending Speed Week, but this had been demolished to encourage them inside to the craps table and roulette wheel installed in the bar at the time.

A block away, on the less prosperous Utah side of town, stood the only gas station, a modest business boasting three pumps and a workshop. Next to the garage was the Western Café, with the Western Motel straight across the road. Burt usually ate at the café and stayed in one of the cabins offered by the motel, and he soon got to know the proprietor of the garage well.

Howard DeVane was a big guy, somewhere in his sixties, who always wore old blue overalls with a baseball cap jammed down on his head. He was a friendly soul who warmed to Burt, giving him the run of his establishment for as long as he was in town. This would prove critically important over the years to come.

Burt also discovered that the old airbase on the edge of town still harboured a fully equipped machine shop, although the place had long been decommissioned, with only a handful of army security and air force personnel remaining. Like their predecessors, they hated the place and keenly encouraged anything that relieved the tedium, including having Burt turn up to use the equipment.

Burt's first task was to pass the technical inspection held in Wendover. As he lined up with his bike many of those he had met over the years came to say hello and have a look. Burt demonstrated the snug fit of his shell, the general consensus being that it looked crazy but quite cool. It was undoubtedly low for a machine you still had to throw a leg over. It was pretty sleek and it looked light. When Burt bent down so that the curve of his back blended with the curve of the shell there was a murmur of appreciation and he climbed out glowing with pride.

He was brought back to earth with a bump when somebody pointed out an area of white canvas on the tyre where he had sanded through the cover. Having had some experience of this problem with inspectors at home, Burt adjusted his stops as he went forward so that when he finally rolled the bike in front of the officials the offending patch was on the ground. Passing the bike through inspection proved easier than passing himself.

Burt's idea of appropriate gear for speed record attempts was clearly very different to the inspectors', although he at least had a decent crash helmet. His old suit pants, check shirt, worn-out sandshoes and battered leather jacket were the subject of a heated exchange, with Burt insisting that he wore the gear because it was comfortable and therefore safer. The argument went back and forth until the senior inspector finally said exasperatedly, 'Look Mr Munro, none of this stuff has a fire rating or offers any real protection if you crash. We just can't let you run like this.'

Burt fixed the man with a hard stare. 'I got married in these pants and they are high quality, pure wool. Everybody knows wool is great for resisting flame. And I wear the sandshoes because otherwise I can't fit in. Besides, it's my flaming skin and bones, so what's your bloody problem?'

By now many of the friends Burt had made over the years of attending Speed Week had gathered around and there were murmurs of support for Burt's stand. He pressed home his advantage. 'Show me the rule that says I can't wear what I like!'

The inspector glared back. 'All right, you do what you want. But don't blame me when they take you away in a box!'

Burt grinned. 'If that happens I'll put in a word of recommendation for you with the old fellow down below! I'll tell him you're just the sort of bloke he's looking for.'

With Tec-spec out of the way there was nothing to do but join the queue of rookies waiting to make a low-speed run in front of Speed Week's senior officials, who wanted to know the riders had control of their machines. Hours passed and the two other riders waiting with Burt became disgruntled and left. Finally, late in the afternoon, a sedan pulled up with three men in it. They all wore white Stetsons and as they clambered out Burt saw that they also wore crisp, white slacks and blue cowboy shirts with the words 'Bonneville Nationals Inc' printed on the back in white script.

The oldest of the three noticed Burt sitting beside his bike in the miniscule spot of shade and walked over. 'Hey fella,' he said, 'you need any help?'

Burt looked up. 'Well, you could get me a gun so I can shoot the bastards who left me waiting out in this sun all day just so I can show them I can ride my little sickle.'

The man looked embarrassed. 'We're the bastards you're talking about and we didn't know anyone was doing a safety check today.'

Burt slowly stood up. 'Well, I am,' he said truculently. 'So are you gentlemen ready or do you need to freshen up?'

The man laughed. 'I guess we deserved that.' He thrust out his hand out. 'I'm Earl Flanders and most folk make a point of keeping me sweet-tempered because it's my call if they run or don't.'

Burt shook his hand and introduced himself. Flanders nodded. 'Sorry about the wait Mr Munro.' He took a long look at the little red streamliner. 'Now this looks real interesting. What you got under the hood?'

'I call her the Munro Special and she's half me and half 1920 Indian Scout.'

Flanders did not try to conceal his surprise. 'And how fast are you hoping to go on this thing. If you want a record it would be, what – the 55 cubic inch modified streamliner class? From memory that's well over 170 miles an hour. You really think your old scooter can run anywhere near that?'

'I reckon we might,' Burt said slowly. 'We ran close to 150 on a road near home before we ran out of room.' He gazed out across the salt flats. 'That won't be a problem around here.'

Flanders nodded, suddenly satisfied. 'Okay, take her up to about 90 and we'll follow. We just want to make sure it's not gonna fall apart and you know what you're doing.' He turned to the others.

'Okay guys, we're doing a safety run.'

And so Burt found himself on the salt, where he discovered that at anything over 120 miles an hour his streamliner developed a sickening speed wobble that threatened to push him out of control at any moment. It was as well that he'd left the car full of officials behind when he opened her up in second gear, as afterwards they seemed to think everything was fine. He had won the right to run, but the idea of running flat out with the thing weaving like a drunken chook was terrifying.

Burt returned with the bike to Howard's garage and pondered his next move. He told Rollie and Marty how the streamliner had started to weave viciously at 140 miles an hour. He had got away with it – as far as being allowed to make a run to quality went – but the bike was handling so waywardly that he was not at all sure he could control it. His two friends listened with growing concern as they realised that Burt was determined to run, no matter how big the risk.

Rollie urged him to take it easy. 'Just feed it a little bit at a time,' he implored his friend. 'See how it responds and if everything is all right feed it a little bit more. But whatever you do don't for Christ's sake go out and nail it!'

Because so many machines turned up each year the racing association aimed to whittle the numbers down to only those with a real shot of breaking a record. They did this by running elimination runs where hopefuls had to exceed the current record in a one-way run, and Burt amazed everyone by turning in a time of 174.75 miles an hour. Throughout the run the bike had again threatened to go out of control. But Burt had experienced worse and he kept the throttle open, marvelling as the bike snaked from one side to the other at the effortless acceleration. By the time he got back to Marty and Rollie he had recovered his enthusiasm and his confidence. 'By God,' he told them, 'if I could just sort the weave out she'd run 200, no worries.'

Earl Flanders wandered over and congratulated Burt on his time.

'You went fast enough to have a go at the 55 cubic inch class,' he told him. 'Do you want to try for it?'

Burt scratched his head. 'Well, I don't see why not.'

'Good,' said Flanders. 'That will be $20.'

'Twenty dollars!' Burt spluttered. 'Where am I supposed to get that?'

Rollie quickly extracted a twenty from his wallet and Burt was official. Next time out he would be riding for a national American record.

There were four basic motorcyle categories in which records could be set, with fifteen different capacity classes. The categories consisted of standard motorcycles running on pump petrol, modified but standard-bodied motorcycles running on other fuels, supercharged bikes, and streamlined machines with modified engines and frames running on other fuels. Naturally Burt was running in this final category, alongside such machines as Joe Dudeski's dual-engined Triumph Streamliner, soon to be ridden by Bill Johnson at 230 miles an hour, the highest speed recorded that year.

The track itself was nine miles long, with each mile marked off by big, easily read boards numbered from nine to one. Competitors aimed to hit their fastest speeds for the timed three miles – miles two, three and four – each of which was measured separately by timing lights. The best speed for any matching miles was the average given. Miles five to nine were used for slowing down. Any record broken was an American national record rather than an international record, the latter requiring FIM-sanctioned officials and timing gear.

Burt knew nothing about any of this. He had been told, of course, by a number of people, including Rollie and Marty. But such was his excitement and anxiety when he turned up for his run the next morning that nothing he heard registered.

The drill for the week was that a number of bikes and cars would make their run one way, gathering at the far end for servicing before running back. The only other critical rule was that the return run had to be made within one hour of the first.

Burt was among the first to run and he was clearly nervous. He climbed awkwardly into the shell, lowering his body carefully so that his legs dropped into their aluminium cradles. As all his controls were hand operated, his legs had nothing to do except follow. While Marty and Rollie waited to push him off, Burt pointed at two tall, well-built young men and said he wanted them as his pushers. A little surprised at being dismissed in this manner, Marty asked Burt why. Because younger men had longer strokes, said Burt.

The two lads were happy to oblige and when the time came they pushed lustily, with Burt yelling at them to go faster. The bike turned over lazily and refused to fire, and the new pushers were soon too exhausted to continue. Rollie and Marty stepped back in, with Burt so close to panic he was now yelling at them to push faster before the wheels had even begun to roll.

They put their backs into it and got the streamliner up to a sprint as the engine turned over. Burt held the valves open with the decompression lever, all the while maintaining his shouted exhortations, until finally he dropped the lever. The bike caught immediately and sped away, leaving Rollie and Marty sprawled face down in the salt. As they picked themselves they saw him accelerate smoothly into the distance, his back level with the contours of the streamliner, head tucked down behind the tiny windscreen.

Burt slipped the clutch until the bike was doing about fifty miles an hour, then he let it out and gave the bike its head. At ninety miles an hour he reached down and slipped the gear lever into second, winding the power back on and rejoicing as the speed built up. At about 100 miles an hour the weaving began again. As the bike accelerated up to about 140 he began to wonder if he might have to button off and abort the mission. At 145 miles an hour he slipped the gear lever into top. The bike was seriously unbalanced now and it took every bit of skill Burt had, from nearly half a century of riding flat out, to keep it from swinging sideways and flipping down the salt. He kept the throttle wide open, desperately hoping the weave might go away at higher speed. It did not, but as he continued to accelerate it no longer seemed to be getting worse. Bugger it, he thought. It's all or nothing.

He was vividly aware that he was going extremely fast now. The interval between markers seemed to be nothing at all. As he approached the end of the timed sections his vision began to fade completely. Something was spattering on to his goggles, coating the lenses with a black, sticky substance. He could feel it stinging the exposed skin on his face, but the discomfort was insignificant compared with the terror of being unable to see the black line on the salt or the marker boards, or anything else for that matter. Thinking now only of survival and with no idea where he was or which direction he was travelling, he slowly wound the throttle off and let the bike coast, fighting the weave as the speed slowly bled away.

By now he had shot past the nine-mile marker where the previous competitors had gathered, and drifted way out into the empty desert. Completely exhausted and disorientated, Burt remembered to lower his landing gear as the bike finally spluttered to a halt, stalling in a patch of soft salt. He lifted his goggles and peered around, squinting against the glare for a clue to where he was. As far as he could see he was alone in the vastness, save for a shimmering black speck in the distance.

Way out on the salt a couple of young guys had been stooging around on a Norton, stopping from time to time to observe the speed attempts through a pair of binoculars. They had watched Burt streak past the finishing area and continue into the desert, correctly concluding that someone was in trouble. They rode over and helped a grateful Burt pull the bike out of the shallow mush. Pointing him in the direction he needed to go, they pushed him off.

Marty and Rollie had waited for the last of the first batch to go through before driving the Nash up to the assembly area to help Burt prepare for his return run. In case he had broken something they towed the trailer and allowed a couple of young guys who had attached themselves to the Munro Special Team to travel with them in the back. At about the five-mile mark one of them gave an excited squawk and pointed to a wheel running along beside them.

The wheel looked familiar to Marty and a quick glance behind confirmed that the trailer was now missing one. To his horror the wheel began to curve off toward the course. 'God almighty,' he yelled. 'If that thing gets on the track we're in big trouble!'

Rollie reefed the wheel over and the old Nash took up the chase as the trailer wheel rolled on with a kind of dumb malice. As they closed the gap it began to run out of steam, executed a tight little turn and flopped over. Everyone in the car breathed out in unison. A quick rifle through Burt's spare parts box yielded a suitable nut with which to fasten it back on to the trailer.

By the time they got to the assembly point Burt had returned from his sojourn in the desert and was busy cleaning the mysterious black substance that had blinded him from his goggles. Rollie removed the cork plug from the tank to refill it and discovered bits of cork floating in the fuel. Burt seemed unworried by the possibility that the cork pieces might block the carburettor – as long as they only floated they couldn't do any harm. He had obviously recovered his equilibrium. He now knew why his vision had failed, and that there was nothing he could do to fix the problem. He decided to press on regardless, hoping for better luck on the return run.

When his turn came the Indian started easily and Rollie and Marty watched it accelerate smoothly away from their usual vantage point sprawled on the salt. To their horror Burt sped past the point he normally picked up his landing gear, and they waited in trepidation for a small trainer wheel to dig in and flip the bike. They were relieved when Burt buttoned off as he struggled to work the landing gear lever inside the tight shell. The little wheels eventually flicked up but Burt was now in more trouble as the bike had slowed and was on the verge of stalling.

To regain speed he pulled in the clutch lever and gave the bike a good handful of revs before dropping it again. Unfortunately he overdid it and the bike flicked sideways as the back tyre spun on the salt. With the streamliner almost at a right angle to the direction of travel Rollie and Marty could only stand and stare. To their amazement Burt recovered the bike and gave it another big burst of power, flicking it sideways in the other direction. Marty began to run down the course, certain now that Burt, whose legs were trapped inside the shell, would fall. Somehow he did not. Once again he caught the bike and flicked it the other way as he fed power into the back wheel. Afterwards Marty could not say exactly how often this happened, but gradually Burt reduced the severity of the broadsides until finally the bike was tracking straight and he disappeared down the track.

It was Rollie who broke the silence. 'What the hell is he? Some kind of alien? Because that was the damndest thing I ever saw!'

Out on the course Burt saw the seven-mile marker flick by and wondered how the devil he could have run that far already. Of course, he had only run two miles. He just did not realise that the numbers were now counting down, not up. As the speed built inexorably the terrible weave returned. To make matters even more hellish his vision was once more beginning to grey.

Inside the machine Burt Munro was fighting for his life, but he did it with the throttle jammed against the stop. He no longer had any idea where he was. He was simply determined to run until the bike broke or crashed. After what felt like many miles the engine faltered and dropped on to one cylinder, but still he kept going, not knowing if he was heading into the vast emptiness of the salt flats or aiming straight at a trailer home. When the bike finally ran out of fuel Burt somehow remembered to deploy his landing gear and the bike slowly coasted to a halt, the diminishing sound of salt crunching under the tyres the only noise to break the perfect silence. Utterly exhausted he pushed his goggles up and once more looked about at a glaring, empty landscape. 'Jesus,' he croaked. 'Don't tell me I'm lost again.'

Wearily he unfolded himself from the shell and examined his leg. For some time he had been vaguely aware that it was hurting; now it began to get really painful. The exhaust, which was shielded only by a minimal metal and asbestos strip, had burnt him badly during the long run. It looked horrible.

In the meantime Rollie, Marty and their two helpers were

making their way to the start line, stopping regularly to tighten the bolt on the trailer wheel, which like its predecessor kept trying to spin itself off. At the start area they could see no sign of Burt, which was a real puzzle. Rollie drove about searching but it was clear he was nowhere around. In exasperation he declared that Burt really must have gone back to whatever strange place he had come from because he was certainly not from any world Rollie was familiar with.

Further enquiry revealed that Burt had in fact come through some time ago, the bike running flat out on one cylinder, and that he had disappeared in the general direction of Wendover. The duty ambulance had taken off after him out of concern at his failure to stop and it had yet to return.

The alarmed Munro Special Team gunned the Nash after Burt and the ambulance, meeting the latter returning after a few miles. Burt was another couple of miles straight ahead. He had a badly burned leg but had refused offers of assistance. As he otherwise seemed all right they had left him to it.

The Nash resumed its dash across the salt, stopping twice more to tighten the trailer wheel, until they finally came across the Indian, standing alone under the blazing sun. There was no sign of Burt, but when they crunched to a stop beside the stranded streamliner his head popped up from behind the bike where he had been sound asleep in the little patch of shade. 'Where have you buggers been hiding?' he demanded. 'I've been asleep here for hours. Gee, my leg hurts.'

They loaded the bike on to the trailer and headed back to the start–finish line where the Indian had to be available for measuring to ensure it met the capacity requirements for its class, should it have broken a record. Burt revealed that he had been blinded on the first run by fried rubber coming off the front tyre, which had grown with the centrifugal force caused by running at three times the speed it was designed for, rubbing on the leaf spring suspension. He had decided to make the return run on the basis that the small amount of rubber in contact with the suspension had probably worn off on the first run. He had been wrong, and his second blind charge into the desert had been the result.

Back at the start area a beaming Earl Flanders told Burt that his bike would have to be measured because his average over two matching miles had been 178.971, a new national speed record.

Burt slumped back against the Nash and let the news sink in. He was a champion; he'd set a record and it was bloody fast by anyone's standards, let alone a geriatric on a middle-aged motorcycle.

'If that's the case,' he said, wincing at the pain in his leg, 'I'm never coming back here again.'

Later that night, back in Howard DeVane's workshop, Burt methodically stripped the motor, his mind returning constantly to the surreal experience on the salt, reliving his battle against the weaving motion, and remembering the way the engine had been singing as it pushed the streamliner ever faster. Yet he was certain that the Indian could go faster, quite a lot faster.

With the burn on his leg properly dressed and the terrors of his two runs receding he began to reconsider his decision to quit. If he needed any encouragement to give up it was right before him on the bench. The melted piston had made an unsightly mess that had to be cut off the connecting rod with a hacksaw. He also had a head full of bent valves that, in the absence of sufficient spares, had to be revived if he was to run again. The question was, should he?

He placed the bent valves in a lathe chuck, giving then a good sharp rap with a hammer at just the right moment, and in just the right place, to straighten them out as they spun. The work went well. By the time the night was at its darkest Burt had decided to run again.

The work on the engine took forty-eight hours and when it was done it was almost time to line up again. Burt headed for the Western Diner to eat and he had just ordered when he noticed two young women, Dorothy Lohn and Jane Nerpel, waiting to be served. He'd seen them a couple of times out on the salt and spoken to them enough to know one was a sales person for a trade magazine and the other for a trade supplier. They asked how he was and he told them he was exhausted from rebuilding his engine non-stop. They noticed that he ordered only a tomato and lettuce sandwich and a glass of milk, the cheapest deal in the house, and watched as he spooned sugar into his milk before downing the lot and leaving. Later the two women asked Marty if Burt was a vegetarian. When it was explained that his eating habits were probably more the result of his finances being stretched to breaking point they decided to do something about it.

By now Burt's run had established him as the wonder of Speed Week. He may have disappointed himself, but thundering along at close to 180 miles an hour on a 1920s Indian showed he had the right stuff. He was much admired. Dorothy and Jane had little trouble getting $20 out of most people they approached and a Burt Munro fund began to swell.

Back on the salt Burt qualified at 179 miles an hour and managed the same speed on his first proper run. The return run was disappointing, with the engine binding up well before the end of the timed section, resulting in a low speed of 162.179. Obviously he had not broken his own record.

On the way back to DeVane's garage the clutch on the Nash suddenly flew apart, slamming the pedal back into Burt's foot with such force that the swelling took over a fortnight to go down. It was just another problem on top of all the others, but it had to be fixed before he could undertake a third engine rebuild. This was even less successful than the first two and afterwards he could not even qualify for an attempt on his own record.

The clutch was just the latest skirmish in the war to keep the old Nash rolling. Among other things, the diaphragm in the fuel pump had failed, emptying gallons of petrol on to the ground. On another occasion, while driving the twenty-five kilometres back to Wendover from the salt with Rollie and Marty on board, the gearbox started making terrible noises. Although Burt claimed not to hear anything, he jacked the front of the car up at Howard's and crawled underneath. He gave a low whistle. Sure enough a broken tooth from the wrecked bottom gear had punched a hole in the casing, letting all the oil out. With no time for a sophisticated repair, Burt whittled another stick with his paring knife and drove it into the hole. Replenished with oil the gearbox was as good as gold.

Dorothy and Jane had again approached Marty and asked how they should present Burt with the money they had collected, as they had no wish to embarrass him. Marty suggested they give it to him as some kind of award. Burt had no idea about any of this when he assembled with various other competitors for what he was told would be a photo shoot. Bob Highby, the official starter, then called Burt to the centre of the circle that had gathered and explained that Burt had been elected Sportsman of the Year. To Burt's delight he was told the award carried a cash component and Bob handed him a small leather purse containing $350. By then it was clear to Burt just whom he had to thank and he advanced on Dorothy, sweeping her off her feet and planting a generous smooch on her mouth. Jane started looking for a way out but the crowd had closed ranks and she had no choice but to submit to the same treatment. All agreed it had to be the highlight of Speed Week.

Burt was slowly packing up after the presentation and idly chatting to Rollie and Marty when they saw his jaw drop. Turning around they were confronted with the vision of sin that had caught Burt's eye. She had big hair, flashing rich ruby in the sun. She was pretty, too, but it was not the face that drew the eyes. With the best will no man could help but be mesmerised by the body. She wore nothing but the smallest white bikini and very high heels, and her skin was a honey tan. She was tall and she was built like an oversize showgirl. She was spectacular.

'Man oh man,' said Burt to no one in particular, 'what a turner on.' As she continued to undulate towards him he whistled softly under his breath. 'She has the female form divine.'

When she stopped before Burt he bowed extravagantly. 'My lady, I have died and gone to heaven. Hallelujah.'

The woman laughed. 'Now Mister, you stand up and look me in the eye. Is that your little scooter over there?'

Burt nodded.

'Well, I would like to sit in it. Would you let me do that?'

'My word, yes, that would be fine. Allow me to assist you. It's quite a tight fit even for a petite damsel like you. And you can call me Burt.'

'And you can call me any time you like, and when you do my name is Valerie.'

'Valerie,' repeated Burt. 'It's a pleasure and an honour.'

He looked her up and down carefully and then glanced over at the streamliner. 'It may be best,' he suggested, 'if I lift you in.'

She considered this for a moment and then slowly raised her arms. 'I'm all yours.'

Rollie nudged Marty in the ribs. 'This is gonna be interesting,' he whispered. 'She must weigh all of 160 pounds.'

Burt manfully took her into his arms, staggering backwards slightly but recovering nicely. He stumped the few paces to the streamliner and slowly lowered her into the cockpit. The process of getting her settled seemed to take an inordinately long time, but Valerie seemed not to mind. Marty and Rollie were crying with laughter by the time she finally stopped cooing and told Burt she was quite comfortable. She leaned forward and squinted over through the tiny windscreen. 'Hey, this is real cool.'

A man wearing a Hawaiian shirt and shorts wandered over. 'There you are,' he said to Burt's new friend.

She waved. 'Hey Leo, come and meet this nice man. His name is Burt.'

Leo shook Burt's hand and then introduced himself to Marty and Rollie. He told them he was a ship's engineer and that he had a couple of weeks off while his ship loaded at Long Beach so he'd hired a car and driven out to have a look at Speed Week. He'd come across Valerie hitch-hiking to Reno and she'd asked to come along.

'And so here we are,' said Valerie, having somehow wriggled out of the streamliner unassisted. 'A sailor and a working girl. The salt of the earth.'

And so they proved for the next few days. Team Indian was growing.

For days after the Sportsman of the Year award Burt had strangers pressing $20 notes in his hand, telling him they had missed the chance to contribute earlier. Before long he had over a thousand dollars in his kick. He was viable again.

With his bank account awash with funds and with the kind offer of the use of a motor-home for a cheap rate, Burt decided to stay on in Wendover to rebuild his engine and do further test runs if the opportunity arose. Although Marty and Rollie had left there would be a number of other friends in the car record business to catch up with and an opportunity to witness the first great battle on the salt between the new breed of record breakers, the jet jockeys. John Cobb's land speed record of 394.2 miles an hour had now stood for fifteen years and it finally looked as if it might fall, almost certainly to an American, the first to hold it since 1929.

There were the usual oddities going after FIM records, including a two-wheeled monster called Big John. Made by Stormy Mangham and Johnny Allen, the same team that had built the successful Triumph-powered streamliner The Texas Cee-gar, it was powered by a small block Chevrolet V8 and it looked plain dangerous.

The real action in 1962, though, was the arrival of no fewer than five jet-powered cars going for the all-out land speed record, the sheer number of contenders being another record in itself.

Since the late 1950s surplus military jet engines from the US air force and navy had been turning up in better junkyards and the price had been steadily dropping. The first jet dragster, Green Monster Number 16, had appeared in 1960, as had the first jet record car. The dragster was the creation of brothers Walt and Art Arfons, and they were both present on the salt this year with separate jet cars.

Dr Nathan Ostich, the man who had built the first jet record car, Flying Caduceus, had brought it back to the salt for one more attempt. Now three years old, the car had been the first to demonstrate the possibilities of jet power in 1960, its construction solving many of the problems that would otherwise have confronted those who followed.

Ostich was already over fifty years old, a successful Los Angeles physician who had been content to build dragsters until he realised that the Model J Ford he'd crammed full of blown Chrysler Hemi just wasn't fast enough. The drag car, known appropriately as The Thing because it was plug-ugly, was topping 170 miles an hour on the salt but it was clear it would never go faster. So, what to do?

Doc, as everyone called him, thought briefly of acquiring a Second World War, piston aero engine, of which there were thousands available for very little money. The Unlimited Hydroplane crowd favoured the Allison V12 – with over 70,000 built, there were plenty to go around. It had powered a range of American fighters including the North American Mustang, the Bell Airacobra and Kingcobra, the Curtiss P40 and the Lockheed Lightning. Of particular interest were the last of the line, the V1710G, which had a redesigned crankshaft capable of spinning faster, and heads with generally better breathing. Although stock V12s delivered only about 2250 horsepower, on full boost 'emergency rating' the C series could be persuaded with extensive tuning to deliver an incredible 4000 horsepower, an output that more than justified its 1.5 tonne weight.

Even that prodigious output paled against the 5200 pounds of thrust offered by a J47-GE-19, the same jet engine that had blasted the North American F-86 to a new air speed record of 670.981 miles an hour in 1948. At Bonneville's altitude one of these engines could be relied on to produce about 6500 horsepower. The jets were now second generation and, like the piston engines they had succeeded, were suddenly available at very low cost. Doc made enquiries and, after $1000 changed hands, he had one in his workshop. Firestone helped by developing 1200-millimetre diameter tyres that would run at up to 600 miles an hour. Although the salt surface always remained cool in spite of the heat beating down on it, the heat generated by the wheels would normally turn the water content of the air inside them to steam, thus over-expanding the tyres. For that reason they would be inflated with nitrogen. The engineering department of the California polytechnic performed extensive tests in their wind tunnel and evolved a big drop tank shape that seemed to work. Using that data Firestone calculated a top speed of 565 miles an hour.

When the car was finally finished it boasted a re-enforced needle-shaped nacelle in which the intrepid physician would sit with air intakes on either side. Heavy-duty, A-arm suspension and steering, assembled from a number of Chevrolet truck components, were welded on, along with a rear fin featuring a moveable rudder. The Doc's calculations showed that any wheel movement over one degree would result in the car simply sledding straight ahead and the rudder was thought necessary for control, even though the wind tunnel tests had suggested a fin would induce yaw.

In 1960, when Doc and his two partners in mayhem, Ak Miller and Ray Brock, towed Flying Caduceus (the name derived from the winged rod carried by Mercury, symbol of the medical profession) on to the salt in front of an astounded crowd, there were no fewer than five aspirants making serious bids for the record. All, including Doc, failed.

Athol Graham, a local Mormon, lost control of his low budget, V12 Allison-engined streamliner Spirit of Salt Lake City at well over 300 miles an hour, the machine tumbling down the track for several miles as it battered itself to bits. Graham died on the way to hospital.

Next to fail had been Doc himself, who finally withdrew with problems of extreme front wheel vibration after the jet car had easily exceeded 300 miles an hour.

It was then the turn of Art Arfons, the grain miller from Ohio. Like the Spirit of Salt Lake City, Art's car was powered by a V12 Allison, this time with a hot turbo-supercharger set-up. It was not to be his moment. First he had trouble with drive shaft bearings and then his clutch blew. Undeterred, he vowed to return the next year.

Next up was Mickey Thompson. After his disappointing showing in 1959, when he had only managed to push his streamliner powered by four Pontiac engines to 362.31 miles an hour, he had told Burt that he would supercharge all four engines and have another go. True to his word and with 700 horsepower pumping out of each engine, and two large humps running down each side of the hood to house the four blowers, he'd clocked 406.6 miles an hour one way. It was a new fastest recorded land speed, beating John Cobb's best one way speed by 3.6 miles an hour. But the return run fizzed out after a $5 drive shaft broke and there was no record.

Last of the quartet to make the attempt was Donald Campbell in the curvaceous and spectacular Bluebird. By far the most expensive and sophisticated machine to attempt the record, the reputedly $4.5 million car used a 4250 horesepower Proteus gas-turbine engine to send drive to all four wheels through two bevel gear-boxes located on both ends of the engine.

It was Friday 16 February, thirteen years to the day since Cobb had set his record, when Campbell took his shot. He followed the black oil line across the salt until he had reached about 350 miles an hour in just 1.7 miles, accelerating faster than any car had before. When it drifted across the line, however, the wheels contacting the oil on the salt momentarily lost traction and the car was driven sideways by the power of the wheels that still had traction. The gleaming blue car rolled to the right and then took off on a 200-metre leap followed by two shorter bounces, hitting its nose and tail on the salt and ripping off three wheels before sliding to a stop. Miraculously Campbell had survived the fastest car accident in history with a collection of cuts and bruises and a fractured skull. And so Cobb's record remained standing.

1961 had been a bit of a washout for a number of reasons. Art Arfons had fixed the problems that had sidelined him the year before and generally beefed up his car, but he was unable to use its power because the record course had shrunk. Once the course had been twenty miles long but years of salt mining had steadily taken its toll, reducing it to just eleven miles. After getting the car up to only 250 miles an hour Art had been forced to deploy his chutes, a sad result for the pugnacious silver car he called the Anteater. Built for just $10,000 Art remained convinced it could have run 450 miles an hour, given enough room, even though it had been scary to drive from a cockpit located right in the nose. 'You can't see nothing except salt rushing at you,' he later said. 'What's bad about sitting so far forward is that if something happens and the back end starts to drift out, you wouldn't know it until it's too late. You wouldn't have the feel.'

Mickey Thompson had also been frustrated by the truncated course and had finally given up before he had an accident. But he was back this year for one last attempt in Challenger, in spite of the fact that the track looked little better than it had the year before. The last real contenders running cars with driven wheels were at a distinct disadvantage. Unlike the jets they relied on traction from the wheels to get up to speed, which meant they needed a lot of room. If they applied too much power they would just spin their tyres. The jets, on the other hand, had no such problems.

Burt had hooked up again with his friend Mickey as soon as he arrived. It was good to see him striding around as full of energy and purpose as ever, as an accident racing his speedboat the previous year had almost cost him his life. He had been thrown out at high speed with the boat then landing on top of him. When he pulled through the first critical days there were further fears he might not walk again, but he was having none of that. There was too much to do.

So far he had enjoyed a fantastic year. He'd broken a raft of international and national records at March Air Force Base, using four different cars in a one day orgy of speed. At the end of the day, counting the records he already had, including the national speed record he'd set while trying to break the land speed record, he now had a grand total of twenty-eight international and national records, a record in itself.

Burt was seriously impressed; he knew he was in the presence of greatness. Mickey had also built the dragster that took the

National Hot Rod Association (NHRA) Nationals away that year from the righteously celebrated Big Daddy Don Garlits. He had also founded a tyre company, specialising in race rubber, that was already a runaway success. Then he had built the first competitive stock block, mid-engined car for the Indianapolis 500, which Dan Gurney had done very well with until an axle oil seal let go halfway through the race. And Mickey was back racing his boat.

Burt and Mickey spent a lot of time together, working on the Challenger or watching the others run. There was certainly a lot to look at this year with four jet cars going for the record. Art Arfons was among them, having sold his Anteater to a wealthy collector of oddball machinery, and Burt soon introduced himself. It was easy to do, since Arfons seemed to spend most of his time working alone on his car. Burt discovered a modest, likeable character very much after his own heart. Art spoke in a soft drawl that disguised a sharp intellect. He had driven a landing barge in the war, taking part in the fiercely opposed invasion of Okinawa, and Burt could tell he had seen a lot and learned a lot from it.

At the centre of the attraction lay the fact that Art was a junkyard man, possibly the king of all junkyard men. The half-Greek, half-Cherokee farmer enjoyed nothing better than turning some cheap, if not worthless, collection of scrap into something that went very fast. He quickly recognized a fellow traveller in the pensioner from Invercargill, especially when Burt offered a hand and proved damned useful. The two men were soon good friends.

Art and his brother Walt, who had now parted to pursue their own speed programmes, had been building cars to run down drag strips and across the salt since shortly after the war. The first one had been an ugly thing created by more or less welding three wheels onto an old Oldsmobile engine. Since the two brothers had painted it with green tractor paint, which was all they had, it had been christened the Green Monster. From that time on a succession of increasingly successful drag cars had raced under the name, although Art called his new jet Cyclops, after the aircraft landing light he'd set in its nose. The two brothers had built at least seventeen Green Monsters in all inside the big tin sheds at the family's Ohio mill. Like everybody else Art was running a J47 jet, although he had modified it with a homemade afterburner. With the afterburner on full song Art calculated the jet was turning out somewhere around 8000 horsepower, sufficient he believed to break through the 400 mile an hour barrier on the way to cracking 500.

It was a brutal thing and he sat right at the front in a little cockpit in the middle of the air intake. The suction from the engine was so strong he had to avoid turning his head at speed, as it was impossible to turn it back again. His goggles had to be stuck in place with race tape for the same reason, otherwise they just blew off. When Burt asked why he had not put a canopy on the cockpit Art just shrugged and said he had thought about it but was afraid it might cut down the flow to the engine and rob a few horsepower. 'It's a bitch,' he said, 'but that's the way it is.'

Because the car was not streamlined, Art was afraid the ground effect air might pick it up and make it light to the point it would not steer. To guard against this Art attached a wing just behind the cockpit and geared it to the suspension. It generated just enough down force to keep the car from trying to take-off.

His first run revealed a distressing problem. The twenty-gallon tank he had installed had insufficient capacity to run the full length of the course with the afterburner spewing its fiery tail. In the end he had to settle for a 330.113 mile an hour average, which was a record in the new Jet Car category but a long way short of where he wanted to be. But the experience had been constructive and he told Burt he would return with a far more powerful engine in a properly streamlined shell. 'I wish I hadn't sold the Anteater. That would have made it when the track came good. These jets are so inefficient they need a whole lot more mumbo. I guess I better start ringing around the junkyards. See if something real fancy has crashed lately.'

The second jet jockey to make a run was a slim young man named

Craig Breedlove. His matinee idol looks were appropriate as he came from a bona fide Hollywood movie family. His mother was a famous dancer who had hoofed it on the silver screen with the likes of Fred Astaire, and his father was a top special effects man. Breedlove had shown no inclination to follow his folks into showbiz, obsessed from a very early age with the pursuit of speed. He bought his first car at thirteen and raced it as soon as he turned sixteen on the Mohave Desert dry lakes. A chopped and channelled supercharged 1934 Ford Coupe, it clocked 154 miles an hour on alcohol fuel. Four years later he constructed and drove a belly tank special to 236 miles an hour on the salt. He had gained a lot of his knowledge and skill working as a structural technician at Douglas Aircraft in Santa Monica before becoming a fire fighter in Costa Mesa. In 1957 he shelled out $500 for a J47 jet engine and started to build a three-wheel record car, which he called Spirit of America, inspired by President Kennedy's speech imploring his fellow citizens to ask what they could do for their country. He quit work and struggled to build his car until he eventually persuaded executives at Shell Oil and Goodyear to back him. Now the twenty five year old was confident he could break Cobb's record.

Alas, the Spirit of America was another disappointment when it had its turn on the salt. Although the three wheeler easily accelerated to 365 miles an hour, it wandered so badly that Breedlove did not attempt the return run and Cobb's record, along with Art's new record, was left intact.

Doc Ostich fared little better than the other jet jockeys when his turn came, spinning the Flying Caduceus at 331 miles an hour on his attempt. Incredibly, the big machine, with the Doc strapped into its droopy needle nose, stayed upright even though one tyre had blown, veering off into the desert where it demolished a large plywood marker, bending the nose but not, fortunately, the physician. The next day the Doc returned with a new tyre and, having performed an overnight nose job, achieved solid runs at 314, 350, 359, 354 and 355 miles an hour, but falling well short of the team's target because the engine would only deliver ninety per cent of its maximum revs. Since twenty-five per cent of the power was made in those final ten per cent of revs, the car refused to go any faster.

None of the team was a jet specialist, so the only thing they could do was huddle over the manual. They reset the throttle stop on the control valve and cleaned out the fuel nozzles to no effect, finally acknowledging that their race was run. To add insult to injury Stormy Mangham and Johnny Allen followed the Doc on to the salt with their motorcycle Big John, and after achieving 310 miles an hour in practice, and with quite a bit of throttle left, looked as if they would eclipse the Flying Caduceus. In the end the torque reaction of the big V8, acting along the roll centre of the pencil-shaped streamliner, rendered the thing unmanageable at higher speeds and they too threw in the towel.

Mickey Thompson was next and he knew he was up against it. The course, at 10.5 miles, was little longer than the previous year and the condition of the surface was poor. It was particularly galling for Mickey, after coming so close in 1960, to once again contemplate failure. But he was determined to give it his best shot. His fears were realised when he was forced to abandon his first attempt after encountering washboard erosion. The Challenger had no suspension and the vicious thumping over corrugations in the salt was threatening to beat Mickey and his car to death. He would have kept the throttle floored anyway, except the same conditions prevented the car from getting traction. He tried again from the northern end of the course and got the Challenger up to 357 miles an hour before again giving up.

On his return to the pit area he announced his car had raced for the last time on the salt and that he would never again attempt the record. Jets, he told Burt, were not for him. He was a driver and he liked driven wheels. It was a bitter disappointment for a man not used to losing. 'Godammit, Burt,' he said ruefully, 'I'd already have had the record for two years if it wasn't for a crummy $5 drive shaft!'

'Well, Mickey,' said Burt, 'maybe you should have bought the $10 one.'

Mickey laughed. 'This from a man who wears his old wedding suit when he's running after records. You and Art would have brought the $2.50 drive shaft and you probably would have gotten away with it. I don't know why I put up with you.'

Burt looked steadily at his friend for a moment. 'Maybe it's so I can remind you that it's only rules made by a bunch of committee men sitting around a table drinking cocktails and eating chips that say you were not the first bloke to go faster than Cobb. You know you did it, Mickey. What else really matters in the end?'

Mickey was mildly astonished. 'You're a dark horse, Burt. A god-damn philosopher.'

He gazed over at his shiny blue streamliner sitting strapped to its trailer. 'But thanks all the same. I needed to hear that.'

The final jet car to take to the salt was possibly the most advanced of the trio. Called Infinity it was beautifully streamlined and the gleaming aluminium body made a stark contrast to the hammered together finish of the other cars. Driver Glenn Leasher sat in an enclosed probe-like cockpit at the front of the car in the middle of the intake. It was powered by a brand-new J47, like Art's engine, fitted with an afterburner. Leasher was a young but experienced drag racer and the car was the work of Romeo Palamides, a respected engineer from Oakland, California, who had built successful jet dragsters in the past. Infinity had appeared on the salt on the last day of Speed Week but had been quickly taken away when initial runs revealed a chassis weakness. Now it was back, and Leasher was impatient to get on with it. He had recently been secretly married and on the morning of the jet record attempt he had learned his wife was pregnant. They decided to announce both the marriage and the pregnancy after the last run, and this may have been the reason he blasted straight after the record rather than gradually working up to it with a number of trial runs – although the car had previously completed a couple at well over 300 miles an hour with no problems.

Infinity accelerated brutally, many thought too brutally, and was already doing about 250 miles an hour after the first mile when it suddenly yawed and went airborne. It came down vertically on its nose, killing Leasher instantly, breaking apart and scattering pieces all over the salt. When what was left finally stopped the fuel exploded and the remains of the machine became a funeral pyre, sending a thick plume of black smoke into the clear blue sky.

It was a grim end to the first battle of the jets, and the tragedy was given one last macabre touch when Utah authorities dumped the molten, battered relic beside the road to the salt flats as a warning against speeding, the crassness of the message apparently evading them. It was there for years, a barely noticed memento of a largely forgotten enterprise.

With Leasher's death the assault on Cobb's record was over for another year. The salt emptied out once again. Yet they were not always silent, for a small red projectile could quite often be seen screaming across the flats. Burt had met the bloke who had the key to the gate, and they were best mates.

CHAPTER EIGHTEEN
ONWARDS AND UPWARDS

The temptation to stay on even longer had proved too much for Burt. With the trailer home, the airbase machine shop and Howard DeVane's garage at his disposal he had everything he needed to track down and eliminate the handling peculiarities that had caused him so much grief. The first task was to thoroughly rebuild the engine, which he managed quite comfortably in the well-equipped air force facility, although he did have to get around a new security guard, who eventually buckled under the usual avalanche of charm and unlocked the door to the workshop for Burt.

Once the engine was finished Burt made a number of runs accompanied by the ever-helpful DeVane, who drew Burt's attention to black skid marks left by the bike, indicating wheel spin. Burt decided to put some weight on the rear of the machine, figuring the loss of traction might be triggering the weave. He smashed up a load of old batteries to make a lead block weighing about thirty kilograms, which he fastened to the frame just in front of the rear wheel. A number of riders with experience piloting streamliners on the salt had suggested to Burt that the three small fins on the Special might be causing the problem, so he and Howard drove to an aeroplane junkyard just out of Salt Lake City and cut the fibreglass wingtip off a small plane. After removing the three smaller fins he glassed the tip oto the shell, then headed back to the salt for a trial run.

Typically, he had made two critical changes to fix the same problem without testing first one and then the other. This was exactly the kind of modification procedure a professional would avoid. But Burt, as always, was in a hurry, relying on intuition to see him through.

A couple of carloads of interested locals followed him to the salt and gathered at the three-mile marker to watch him go by. By the time he reached them Burt was in serious trouble. As he hit 150 miles an hour the bike began to handle like an angry bronco, slamming from one side to the other with such violence that it was only the tightness of the shell that kept Burt on board. He tried to ride through the problem by keeping the throttle wide open but the faster he went the worse it got. By the time he was doing 180 miles an hour the bike was weaving spectacularly. Examination of tyre marks later revealed the weave to be almost one metre every 180 metres – at the level of Burt's head the machine was being thrown about 1.5 metres from side to side. Somehow he managed to slow it down to the point he could sit up with his head in the slipstream when the Special once again ran true.

One of the observers later mentioned that he had been so mesmerised by the violent action he had neglected to take any photographs. His request that Burt go again so he could take a few shots was met, for once, with a stunned silence. Burt said the run had been so terrifying that if the butterflies in his stomach had been cows he could have started a dairy farm.

When Burt dropped into the airbase for the last time before going home he met an overnighting pilot with little better to do than hang out in the machine shop and chat. It turned out he had more than a passing interest in aerodynamics. When Burt told him about the way the streamliner was weaving at speed the pilot asked how he had eventually extricated himself from the situation. When Burt told him that the machine had run straight after he sat up, the pilot nodded. 'What you did was move the centre of pressure forward. That stabilised the machine and made it run true. If you can modify the body to achieve that you won't have to mess about with adding weight here and there, which won't work anyway. I'm guessing you want to keep everything as light as possible in any case.'

Burt listened carefully. He recognised the sense of what the pilot was telling him and filed it away for future reference. The lead block came out and was put on a shelf at DeVane's garage, with the words 'Sacrificed to the God of Speed' painted on its side, where it would gather dust for many years.

It was time to leave and Burt worked furiously on the Nash to make it roadworthy, scrounging what he needed from a junkyard in Salt Lake City, where he was offered $10 for the car. Refusing the offer he bought an uncracked windscreen, a watertight radiator and a couple of new headlights. Back at Howard's he fitted the new parts and welded up the hole in the gearbox.

He had booked passage for the Special on a ship leaving from Seattle and would have to push hard to get there on time. The Nash was predictably difficult, breaking down en route to San Francisco and incurring a heavy towing fee and fine for leaving a vehicle unattended on a freeway. Without a backup vehicle to get him over the Cascade Mountains, Burt was forced to search a number of junkyards for a replacement gearbox, which he persuaded the owner to allow him to fit there and then. It was a huge relief to get the bike to Seattle in time.

The trip back to Los Angeles, from where Burt was catching his liner home, was comparatively trouble free. When he called in to see his friend Ed Iskanderian, the famous and eccentric designer and manufacturer of performance camshafts, Ed was sufficiently impressed to pay Burt the $50 he wanted for the Nash. Ed kept a row of old jalopies outside his factory, which were full of the junk he could not bring himself to throw away, and Burt fully expected that the Nash would become another storage unit. Such was Ed's high opinion of Burt's mechanical skill, however, that he actually on sold it for $60 to a friend, who then enjoyed years of trouble-free motoring. For Burt, though, it was the end of a less than beautiful friendship and he was happy to see the last of it.

Ed was a master in the art of cam profiling and was highly respected by the few people he met who could demonstrate a similar facility. He had already bought one of Burt's camshafts for the princely sum of $350, and even after careful study could not work out how it created so much power. It made him respect Burt more than ever. There was just time for a last visit with Marty and Rollie before they dropped him at his ship. By now he was pretty tuckered out. It had been a long and gruelling voyage, his time on the salt disappointing and often frightening. His burnt leg was still hurting and his foot still tender from being walloped by the Nash clutch.

He had spent a few days with a doctor in Del Mar, just north of San Diego, on the way south from Seattle and the visit had left him somewhat shaken. The doctor was an Indian enthusiast and had invited Burt to stay after corresponding for some years. Burt was always careful to reply to letters and, although he did it out of respect and good manners, the effort often paid off in unexpected ways. On this occasion the doctor took one look at him and immediately prescribed a complete physical check-up. His findings were disturbing. Burt was suffering heart shock, a result of the terrible frights he had endured on the salt. He was prescribed heart tablets, which he referred to from then on as his 'nitroglycerine' pills. He was also advised to take a good long rest.

A relaxing sea voyage was just the ticket and when Burt arrived back in Invercargill it was to a rousing civic and private welcome, which did even more to restore his spirits. Once more he was ready to take up the challenge in pursuit of that one perfect run. A run he was sure would give him an average of over 200 miles an hour.

It was good to be out of the limelight and back in the shed. As much as Burt enjoyed the community of the salt he missed the simple solitude of 105 Bainfield Road. He still received a constant trickle of visitors, but they were on his turf and he did not feel an obligation to down tools to talk to them.

He had been thinking a lot about ways of making the engine stronger, more powerful and less stressed. One way to achieve the last two objectives would be to increase the capacity, offering as it did a way of making more power at lower revs. Another way to make more power was to improve the efficiency of the breathing, a significant challenge given the cam set up on the engine. Because the Indian system operated the inlet and exhaust valves from the same cam there would always be compromises with valve actuation. The reality was that high-performance motors require individual lobes for exhaust and inlet valves, as they in turn require differing profiles and differing opening and closing points for peak performance. In spite of the fact that this would entail the creation of numerous precision parts from scratch and a great deal of intensely challenging design, Burt decided to go ahead.

He ground off the single wide cam from the cam drive shaft and made two very narrow cams, one for the inlet valves and one for the exhaust valves. To make the cams he first created a cam grinder, using an old washing machine motor. Prior to this Burt had always shaped his cams by hand with hacksaws and files, demonstrating a remarkable facility with the simplest tools. His new machine worked well and saved a lot of time and effort, even though most who saw it were hard pressed to decipher how exactly the thing worked.

The two new narrow cams ran side by side on the cam drive shaft and activated appropriately narrow cam followers. He carved the four L-shaped cam followers from high-tensile steel, each forked at the cam end to take a twenty-millimetre needle bearing roller, just six millimetres wide. When the cams were finished he drilled a hole through them so they slipped over the cam drive shaft. Once he had the timing right a high tensile bolt was screwed through the cam wheel via a six millimetre threaded hole, locking the cam on the shaft. He organised a healthy supply of oil to keep the cams and followers well lubricated by mounting an oil pump from a 1933 Indian, which also supplied the big ends and main bearings.

The work took approximately 800 hours of 16-hour days and when it was done the valve set up was capable of sustaining high revs without any real problems. Burt had created another unique engineering solution to a complicated problem without drawing a line on a piece of paper.

He also carved a new set of connecting rods and cast a load of fresh pistons. Unable to find the Caterpillar axle he preferred, he made the rods from steel of uncertain pedigree. He then turned his attention to the shell, remembering the words of the pilot in Wendover. To shift the centre of pressure forward he decided to lower the nose, thereby increasing the down force on the front wheel. Rather than hacking straight into the shell he first made an accurate model of the streamliner, which he mounted on gimbals on the hood of his old black Vauxhall, rather like an ornament. After observing the way it reacted to the flow of air over it he carved a little off the nose and was pleased to see it assume a more nose-down attitude. With his theory thus supported he cut a thin wedge out of both sides of the shell. The wedge met at the tail and grew wider as it ran forward, being fifty millimetres across at the front. Once the shell was glassed back together the nose was naturally fifty millimetres lower. The rear also received attention with a carefully shaped single tail replacing the aircraft wingtip grafted on in Wendover.

Having burned his leg painfully twice now he improved the heat protection, painstakingly stripping the asbestos insulation around the electrical wiring in an electric blanket and wrapping it carefully around the exhaust pipes. He did not bother testing his improvements, as he knew he could never achieve sufficient speed on the beaches and roads of New Zealand to learn anything. Instead, he took the Velocette to flying and standing quarter-mile sprints, doing very well as always.

After investing 2000 hours in the Indian, and having delayed his last return from America for so long, the time to once again crate up the bike seemed to roll around quickly. The box was loaded onto a ship bound for San Diego, also the destination of Burt's passenger liner. Once more, however, he discovered that the freighter was running late and had docked at Eureka, some 1200 kilometres north. He jumped on a bus north to Los Angeles and again went hunting for a good $50 car, discovering they were now scarce on the ground. The United States economy was booming and scrap steel was worth real money; old automobiles were going to the crushers in record numbers. Finally he spotted a decrepit 1946 Chrysler parked on the side of a road. He found the elderly lady owner in the house behind it, a kindly soul who said she had given up driving some time ago. She assured him the car had a perfect engine and used not a skerrick of oil.

Three hundred miles and five gallons of oil later he was pulled over by two highway patrolmen complaining angrily that the car had thrown dirty old oil right out of its tail pipe and on to their windscreen. Burt protested that the little old lady he had bought the car from had promised it wouldn't, but the jig was up and he knew it. The officers accepted his assurance that he would get the car fixed immediately and he hauled off behind a friendly gas station to strip the engine, removing all the bearings, filing the ends and scraping them with his fruit knife. The motor ran faultlessly after that.

There was no sign of the ship at Eureka but he found the shipping agent who told him it was in Vancouver, 950 kilometres hard driving north. At the Vancouver dock Burt's concern turned to near panic when he found the ship but not his crate. He bent the captain's ear until the entire crew was rousted out to look. They finally found it, buried under twenty-five tonnes of bagged fertiliser. To Burt's consternation the shell had been damaged, with one crack thirty centimetres long, and buckled in places. It was a very concerned Burt who finally began his trek south but, to his delight, the hot sun popped all the dents out. With five days to spare after his arrival in Wendover there was time to complete the repairs.

He had driven straight to Howard DeVane's garage, only to find the place locked and looking somewhat abandoned. The waitress in the Western Café next door was silent when Burt asked where Howard was. When he was sitting down she told him that Howard had died. Burt gasped. Howard gone? He walked over to the gas station and stood staring at the worn old clapboard building. Howard had been so much more than an acquaintance. Like everyone with whom Burt became close, he had been a straightforward, decent man who recognised the same qualities in Burt.

Burt settled quietly into his cabin at the Western Motel but his downcast spirits were lifted a few days later by the arrival of Rollie and Marty. To Burt's delight they had a supercharged Vincent Lightning on the back of Marty's pickup.

'Which one of you roosters is having a go,' Burt demanded before they could ease their cramped limbs from the cab. Marty replied that he was riding the bike for its owner, Joe Simpson. 'Up until now Joe's done all his own riding, but he wanted me to do this and I said yes.'

Burt had a close look at the Paxton blower set up and whistled. 'It sure looks flash,' he said. Marty grimaced. 'It looks good but I don't know about this blower. It looks like it's going to take a lot of power to turn it. I liked the Shorrocks it used to run with but that was damaged. I guess we'll see.'

Burt went out on the salt to qualify, hating the long wait to get the call as much as ever. He complained about it to Marty, telling him the sitting around was stirring him up so much he wasn't sure he wanted to come back again. 'I'm sixty-four years old, Marty. Maybe I should just call it quits.'

Marty shook his head. 'You'll stop coming when you forget where it is.'

Burt's qualifying run went well and he was comfortably in with a speed of 183.673 miles an hour. By the time Marty and Rollie caught up with him to return the bike to the start area he was jittery with excitement. He said the engine was going like a bomb and the handling problems seemed a thing of the past. 'She gets a bit wayward at about ninety, but after that she just settles down like an angel and runs as straight as a die. I reckon we'll do 200 this time by crickey!'

The first run at the record started well, the bike humming along with everything in perfect harmony. He accelerated smoothly to minimise the moments when the back wheel broke traction. Whenever this happened the revs soared into the red zone and he was conscious of the valves bouncing, but he knew his valve gear was good and strong. By the two mile mark the bike was going better than it ever had. Burt was certain he was only five miles an hour from the magic 200 mark, with the salt whizzing by under the red nose so fast it looked just like an ironed table cloth; featureless, no longer even blurred. He kept the throttle open, exalting in the certainty that in just a few seconds he would pass through the magic barrier that had been his target for so long.

The split second the engine began to blow Burt had the clutch lever hard against the stubby left handlebar, fast enough to avoid a lock-up and crash that would almost certainly have killed him. The bike coasted for another mile before he lowered his gear and crunched to a halt. The front connecting rod had broken, shattering the cylinder barrel and wrecking the camshaft and followers he had so carefully laboured over. One glance and he knew it was over.

Back at the start Burt's disappointment lasted only a few minutes. A timing official rushed over to say he had been clocked at 183.667 miles an hour in spite of the blow-up; by his estimate he had been doing over 190 when it happened. Burt was considerably cheered. He had set the fastest speed of the week for any competitor. He might not have any idea how to extract more horsepower from his old Indian engine, but the run had shown he clearly had enough. The conrods he had carved from suspect material had been the only thing to deny him triumph. His leg was again throbbing with pain after being burned by escaping hot engine parts, but after having it dressed by the paramedics he thought no more of it. He was now part of Marty's support crew.

Marty's run on the Vincent was a disappointment. He could not get it to exceed 164 miles an hour, just one mile an hour faster than the same machine had run without a blower. As he had feared, the Paxton swallowed nearly as much power as it delivered. Still, he had succeeded in breaking a supercharged 1000cc, non-streamlined motorcycle record. A powerful group of senior AMA officials then made it clear they would oppose such a record being granted on the grounds that there was no such class. Marty argued that they had accepted his entry fee for such an attempt but they would not budge, even when the acting AMA referee rejected their argument. Despite being a Harley dealer himself, Marty accused them of being in the pocket of Harley Davison, which had apparently failed to set just such a record themselves. Marty left Bonneville empty-handed.

As usual Burt stayed on to watch the land speed record action, this time between the Flying Caduceus, Spirit of America and a new car built by Walt Arfons called Wingfoot Express. Art was sitting 1963 out, hard at work in his barn on a more powerful Green Monster, but his brother had teamed up with a torque wrench manufacturer named Tom Green to build an impressive jet car.

Green was an aerodynamics buff, able to accurately calculate the wind resistance of a given shape, even if it was only drawn on paper. Like Breedlove, he believed that a single wheeled streamliner was the way to go, but when Walt objected that such a machine would not be judged to be a car, he came up with a design offering closely spaced front wheels faired into the body along with outrigged rear wheels. He figured this offered the slipperiest and most stable set up for a four-wheeled jet car, one that would allow the J47 engine to push it over the 400 mile an hour mark. His final design had the smallest frontal area of any current jet car and weighed just half as much as Breedlove's. Also unlike the Spirit of America, the J47 in Wingfoot Express had an afterburner giving an extra 2600 pounds of thrust. On paper at least the car looked more than competitive.

Walt had built the car on an extremely modest budget after a chance meeting with Green at a trade show. Although already a grandfather, he intended driving it, but those plans changed when an accident during power tests resulted in a stand-in driver launching the car at 200 miles an hour through a chain link fence, across a highway, over two 1.2-metre ditches and into a forest. The ninety metres of fence the car was dragging snagged it to a halt without major damage or injury – except to Walt, who had suffered a heart attack on the spot.

Walt discharged himself from hospital to finish preparations on the car, but it was now up to Green to take the wheel. His experience of motor sport was limited to a brief foray into stock cars some years before, but he gamely learned to drive the beast by cruising around the parking area before taking his first trial run at 236 miles an hour. The first all out run became a surreal experience at about 275 miles an hour, when the cockpit filled with what looked like gently drifting snow. The white flakes turned out to be salt crystals sucked into the now pressurised cockpit, leading to fears that the plexiglass might implode, a possibility Green decided simply not to think about. A problem with an oscillating front axle was cured and the car made its first run with the afterburner, cruising easily to 335 miles an hour before salt crystals ingested into the engine threw the balance out. With their allotted time now used up they had no choice but to abandon the record attempt for another year while Breedlove made his runs. This time the Spirit of America, now equipped with a steering front wheel and a tall, elegant tail, whooshed down the course with a two-way average of exactly 400 miles an hour, a new land speed record – for motorcycles.

The FIA decision that his car was actually a motorcycle did not come as a surprise to Breedlove, who had been fighting against such a ruling for some time. In truth he was now the fastest man on earth, so categories were somewhat academic. Meanwhile, Doc Ostich had gone out in the Flying Caduceus but found the car could not be coaxed beyond 360 miles an hour. He decided it was time to retire and enjoy gentler pursuits.

After watching the jet cars battle it out Burt packed up and was about to leave Wendover when a posse of railroad officials arrived, looking for every able-bodied man they could find. There had been a major derailment, with a trainload of shiny new cars scattered about, and they were offering good money to anyone who could help untangle the mess. Burt was among the first to put his hand up, and for the next ten days he toiled mightily under the hot sun, earning such respect from the railroad officials that they arranged a social security number for him. In the days before Green Cards this was the next best thing to being granted citizenship, and although he never worked again in the United States, the standing his social security number gave him would prove most useful.

Burt had recently made the acquaintance of one Sam Pierce, a motorcycle shop owner in San Gabriel, a Los Angeles suburb, who specialised in servicing Indians and supplying parts. Sam would prove a generous ally over the years, though Burt would occasionally become irked at Sam's portrayal of himself as his sponsor, a claim he vigorously denied. But if Sam extracted a certain amount of publicity from the association it did no real harm. In fact, he was immediately helpful, since Burt had tired of the shipping dramas he always endured and needed the bike stored in America. He would take only the engine and gearbox home in an old wooden ammunition crate with rope handles. There was no doubt in his mind that he was coming back. Two hundred miles an hour beckoned irresistably. He had come so close; there was no way he was going to give up when just one good run would do the trick.

CHAPTER NINETEEN
FEAR

Back home Burt set about making a new set of conrods, having finally secured the Caterpillar axle steel he had learned to trust. He had also decided to increase the capacity of the engine, which was still less than the maximum 55 cubic inches mandated by the class he ran in. He fashioned a new pair of barrels, increasing the bore from 74.4 millimetres to 76 to give a volume of 871cc. Next he modified his piston dies to allow for the increased bore, and added larger valves for the expanded combustion chamber.

The crankcases were looking decidedly worse for wear after the blow-up on the salt – itself merely the last in a long line of blow-ups going back forty years. Successive repairs had left them considerably weakened. The Silver Dolphin sheet metal works in town had recently acquired TIG welding whose best welder, Ross Young, glued everything back together so that the cases were as strong as ever, if not stronger. This was impossible without shifting the bearing housings, so Burt took the finished cases to Melhop Engineering where the housings were line bored in a vertical milling machine. He bored them oversize to realign everything and allow appropriately oversized needle roller bearings to be fitted. Once all this had been done the bottom end of the engine was actually better than new.

A delighted Burt installed the engine in the stretched Velocette frame after changing the back wheel for an Indian unit, as the drive was on the other side, and making up new engine plates. Now he could run the engine again, Burt discovered that the clutch was failing, a problem he thought he had permanently banished. With his usual equanimity he made up a set of even stronger clutch springs and inserted an additional pair of clutch plates in the cluster. It was then time to head for Auckland to catch a boat back to America. Sailings were few and far between and this time the schedule would be very tight.

One of his mates called around to say goodbye and found him sitting in the sun outside his shed reading a letter. Burt carefully folded and put it away with a sigh, prompting his friend to ask if it contained bad news. Burt shook his head.

'Not really. It's from young Donald Campbell. He's decided to go for a land speed record in a dry South Australian lake bed and he wants to know if I'd like to have a crack at the same time.'

The friend was suitably impressed. 'You know Donald Campbell?'

Burt nodded vaguely. 'We have written a bit. But I'm buggered if I want to go over there. I don't reckon you can beat Bonneville for that sort of thing. I'll have to tell him no thanks.'

Burt's liner berthed at Vancouver where he grabbed a Greyhound for Los Angeles. He enjoyed a quick catch up with Marty, Jackie and Rollie before heading for Sam Pierce's shop where he reunited frame and engine and hooked up his outfit behind a 1952 Chevrolet panel van Sam had lent him. He drove straight through to Wendover, almost 1300 kilometres, stopping only for fuel and food.

He was just in time to qualify but found to his consternation that the rear wheel bearing was shot. In all the years he'd owned the Indian it had never occurred to him to check the wheel bearings and for forty-four years they had never given him any trouble. Now, each time he rode the bike the locking nut securing the wheel bearing came loose. It took a frustratingly long time to fix and Speed Week was nearly over, the normally dry conditions breaking down with squalls of rain that left the salt heavy and unsuitable for record attempts.

Despite Earl Flanders warning Burt against running, he took advantage of a break in the weather to have a go. At 125 miles an hour the rear wheel was still spinning on the slippery salt whenever he tried to open the bike up, but he gradually wound up to 170 miles an hour. At that point the bike began sliding so badly he was forced to sit up to regain control before once more accelerating for the last of the timed miles. Somehow he managed 184 miles an hour and became the only racer out of the 230 that year to better his previous best recorded time. It was an impressive exhibition of motorcycle control but it did him no good. As he sat waiting to run the next day a rainstorm dumped 100 millimetres of water over the course. It would be two months before it could be used again. There was nothing for it but to head back to Los Angeles, drop the bike off at Sam's and hit the highway for another round of sightseeing, wandering from one state to another as the fancy took him.

Burt was not the only one disappointed by the weather. The jet jockeys' carnival had also been rained out and would not run again until October when the land speed record would be broken an incredible eight times in just two months. By then Burt was safely ensconced back in the shed at Bainfield Road, happily tinkering with the Velocette. For once there was little to do. The Indian was running beautifully and the occasional sprints he undertook on the Velocette required little more than an oil check.

He returned to Wendover in July 1965 for Speed Week but unseasonable rain again ruined the course. When he returned to New Zealand he decided to enlarge the engine. His goal was the 1000cc class, where he was confident he could set a new record, since the existing one was only 178.971, lower than the record he held in the smaller capacity class.

Again he made new barrels, increasing the bore to 77.5

millimetres, which with the standard ninety-six-millimetre stroke gave a new capacity of 905cc. After further modifying the piston die he spent hours reducing the weight of the new, larger pistons so as not to upset the sixty-six per cent balance factor he liked. To handle the extra power he made a pair of slightly beefier conrods and went up a size on the gudgeon pins, from nineteen millimetres to 20.2. The larger bore allowed for larger valves and to accommodate them he cast a new pair of cylinder heads. He wanted to position the spark plugs between the valves but there was insufficient space even for the tiny ten millimetre models Champion had given him. His solution was typically ingenious. He bored the spark-plug hole short of the combustion chamber and had the plug fire through a slot between the valves. It was a strange arrangement but it seemed to work and that was all that mattered to Burt. After fitting the engine into the Velocette he made a few runs on Oreti Beach with Duncan in attendance. Everything seemed well, so he put it in its box.

Back in Wendover Burt was full of confidence that he could not only set the record he wanted, but also shatter the 200 mile an hour barrier. But the God of Speed is a capricious fellow. During his qualifying run Burt was horrified to discover the streamliner was again shaking and weaving, even at his comparatively modest qualifying speed of 172 miles an hour. The next day he lined up to take his first serious run with frayed nerves and a sense of dread. Neither Marty nor Rollie had made it to Speed Week that year and Burt missed them both. He still had the small but dedicated band of helpers that had formed over the years, always designating whatever car Burt was driving as Team Indian HQ. They even had Team Indian T-shirts printed. They treated Burt like a guru and could not do enough for him. Like Rollie, they were convinced he was from another planet where the normal rules of ageing did not hold. Even so, as they pushed him off, Burt could not shake his anxiety. But Burt always found confidence once he was under way. He took the bike up to about 180 miles an hour in spite of the shaking and weaving. It was an heroic effort, and far more than most mortals would have attempted. Still the God of Speed wanted more. As he approached the timed sections Burt had a split second to make his choice. Did he back off and hope he could slow the bike down without crashing, or did he go for it and hope it became more stable in the mysterious world that waited behind the door?

It was never really an issue. He kept the throttle wound hard against the stop. As he hit the timed miles the bike was going faster than it ever had before. At over 200 miles an hour, the first quarter mile – clearly marked because it was used in setting qualifying times – went past in just four seconds. But the bike was not becoming more stable. Far from it. Burt knew he was rapidly losing control and a fatal crash was just seconds away.

He had used every bit of his skill to keep it on track but the weave and vibrations were now so bad he was beginning to grey out. In desperation he did the only thing he could do – he sat up. The terrific slipstream immediately tore his goggles off and tried to rip the helmet off his head, strangling him with the chinstrap. Blinded by the 200 mile an hour blast and by stinging salt flying off the front wheel Burt lost track and the streamliner veered off into the salt flats, heading like a guided missile for a steel pylon standing all by itself in the distance.

The bike missed it – and certain destruction – by just twenty centimetres, streaking into the emptiness with Burt riding completely blind. It seemed to take forever to slow but he finally reached a speed where he could put the landing gear down. Burt was so dazed by this stage, however, that he could not locate the handle to drop the little wheels. When the bike stopped it just flopped on its side, badly tearing his shoulder muscles.

When the team arrived in the panel van he was still stuck in the shell, mute with shock. They heaved the bike up on its tyres and managed to get the landing gear down before extracting Burt. Someone carefully cleaned the caked salt out of his eyes while Burt worked his shoulder, trying to ease the pain and regain some mobility. When at last his vision returned the first thing he saw was a long split in the shell, stretching from the back of the cockpit to the tail, up to fifty millimetres wide in parts. Obviously it could not be ridden again.

Many people would have admitted defeat at this point, proclaiming disappointment while inwardly rejoicing, but not Burt. He gathered his little team around him and sent one to the panel van for a roll of thin wire. Next they kneed, shoved and bashed the shell back together before winding the wire around it and twisting it tight. A car rolled up and Earl Flanders got out wearing his customary white cowboy hat. Burt walked over to him, standing casually between Earl and the activities going on behind. Luckily Earl did not seem much interested in getting closer, just in finding out what had happened. 'What the hell are you doing way up here Burt?'

Burt scuffed his feet. 'I guess I overshot, Earl.' Flanders stared at him while Burt scratched his ear and stared across the salt.

'You need to get back over there pronto, Burt. You'll have to run last but the record is yours if you can keep it up on the way back.'

Burt thanked him and Earl got back in his car with one final look at the crew gathered around the bike. He seemed about to say something more but changed his mind and with a casual wave he was gone. The team towed the bike back to the gathering point, making sure to keep a distance from the curious eyes of any officials. One of Burt's helpers was a slight young man named Darrel Packard, a member of the famous car manufacturing family. On Burt's instructions Darrel tightened the helmet straps until they were almost choking him and pulled the goggles as tight as they would go, too. He patted Burt on the helmet and wished him luck. With the last minutes of Burt's allotted turn-around hour ticking away the team pushed him off.

Burt knew that his fastest section had been six miles back down the track, so he let the speed build slowly, aiming to run flat out for the minimum amount of time. Approaching mile seven Burt opened up the machine and felt it accelerate smoothly toward 200 miles an hour. He experienced a wild moment of hope. Maybe the mysterious imbalance that had upset the streamliner had somehow fixed itself. The weave, when it began, was so slight as to be almost imperceptible, but as the speed continued to build it was soon as bad as the last time, battering Burt against the sides of the cockpit. Once again he sat up just as the machine began to go completely out of control. A press photographer took a shot that was later published with the caption: 'Burt looks happy, he's just broken the 61 cubic inch National record.' Even a cursory look at the photo, however, revealed that Burt's helmet was trying to tear his head off and that his goggles were dangling around his neck. He was not happy, he was fighting for his life, running completely blind down a course that led not to the open salt flats but a collection of parked trucks, trailers, cars, record machines, trailer homes, temporary shelters and a lot of people.

Somehow he guided the bike right down the black line until it stopped, flopping over on its side again. The streamliner was hauled back on its tyres and Burt, who had again badly wrenched his shoulder, was helped out. Earl Flanders arrived to tell him he had broken the record with an average of 168.066 miles an hour.

Throughout the day people told Burt that the chief timekeeper, Otto Crocker, had announced over the PA system that Burt had been travelling at well over 200 miles an hour through the timed quarter-mile section. Some said he'd put it at 212 miles an hour. Burt had another national record but he was far from happy. The terrifying run had been bad enough. But to go through all that and settle for such a disappointingly slow average, record or not, was hard to take.

If Marty and Rollie had been there they might have dissuaded him from going out and repeating the nightmare, but they were not. He spent three days in bed with torn shoulder muscles, a cut eyebrow and a painfully bruised hip. But his physical injuries were not the worst of it. His biggest problem was that he could not stop shaking.

The condition had not improved when he climbed into the streamliner for a last attempt on his own record for the season. For the first time in his life he forgot to oil the exposed rockers and push-rod ends, an essential task as this was their only lubrication. His general lack of fitness was also obvious when he stalled the engine. A second push-start saw him safely under-way but he failed to engage second gear properly and buzzed the motor. When the revs howled off into the danger zone a bone-dry pushrod end jumped out of its rocker cup and ended Burt's record runs for the year. Finally he could give up.

He stayed on the salt long enough to witness the Gyronaut, a new mid-engined streamliner with twin Triumph 650cc engines, break the motorcycle land speed record on 25 August, forgetting for the moment the absurd ruling that Craig Breedlove's jet car held it. With rider Robert Leppan nestled in the enclosed cockpit, his feet stretched out in front of him, the low projectile streaked down the track and back at an average speed of 245.616 miles an hour – with nary a wobble, arrow-straight all the way.

Burt was determined to catch up with Art Arfons before returning home, as so much had happened in land speed racing since they had last met. In July 1964 Donald Campbell had finally succeeded in getting a run on Lake Eyre, having been frustrated for months when the dry lake-bed was submerged by once-every-twenty-year rains. He had managed 403.10 miles an hour – slower than the record set by Breedlove the year before, but the fastest speed a car with driving wheels had ever achieved. From then on the driven-wheel record had existed as a separate target for record breakers, one that would be increasingly difficult to break even as it became a sideshow.

The almighty battle between Arfons and Breedlove that had raged through 1964 had ignited much public interest and a great deal was written about it in the American and international press. Ironically, the first shot had not been fired by either of them, but by Tom Green and Walt Arfons. The pair had been first to run when the salt finally dried out in October 1964. With Green at the wheel the Wingfoot Express had broken Breedlove's record with an average of 413.2 miles an hour. It had been a near run thing, as the engine would not deliver full power and, after a week of cruising up and down, they were almost out of time. It was only after Walt's little brother Art suggested they open the exhaust clams by several centimetres and make one sixteenth of a turn adjustment to the idler jet that the car finally ran on full power. Green had only three days to enjoy his record, however, before Art raised it to 434 miles an hour with his new Green Monster.

Six days later Breedlove took it from him, raising it first to 468 miles an hour and then, on 16 October, to 526 miles an hour. In setting this last record he had also written off his car in spectacular fashion when, after completing the final timed section, Spirit of America began to slide out of control. He had immediately buttoned off the jet and hit the chutes, both of which were torn away. Seconds later the brakes burned up while the car careered off course, clipping a power pole at over 400 miles an hour and skating across a shallow pond before shooting over a two-metre high dirt bank. It was still doing well over 200 miles an hour when it finally speared into a six-metre deep brine pool. Breedlove, who had somehow escaped injury, popped the canopy and clambered out, swimming to safety as his car sank. He was now the fastest man in the world.

But not for long. Art Arfons returned eleven days later and on his first two runs, using full afterburner for the first time, he set a new record at 536 miles an hour, surviving a blown tyre during the last stages of his final run at over 600 miles an hour. Only his second chute, deployed by a $30 second-hand shotgun, held the car stable after the first was blown away, dragging the car to a stop without further damage.

The battle continued in 1965 when Breedlove, still nominally the fastest motorcyclist in the world, returned with a new four-wheel car powered by the same J79 Art was running. Spirit of America – Sonic 1 set a new average at 555 miles an hour in November. A week later, while Breedlove was in New York attending various celebrity functions, Art hauled his car back to the salt and raised the mark to 576 miles an hour. It looked certain he would keep it until the next season as freezing rains were already falling. Then

Breedlove, who simply ignored the pools of standing water all over the course, came back again and smashed Art's record with an average that was .601 of a mile an hour over the 600 mile an hour barrier. The duel was getting serious.

Burt knew Art was not due at Bonneville until mid-November, so he went for another of his sightseeing trips, racking up the miles in Sam's old panel wagon, which he had made very comfortable. When he made it back the first thing he saw was Art's big old bus parked out on the salt. The jet had already been unloaded and was sitting in the shade of a tarpaulin with a number of people working on it. As soon as Art saw Burt his face creased into the familiar friendly grin. Burt was struck by the contrast between the relaxed atmosphere around Art and the frantic bustle he associated with Craig Breedlove, who always seemed to be surrounded by techni-cians, engineers, public relations men, media people and the scent of big money. Art, on the other hand, was largely ignored by the media. The few who lent him a hand did so because they wanted to be part of his grand adventure.

Art introduced Burt to his team: his right hand man Ed Snyder, a mechanic who Art never failed to publicly acknowledge; Pop Groff, a sixty-year-old painter who had walked into the shed one day and volunteered his services; and Charley Mayenschiem, a civilian jet engineer along for the ride. Charley had actually snuck into the left hand cockpit of the Green Monster when Art was doing a 400 mile an hour shake down run in front of Firestone executives. 'You wouldn't get me in there with a gun and a crow bar,' Burt said. 'I'm strictly a shy pensioner when it comes to cars.'

Art showed Burt over the big barrel-like car, which had been painted by Pop in a splendid red and green colour scheme. He called it 'my baby' and was very proud of the job he and his team had made of it. And it did look good. The big jet engine had been streamlined with an aluminium body featuring two cockpits about halfway back on either side. Art occupied the right hand one while the other was really only there to make the car symmetrical. The driving position put Art right beside the spinning turbine blades but he shrugged off the danger. Turbine blades hardly ever flew off.

The engine itself was massive, capable of producing 17,500 horse-power with the multi-stage afterburner lit up, enough to fire an F104 jetfighter to 1600 miles an hour. Art chuckled as he replaced the light alloy access panels. 'Every time we test fired it we broke windows up to half a mile away and had the police come round. In the end everybody kinda accepted what we were trying to achieve and mostly they were real good about it.'

Burt nodded. 'Yep, its amazing what neighbours will accept eventually.' 'I heard this thing was for sale in Miami,' explained Art, 'so I drove the bus down, gave the junkyard guy the 600 bucks he wanted without quibbling and hauled it away. When I wrote to General Electric and asked for a manual for it they told me I didn't own one. Nobody owned one, they said, except the military. So I wrote and gave them the numbers we found on it and the next thing this air force colonel arrives and tells me I have to give it back to them. Well I showed him my receipt and told him I bought it fair and square and I intended running it in my car. He stormed off but I haven't heard anything since.'

Burt took time off from helping Art to watch the duel for fastest single-piston-engined car in the world between two extraordinary machines. The Herda-Knapp-Milodon Streamliner, resplendent in a brooding blue-black livery, looked like something Batman would have loved to drive. Bob Herda, the driver and engineer behind the car, was an aerodynamics expert, widely recognised by the hot rod community as the best in the business. He had built an advanced space frame and clothed it with a flawless body that he made as slippery as possible, even installing onboard oxygen to eliminate the need for an air intake. From its first outing in 1965, running alternately a big block and small block V8, the car had established eighteen national records. In 1967 Ford, as a tribute to founder Henry's land speed record set forty years before, had asked Herda to run a special single overhead cam engine to attempt various class records. The streamliner had done so with an incredible average of 357 miles an hour.

Bob had always been friendly to Burt and Burt was keen to see how he went against Red Head, another extraordinary streamliner that had first rolled on the salt in 1962. Red Head made a dramatic contrast to Herda's sinister looking beauty. Painted flame red it had a dramatic wasp waist that had earned it the nickname the 'Coke bottle'. Taken over as an unfinished Romeo Palamides project by its first owner, it had since set various class records with a variety of engines and drivers. Driven by Bob McGrath the car's highest recorded speed had been 331 miles an hour in 1966 with a blown Chrysler engine.

In the end the duel fizzed out when Red Head had a bearing fail in its overdrive unit, while Herda cooked his big block Chrysler motor. At well over 300 miles an hour a body panel had collapsed, jamming his foot on the accelerator. Afraid that the entire body might break up Herda had slipped the automatic gearbox into neutral and coasted to a stop. Unable to take his foot off the accelerator he could only sit and wince as the 5900cc V8 screamed up to 11,000 revs, stopping only when a cylinder wall collapsed. He had no luck with his smaller engine, either, as the anti-detonation additive they put in the nitro-methane fuel caused the valves to warp. As always the congenial engineer was philosophic about the various failures, telling Burt he'd be back the next year for another go.

Art's own preparations were frustrated by the afterburner refusing to light and a patch of squally weather, but Thursday 17 October dawned fine and still. It was time to go.

Art had confided to Burt that he had dreamed he was going to crash, and had made the further mistake of telling his wife June about his dream. She had been badly frightened and tried to dissuade Art from going but he'd packed his bags anyway. 'You can't take too much notice of that negative stuff,' he told Burt, 'or you'd never do a danged thing.' They had laughed at him when he started to build his car, he said. Breedlove had nearly half a million dollars in sponsorship to Art's ten thousand of his own money, plus a deal with Firestone to supply the tyres and the wheels. 'But here we are, ready to roll.' The plan was simple. Art intended to get under way and then light up all four stages of the afterburner, accelerating to over six hundred miles an hour as quickly as possible to leave himself as much room as he could to slow down. As he walked to the jet, surrounded by his small team, he told them he was going to stand on the accelerator through the first mile. This was a high stakes decision. He would be accelerating much faster than any car previously, the stresses on both the machine and driver being almost impossible to anticipate.

It was peaceful out on the salt; the only sound being the distant beat of a press helicopter hovering over the course a few miles down the track. With a final adjustment of his helmet Art climbed aboard and strapped himself in. The Green Monster started with a low whine that quickly became a high-pitched scream as it reached operating temperatures. Art increased the revs, holding the car on the brakes. When he was ready he let go the brakes and hit the afterburner, blasting a great sheet of orange flame from the tail pipes as the car rocketed forward. The first timer recorded a speed of 585 miles an hour and the car was still accelerating strongly. He cleared the final timing trap at 610 miles an hour but as he closed the throttle for the slow down the car suddenly swerved to the left.

Art turned hard right but the vehicle pitched abruptly onto its right side and dug its nose in. Art had already cut the fuel to the jet and punched the chute release but it was too late. He was still conscious as the car flipped high in the air, flying over 150 metres before bouncing. By then Art was unconscious, mercifully oblivious to the next slamming landing and the sickening slide that ended over 1.5 kilometres from the point the jet first went airborne.

Parts of the Green Monster were scattered all over the salt and many had torn great chunks out of the surface. A wheel had flown into the air and passed between the rotors of the press helicopter, miraculously without touching them. When the team got to the crash site rescue workers were already prizing the wreckage apart to get to Art. Incredibly he was conscious again, lying in the blood-spattered cockpit with bits of the smashed instrument panel in lap, insisting he was all right and that they take their time freeing him. In a few minutes he was on a stretcher, ready to be flown to hospital in Salt Lake City.

He was back the next day, his eyes covered in gauze and his face raw from salt burn and flying plexiglass. His entire body felt like it had spent a few days in a concrete mixer, but he had no broken bones and was already talking about a lighter, more streamlined Green Monster. Ed Snyder had determined the probable cause of the crash: a frozen wheel bearing. At the speeds Art was doing the wheels were turning at about 7000 revolutions every minute. It looked like the right front wheel had cooked off all its grease and welded itself to the hub before tearing off the entire front wheel assembly and gunning for the press helicopter. Art and Burt had time for just a few words. 'You want to buy a used car?' he asked Burt softly. 'Only done a few miles.' Burt shook his head. 'I hear the last owner was a bit rough on it.'

Burt carefully shook his friend's hand and Art walked stiffly to the aircraft waiting for him on the salt. As Art reached the steps Burt called, 'I guess your dream was right.' It was Art's turn to shake his head. 'Nope,' he called back. 'In the dream I got killed.'

A week later Burt was on a ship going home. He finally had time to reflect on what had been a crammed few months. He remembered what he had said to Mickey Thompson when the American was disappointed at not taking the land speed record, and becoming the first to set an average time over 400 miles an hour, all for the sake of a broken drive shaft. 'You know you did it,' Burt had told him. 'What else really matters?' It was true then and it was true now. Burt had pushed the Indian over 200 miles an hour. He knew it, and in the end that should have been all that mattered. Except, of course, it wasn't. He wanted the number 200 written against his name in the record books.

CHAPTER TWENTY
BLUBBER AND SURGE

Burt had thought carefully about his next steps. As soon as he was home in his shed he began work. The shell was still in America, so there was little he could do about the stability problem other than formulate a plan to overcome it, something he had already done. The other steps involved increasing the size of the engine again and making it stronger, particularly around the bottom end.

His plan was about more than simply increasing power. Burt had realised some time ago that his engine would be more reliable if he could generate the power at lower revs, reducing the stresses on all the reciprocating parts. His aim now was to produce sufficient power to run at 200 miles an hour pulling 6500 revs, a long way short of the past when the engine had frequently gone over 7000.

He calculated that there was enough metal in the existing cylinder liners to bore the engine to 79.5 millimetres, yielding a capacity of 953cc. He knew that with careful machining he could make big enough pistons without modifying his die. To beef up the bottom end he adapted the crankpin he had been given at the Indian factory, mating it to the flywheel at one end and the timing gear at the other. He installed a caged roller bearing, using the Indian needle rollers he had also been given, and then turned his attention to the drive side of the mainshaft. Selecting a suitably sized gearbox shaft from his spares he annealed and cut it to size, grinding off the splines. He then had it re-hardened and ground to the correct size. The new mainshaft now looked beefy enough to handle the power the engine was making, which was somewhere around six times more than when it left the Indian factory forty-seven years earlier.

At the same time he enlarged the bore on the Velocette for a capacity of about 600cc and raced at a number of speed trials. For the National Standing Start Championship, held at Mosgiel just out of Dunedin, he went back to 500cc and set the fastest time of the day in his class for the standing quarter mile, at just 13.93 seconds. This was really smoking for such an old bike and easily blitzed a large number of more youthful riders and machines.

The time to return to Bonneville had rolled around again, but Burt had comfortably achieved his objectives by the time he drove out of Sam Pierce's shop in the panel wagon. He had attacked the stability problem by cutting an 203-millimetre diameter hole in the nose of the streamliner which channeled air into the body through a ten-kilogram lead tunnel, cast from the old weight he had once attached to the front of the frame. He also created outlets towards the rear of the shell, hoping his modifications would reduce the pressure wave coming off the front, which he thought had prevented the tail from stabilising the bike. He also hoped the extra weight at the very tip of the nose would help it run true, like an arrow. Fibreglass at the base of the tail was cut away and a parachute mounted, a new requirement that was actually rescinded for motorcycles before he arrived at Bonneville.

This time he was travelling with Marty and Rollie and was in high spirits as they cruised toward Wendover. Perhaps that was why he began pulling waitresses onto his lap in the diners where they stopped to eat, a habit his two friends could not persuade him to abandon. A waitress who avoided his lunge and dumped a cup of scalding coffee in his lap succeeded where they had failed, however, and a chastened Burt left that particular dinner. To add to his despondency he came down with a virus that badly sapped his energy. He was glad to arrive early at Wendover as it gave him some time to rest.

He bounced back to enjoy the customary enthusiastic welcome from his support club, and by the time he hit the salt he was feeling a lot better. His first qualifying run went well with a recorded speed of 184 miles an hour. He was relieved to find that the shell seemed a great deal more stable, although the engine had nipped up during the run and he let it cool right down before the next one. Alas it was not running well and he could manage only 162 miles an hour the next time.

A quick strip down revealed a piston had seized and the cylinder liner had split, no doubt as a result of all the metal he had machined off it. With no spare cylinder liner he was stumped. A gloom settled on the team as they sat around outside the Western Motel. Then Burt suddenly noticed that the water downpipe was made of cast iron. His crew quickly removed it and sure enough it was just right for the job. After a quick word with the owner Burt shot off to Wendover Airbase, with a bottle of bourbon for the boys, where he cut off a length of pipe and machined up a new liner. By the early evening he had removed the muff from the split liner and heat-shrunk it around the new one.

Back at the motel he hung the truncated downpipe back on the wall and began to reassemble his engine. Unfortunately the long hours had taken their toll and the virus he had been fighting kicked back in. Utterly exhausted he was forced to stop work. By the time he arrived back at the salt he had gone thirty minutes over the twenty-four-hour maximum allowed between qualifying and attempting a record, and had to queue again in the blazing sun to re-qualify. When it was his turn he was in a bad way. He started well enough, but failed to engage top gear properly and the motor screamed up to about 8000 revs, bending the valves and damaging a camshaft.

Back at the airbase he searched through the accumulated junk until he had found enough old valves he could machine to replace those he had ruined. He generally carried at least eight spare pistons, but there was still the matter of the bent camshaft. A broken torsion bar, probably from a Chrysler suspension system, machined down to size just fine. He was ready to reassemble his engine again.

At his qualifying run on Friday he clocked 190.06 miles an hour. The next day, feeling better than he had since arriving at Bonneville, he arrived bright and early to attempt the record. Conditions were far from ideal, the surface wet and heavy, and with so much salt sticking to the machine by the end of each run, speeds were well below the bike's potential. He lined up for the attempt anyway, determined not to run the engine above 6500 revs, and to let the bike flow up to speed with only moderate acceleration. He kept to the plan and, after running both ways comfortably, learned he had set a new national record with a two-way average of 183.586, some 15 miles an hour over his old record.

The run earned him the trophy for Top Record Breaker for 1967, a signal honour and cause for much congratulation and celebration. It was a splendid recognition of his efforts, and there was more to come.

In late October Burt returned to a warm welcome in Invercargill, settling down to make two new cylinder barrels with thicker liners for the Indian, enlarging the bore to eighty millimetres and a capacity of 965cc. He also decided to build another identical frame to the modified Scout one the Special used, and had just started the work in December when he was voted American Motorcyclist of the Year. It was a strange thing to be 'old Burt' at home, puttering away in his humble shed, and a celebrity abroad, at least within the motorcycle fraternity in America. But Burt simply accepted the accolade gracefully and got on with it.

Once he had finished making his second Indian frame he installed the engine and made an attempt on the national beach record. Unfortunately, the engine played up on the day and he left Oreti Beach empty-handed. He had better luck in June 1968 with the Velocette, setting the fastest time of the day for the flying quarter mile at 130 miles an hour. It was now clear that he could not really develop his engines further without a dynamometer, which would allow him to methodically test his improvements to the bikes without the complicating variables that racing introduced.

He had talked with a number of people over the years about building such a machine, and he now set out to do it. It was a fearsome looking device when finished, with two flat thirty-five by twenty-centimetre plywood paddles, driven by a long chain from the engine running though exhaust pipe to stop it flying off the sprockets at either end. When the dynamometer was in use both the bike, with its rear wheel removed, and the paddles were mounted securely to a heavy steel frame.

Burt had also made an electric starter (using an old Ford starter motor) with handles on either side that fitted over the drive side mainshaft nut on both the Indian and the Velocette. He had first seen such a thing when a local grass track hotshot named Earl Bryan built one. Earl was asthmatic and had trouble push-starting his speedway JAP. There were a number of copies about that Burt would borrow, until their various owners decided he could build his own, which he finally did. He could now start the bike while it was hooked up to the dynamometer and run his tests.

Burt persuaded Norman Hayes to help with the first trial run, something Norman, who had followed the construction of the machine, was reluctant to do. Burt kept at him until he relented and Burt soon had the paddles whizzing around creating what to Norman felt like a hurricane in the confines of Burt's little shed. He was relieved when the engine refused to run properly and the trial was aborted.

The bike might not have performed but Burt was happy with his dynamometer. The only further equipment he needed was a hand-held rev counter to ensure the one on the bike was accurate, and without which he could not accurately calculate the horsepower the engine was developing. Luckily a friend named Vern Russell had just such a thing, which worked by holding it over the end of the crankshaft, and he agreed to help Burt. He soon regretted it.

Having operated the starter motor to get the engine running, Vern held the rev counter over the end of the crankshaft and Burt slipped the bike into second gear. As he let the clutch out, the unshielded paddles began to revolve, horribly close to where Vern was crouched beside the bike. Burt opened the throttle until the paddles were spinning at about 2000 revs, at which point the din from the open megaphones on the bike combined with the clatter of the chain in the pipes and the roar of the wind generated by the paddles was enough to daunt the stoutest heart. Papers and dust were flying around the workshop and just as Vern thought matters could not possibly become any more unpleasant, the bike slipped out of gear, the revs went through the roof, and the engine blew up. Vern was shaking violently as Burt calmly leaned over to have a look at the damage and announced, 'That's the first time that has happened in the history of this church!'

Although he would thereafter allow Burt to borrow the rev counter whenever he asked for it, Vern was always too busy to help out in person. Duncan and Ashley had also heard enough to avoid being roped into a session, and Burt was forced to recruit others.

The last such victim was a general practitioner by the name of Dave Bruton, a motor racing enthusiast who had turned up at the shed on numerous occasions to talk to Burt. Little suspecting the drama in store, the doctor arrived with an old 1920s textbook on calculating horsepower from paddle-type dynamometers. After enduring a session, holding the rev counter in place with stalwart courage, he sat down and calculated the horsepower generated at 6000 revs. His final figure, after making allowances for power loss in the chains and mechanism, was ninety horsepower. This was a lot less than Burt had persuaded himself the engine made and he immediately gave up on the dynamometer, deciding there and then that he now had enough power. He would concentrate on making the bike run true so that he could actually use all the power he had.

Now just a year shy of seventy Burt was aware that his time was running out. 'Old age is sort of sneaking up on me,' he told one interviewer. Pain from angina was kept at bay only with his 'nitro' pills, and he now had an active thyroid, which he claimed kept him young. But he easily passed the mandatory driving test required for his age as well as the medical examination he needed to run at Bonneville. His hearing was getting worse but, like many in that position, he compensated by raising his voice, encouraging those he was shouting at to reciprocate.

In 1968 a rainstorm blew in and ruined the surface at Bonneville. No sooner had Speed Week been postponed for a month than the sun came out and dried the track off beautifully, but it was too late. The salt remained unused until the Ford Motor Company arrived to run their new Mustangs on the ten-mile oval in pursuit of endurance records. None other than Mickey Thomson had been hired to do the driving, along with well-known American racer Danny Ongias. Burt soon had a job as an observer for the US Auto Club. Mickey intended running night and day and decided to run a few trial laps at night.

'Hey Burt,' he said, 'what say I take you for a bit of a skid?' Burt fidgeted and tried to think of an excuse, but Mickey had a way of blowing past objections and he soon found himself strapped into the passenger seat. 'Don't worry,' said Mickey, 'these things won't run much more than 145 miles an hour. It'll just be a drive in the country.'

They had been humming along for a couple of miles when they encountered two cars coming straight at them. Mickey kept his course and the two cars swerved to either side while Burt sat with his eyes screwed shut. Mickey grunted something about tourists and kept the accelerator buried in the carpet as they approached the huge sweeping turn at the top of the elongated oval. The back end began to slide but Mickey just applied more and more opposite lock until the Mustang was running broadside at about 140 miles an hour. Every now and then the back would slide out a little further, threatening to turn the car around and Mickey would deftly catch it, talking softly to it as he did so. 'Oh no you don't, sweetheart. You come right back here, there's a good girl.'

As they slid around the final part of the turn the headlights cut out. Burt felt a surge of relief – they would have to give up now. Then the lights flickered back on illuminating the 1.2-metre high heavy wooden pegs marking the inside of the course, flicking past the nose of the car. Burt squeezed his eyes shut again as Mickey twitched the Mustang's tail the other way, only to open them and find they were once again running in the dark at full speed. 'Kinda peaceful, isn't it,' said Mickey.

The final turn was the worst. The salt was wet in places and it seemed to Burt that the car was about to spin and roll at any moment. As they approached the pit area Mickey apologised for not doing another lap due to the failing headlights. 'Don't worry,' he said. 'When it's ready you can come on out again.' Burt was already out of the car. 'That's all right, Mickey. To tell you the truth I find these low speeds a bit boring. I reckon I'll just have a cup of tea and take it easy.'

He never did get back in the Mustang and was content to watch as Mickey and Danny set several national records before the re-sumption of the rescheduled Speed Week.

Burt had gone over the Indian a number of times and was confident all was ready for the one good run he lived for. But the God of Speed wanted to test him some more, and the engine refused to run properly. 'It just blubbered and surged,' Burt complained later. 'It would only run a lousy 155 miles an hour.'

In desperation he rechecked everything. The bike persisted in running rich, even when the main jet in the carburettor was nearly closed completely. Time finally ran out but Burt stayed on in case he could get a run. Then Craig Breedlove turned up to race an American Motors AMX Javelin. Breedlove had already set 106 national and international records with an AMX earlier in the year on a track in Texas, but the ailing company was keen to set an all out speed record. Breedlove quickly clocked 189 miles an hour, but

Burt had still not eliminated the gremlins in his engine. Time was rapidly running out.

Finally one bright morning Burt felt he might have solved the problem. The engine seemed to be running like its old self and he decided to attempt a quick run just to make sure before he went back out on the salt. The only place to do this was on the splendid highway that ran through to Reno on the Nevada side of the border. Unlike Utah, which had strictly enforced speed limits, Nevada allowed its citizens to drive as fast as they liked as long as they did so safely.

Of course, what was safe and what was plain foolish was something for the Nevada Highway Patrol to determine. The officer who saw the red projectile flash past at well over 100 miles an hour was in no doubt he'd seen something foolish. He wheeled his car round and gave chase, finally coming across the red missile on the side of the road about four kilometres away. He took a good look at the rider, who seemed to be an elderly man, tinkering with something inside the strange red body, oblivious to the officer's approach. 'Any idea how fast you were going, sir?' he asked.

'I sure do,' the old guy replied. 'It was a lousy 160 miles an hour at best.'

The officer was taken aback. 'Were you wanting to go faster?' He took a closer look at the machine. 'On that?'

Burt stood up and pulled a piece of cloth out of his pocket. He wiped his hands and mopped his face. 'I was hoping to, yes. But there's a problem I can't fix. I might as well go home to New Zealand and come back next year.' He sighed and shook his head. 'At least you can give me a ride back to my car. I'll drive back and put the Indian on the trailer. It's going like a hat full of busted arseholes so there's no point in running it any further.'

The officer was incredulous. 'You mean that thing is an Indian motorcycle? And you want to go faster than 160 miles an hour on it?'

Burt laughed. 'I've already run at over 200 miles an hour. One hundred and sixty is like a stroll in the bloody park.'

The patrolman took another long look at the red streamliner, noting the narrow front tyre and the leaf-spring suspension. 'What year was this thing made?'

'I've made bits and pieces over the years,' replied Burt, 'but the bike was built in 1920.'

'And what about you?'

'1899. Queen Victoria was on the throne and the sun was shining on the Empire!'

The officer shook his head. 'I should be throwing you in the pokey but I guess I'll just give you a ride back to your car. No one would believe it if I told them what you just told me anyway.'

They were soon rolling back down the highway. The officer looked over at his passenger who seemed somewhat downcast. 'Listen old timer,' he said. 'I have a feeling you'll fix whatever it is and have that thing doing 200 miles an hour in no time. Just promise me you won't do it on my highway.'

Later that night Burt finally gave up. The bike was still blubbering and surging and he'd completely run out of ideas. He would head back to Invercargill and get to the bottom of it. Then he'd come back and have one last shot at 200 miles an hour. It would be a close run thing. Not only was age catching up but money was also running out. His days of travelling were almost over.

CHAPTER TWENTY-ONE
POP

Burt concentrated on the engine problems, building up a new Schleber De Lux carburettor from his stock of spares and rebuilding the magneto, which going by the symptoms he had experienced in Bonneville, could have been the culprit. Faulty magnetos are hard to diagnose as they can function perfectly one moment and hardly function the next. Testing a magneto is therefore no guarantee, but Burt was loathe to throw away the English ML magneto that had given such sterling service for so long. In any event, replacing it would not be easy and, in the same way that he had ignored the inadequacy of splash lubrication for so long, he now put the magneto issue aside and turned to the bike's wheels and tyres. The narrow 482-millimetre racing tyres were no longer available so he switched to 457-millimetre rims, for which he could find any number of racing rubber (usually for free, since he did not need good tread, filing and sanding them to his customary smooth finish).

In April the motorcycle club running trials on Muriwai Beach near Auckland offered to pay his expenses if he wanted a run. He took the front wheel off the Indian and hooked the forks onto the Vauxhall's tow ball. After removing its chain he towed the bike the 1700 kilometres north without the extra burden of a trailer.

The meeting turned into a disaster when the engine blew, scattering hot parts all over the sand. A piston had broken up and, as the gudgeon whizzed up and down, it had split the cylinder liner. A conrod had then punched a hole in the front of the crankcase and smashed into the magneto, bending the armature arm and damaging the slip ring. Burt was characteristically philosophical, proclaiming as usual to those who gathered to inspect the damage that it was 'the first time that has happened in the history of this church'. There was now a serious amount of work to do, however, and his departure for America was just eight weeks away.

After driving home Burt knuckled down to create a new pair of conrods, two new cylinders and eight pistons. He also repaired the crankcase and fixed the magneto using magnets from an old Bosch unit. He finished with days to spare. A few weeks later he was back on the salt.

As he waited in line for his qualifying run he chatted to Bob Herda. Herda's car looked as menacing and immaculate as ever, but the team had been experiencing trouble with the nitromethane fuel, commonly known as 'pop', which for some reason was clogging the fuel lines and had to be flushed out regularly. With the engine now running clean again Bob was confident of a good run. Burt's turn came and Bob wished him luck, saying he would see him at the other end.

The qualifying run went well for Burt. He was sure he had beaten his old best time and was waiting for confirmation when Herda's wicked little projectile rolled through with its chute billowing behind. The car stopped and Burt waited for the canopy to open. When it stayed shut a couple of officials wondered over. It was only when they were within a few feet of the car that they started yelling.

The gunk Bob had been flushing out of the fuel system was actually the sealant from the fuel tank. Alcohol could not eat it but nitromethane could. The back of the streamliner had been filling with leaking fuel. When the car got up to about 300 miles an hour the belly pan had been sucked toward the salt, opening a gap in the firewall behind Herda's back. As soon as the chute slowed the car, the leaked fuel had sloshed forwards through the gap into the cockpit, where the tiny drain holes in the floor could not dump it fast enough. In just a split second a drop of pop splashed onto the hot exhaust, igniting the whole lot and burning through the oxygen feed line to complete the cycle of horror. Bob Herda had been incinerated so completely there was almost nothing left of him.

Burt had seen many shiny machines reduced to mangled wreckage in the years he had been visiting the salt, but there was something especially eerie about the death of his friend. In the shocked hush that settled over the assembly area as the dreadful news spread, a timing official made his way over to Burt and quietly told him he'd clocked 191 miles an hour, his fastest ever recorded speed.

In his first record attempt run the following day all went well. Burt again recorded a time of 191 miles an hour. But on the return run the engine began to blubber and surge again and continued to for the rest of Speed Week. Burt kept fiddling with the mixture and ran down the strip fourteen times in four days in his attempt to get it right. To no avail. He was forced to admit that those who had told him the magneto was faulty were probably right.

Arriving back at Bainfield Road a month later he immediately began work to replace the magneto. Years before, Joe Hunt, an American specialist, had given him a Bosch magneto. The item was probably from a BMW and Burt had been dissuaded from fitting it because it ran the wrong way. Once he'd decided to use it, however, he quickly solved the problem by dispensing with the two idler pinions in the gear train driving the magneto. He replaced these with a single large cam gear mounted on an eccentric shaft, to allow an accurate meshing of the gears. He had to move the magneto closer to the gear and to do this he cut about four millimetres off the base of the magneto and about the same amount off the crankcase mounting. He drilled and tapped new holes to mount the magneto. Because it was designed to fire a flat four-cylinder engine, rather than a forty-two V-twin, he next made a new brass cam ring and a set of cams to work the points. The latter he created from an old ball race that he annealed before filing it to the correct shape to achieve the timing he needed. Once he'd annealed it again it was ready.

Burt's next job was something entirely new. He had seen a pair of Triumph motorcycle conrods made of aluminium alloy and had set his heart on making three, one for the Velocette and a pair for the Indian. His main purpose was to reduce the reciprocating weight in the engine – plus the alloy was easy to work. Unfortunately, the piece of aluminium plate he bludged off George Begg was nothing special, but he would not listen to George's warning, only learning the error of his ways when it broke almost immediately he tried it in the Velocette.

Burt would not abandon the idea of alloy conrods. When someone gave him the propeller blades off a DC4 aircraft he carved into one of them with his usual array of hacksaws and files, and made a fine looking pair of conrods. Once they were finished, though, he had second thoughts, returning to his tried and true Caterpillar axle steel. He made another pair of cylinders, taking the bore out to eighty-one millimetres to give a capacity of 985cc. He was still within the 1000cc class but the cylinder liners were now extremely thin and they relied on a snug fit in the crankcase to support them.

In June 1970 Burt was back at Bonneville where his next decision seemed, on the face of it, to defy all logic. For years he had run his bike on methanol, a fuel whose many qualities included a very low burning temperature. Why he would decide at the last minute to switch to pop, a difficult fuel that was notoriously hard on engines, was hard to fathom. Rollie and Marty, at Bonneville to keep him company, cautioned against it, but Burt would never take advice, and often seemed to resent it being given. Two well-wishers had bought a can of Mickey Thomson's finest pop, at some considerable expense, which they presented to Burt to help him out. One of the reasons he had never bothered with it before was the cost.

Now that he had some it was more than his nature could stand not to use it.

Nitromethane requires a very rich mixture to work or it will simply blow holes in pistons. Burt made the adjustments he thought were needed and went for a run. The bike went well for a brief time and then stopped. A quick strip down revealed that the entire top of one piston had been completely vaporised. Burt tweaked the mixture to run richer, replaced the piston and went for another run, ruining both pistons almost immediately. He quickly undertook another strip down, fitted another set of pistons and in half a mile two more were totalled. By now Burt was getting cranky, but he still refused to listen to Rollie and Marty. His final set of good pistons was sacrificed. He then began to weld up the least damaged ones in his pile of burnt-out wrecks, but it was too late. He had thrown away his last, and possibly best chance to take a record at more than 200 miles an hour. It was all over.

Later that year Burt was invited to attend a function at the Southland Motorcycle Club where he was presented with a plaque from the New Zealand Auto Cycle Union, honouring him for his contribution to motorcycling. It had only been awarded twice before, once to Ivan Mauger, the world speedway champion, and once to Hugh Anderson, a former 50cc and 125cc world grand prix champion. Burt was deeply moved, and he enjoyed one of the best nights of his life, surrounded by some of his closest friends.

Burt was now taking life a lot easier, although he still turned up for any race meeting within range. He had reconciled himself to the idea that he would never see his beloved salt flats again when two young filmmakers walked into his life and everything changed. Mike Smith and Roger Donaldson had telephoned him from Auckland, to say their company Aardvark Films wanted to make a television documentary about him. Burt was delighted and the two men turned up late the following night. Burt greeted them warmly and fired up the Indian. The noise in the little shed was deafening and the filmmakers retreated to the door, from where they could see lights going on up and down the street. Windows were thrown open and angry voices joined the cacophony from the shed.

'Turn that bloody thing off you silly old bugger!

'Go back to bed you idiot!'

Burt made them a cup of tea and his guests exchanged surreptitious glances when they tasted something metallic in the brew.

Aardvark Films accompanied Burt to a meeting at Oreti Beach where Burt and the Velocette posted an average speed of 132.35 miles an hour, a new national beach record. They also recorded him setting the fastest flying quarter-mile of the day at a meeting at Mosgiel, against the fastest modern motorcycles available. Clearly the spirit was still willing and so was the rest of Burt. When Roger asked him if he would like to go back to Bonneville so they could film him running on the salt he did not need to be asked twice.

Burt's tenth and final visit to Bonneville was in July 1971. He was disgusted to learn that the rules had been changed and that all streamliners now had to have separate engine compartments. The year before had seen a flurry of activity as three contenders chased the all out motorcycle land speed record. Don Vesco had fired his twin engined 700cc, two-stroke Yamaha, feet-forward streamliner across the salt to take the record with an average of 251.6 miles an hour. A month later his good friend Cal Rayborn broke it again with a speed of 265.5. Rayborn's head-first streamliner, powered by a 1480cc Harley Davidson twin, had been a handful to drive and he had a few high-speed slides before he got the hang of it. Less fortunate had been the third contender Robert Leppan, who had set a time one-way of 266 miles an hour in his twin Triumph 650cc powered streamliner Gyronaut X-1. On his return run the streamliner had become airborne at about 280 miles an hour, finally sliding for about 2.5 kilometres with a badly injured Leppan in the cockpit.

The high speeds had prompted the new safety rules, but they effectively ended any participation by streamlined machines that were conventionally ridden. Burt was allowed to make a few half-hearted passes in the streamliner for the Aardvark cameraman, probably the most frustrating thing he had ever done in his life. He was also allowed to run his bike without the shell, but the gearing was far too high for him to do well. On the way back to Los Angeles, alone once again, an axle broke on his old trailer which then collapsed. He had to lash a tree branch underneath it, dragging it for miles until he found a truck stop and some assistance to slide the streamliner into the back of the $90 Pontiac station-wagon he had bought for the trip. Once back in Los Angeles he spent time with Marty and Jackie at their home in Thousand Oaks. Rollie came over and they talked about old times, each of them facing the reality that Burt's record-chasing days really were over. It was a sad farewell.

Back home Burt was soon in the thick of it again. He and Duncan still thought nothing of driving 600 kilometres to compete in a speed trial near Christchurch, then home again for a trial the next day. At a quarter-mile sprint along School Road in Invercargill, he kept the power on too long for his feeble brakes to pull him up, yelling as he careered down the road for someone to pull the traffic barrier out of the way. Just in time it was whisked away, and Burt hurtled past. Then he turned right around and lined up for another run. He was seventy-three years old.

At another speed trial he took off at about 120 miles an hour over a slightly humped bridge, smacking his nose on the tank. At the end of the run he was streaming blood but dismissed all expressions of concern. 'Never mind that,' he said. 'What's my time?'

He still blew up his engines regularly, the mangled parts joining all the other offerings to the God of Speed on the shelves in the shed. He also continued to turn out the most amazing inventory of parts for the Indian and the Velocette, sometimes expressing regret that he could not take the latter to Bonneville to set the time for fastest Velocette ever, just as he had with the Indian. Somehow it did not occur to him that he might have already achieved that goal; he almost certainly had.

He also gave in to council pressure and built himself a comfortable little home next to the workshop. When he found out how much money he could make renting it, however, he stayed put in the shed. It is probable that the council did not know, and almost certain that they would not wanted to have known.

And then, at the age of seventy-six, he broke his own beach record at Oreti Beach on the Indian, with frame number two. He achieved a blistering two-way average of 136.15 miles an hour, in spite of the fact that the course was curved, due to the intrusion of a couple of flooded streams, and the sand was unusually wet and heavy. For some reason the record was never ratified, but the press made much of it, as did Burt's friends, and he was happy.

The unexpected income from the rented house, and an offer by an American enthusiast to buy the streamliner, prompted one final trip to Los Angeles to say goodbye to all his friends. He could not bear to part with his original engine, so he built up a second with help from Norman Hayes. The buyer was happy with the arrangement and in 1975 Burt flew to America.

Burt, Marty, Jackie and Rollie had a wonderful time, sitting around the table in Marty and Jackie's cosy kitchen, eating ice-cream and reminiscing. As usual Burt did most of the talking, often about a past his friends had not shared, and he was more reflective now. One morning over coffee he asked them if he had ever told them about his friend Archie Prentice, whom none of them could recall him mentioning.

'Oh well then,' said Burt, 'I'll tell you about him. Archie Prentice was woman shy. He had an Indian Chief and he'd ride it on the back streets just to avoid seeing women on the main street in town. They'd be all done up and Archie just could not face them.'

'He must have hated his mother,' offered Jackie.

'No,' said Burt, 'I think he was afraid of them.'

'Well, you made up for it,' said Marty.

Burt grinned. 'I did my best. So did Archie's two brothers. They used to chase them! But old Archie had a great handle on life and he used to say something that I have come to see as the simple truth. He used to say a man is like a blade of grass. In the spring he grows up and in the summer he is at his best, spreading his seed. In the autumn he begins to wither and in the winter he just fades away.'

'Well Burt, you were sure spreading away long past summer time,' said Rollie.

Burt's braying laugh echoed around the house. 'You know I was asked to address the 200 Mile an Hour Club at their annual dinner in Los Angeles and I asked, "How long have I got?" They said an hour and a half, if you want it. I said that there obviously wouldn't be time to talk about my love life!'

Burt gave them news of people they had long forgotten, including Leo, the ship's engineer they had met in Bonneville. Burt had fallen ill in Auckland while waiting to catch a boat to Taiwan. 'He was working on a ship trading around China and Japan and he had a place in Taiwan. I was going to stay with him and sail around the place but getting sick scuppered the trip.'

Marty was incredulous. You mean the guy who turned up with that real looker, the working girl from Reno? Are you saying you kept in touch with him all these years?'

Burt nodded. 'Yep, that's the guy. Her name is Valerie. They got married.'

When it was time to go there was no sadness. The final meeting had been such an unexpected bonus, and all the sadness had been used up last time when Burt had climbed up the ship's companionway in Long Beach. This time they waved him off at Los Angeles airport with a sense of completion. He was ready to go home and they were ready to say farewell.

Working on motorcycles and racing them carried on for a few years more, but Burt knew it could not last for ever. His eyesight was failing and he could no longer read the settings on his Myford lathe or the numbers on his micrometer. Duncan, whose near sight remained as sharp as ever, would come over and help him set up a piece to machine, but Burt finally sold his tools and called it a day.

On hearing that he was packing it in Irving and Norman Hayes came by and bought both bikes. They were determined to keep them in Southland and put them on display in their shop for all to enjoy. By then Burt had moved into his little house, which was rather like a shrine, with shining silver trophies packed on every shelf. He appeared on a television special hosted by David Frost, along with half a dozen outstanding New Zealanders, recorded in Auckland. He charmed Frost and became the star of the show when he told the famous host he could not hear him, demanding he come and sit next to him. Frost talked to Burt with his arm around his shoulder, staying beside him for the rest of the show.

He complained in a letter to Marty that he was not paid to appear, but he did at least get a free trip to Auckland and the chance to catch up with his son John and his family. He enjoyed his grandchildren and the neighborhood kids continued to drop by whenever they liked for a biscuit and a yarn.

He was lucid but increasingly absent-minded, once placing an advertisement in the local paper asking if anyone had come across a spare tyre that must have fallen out of his Vauxhall. A man from the local garage, where Burt had taken it to have a puncture repaired, returned it.

He suffered a heart attack but made a good recovery, teasing the nurses with all his youthful enthusiasm, and returned to his little house where he spent his days in a comfortable chair with a two-bar electric heater always going. He had rigged up a special wire holder on the heater for his teapot, and the many visitors were always offered a cup. His tea no longer tasted metallic.

With the sun streaming into his cosy little house, he would sit in his old armchair, close his eyes and find himself back on the salt. The Indian would be humming along, everything operating in perfect harmony. The black line would be flickering under the bike as it hurtled along, rock steady at maximum revs in top, doing well over 200 miles an hour. He would raise his head just a bit against the pressure of the slipstream and lift his eyes to take in the cobalt sky. As he drifted into sleep his perfect run would slowly fade, until there was nothing but the glittering white plain and the distant purple hills and perfect, eternal silence.

On 11 January 1978, in the late afternoon, the woman next door rang emergency services to say she had not seen Burt all day. He always came out to wave to her around midday and she was worried. An ambulance arrived and the two officers let themselves in. They found Burt sitting in his chair, his slippers stretched towards the heater. The sole of the nearest slipper was smoking.

Scarcely a soul among the 75,000 living in Invercargill did not note Burt's passing. For many it was the loss of a friend. For a few it was more than that. When Ashley next encountered the normally glum-looking Duncan Meikle he looked even glummer. 'It's just not the same,' he confessed to Ashley. 'I miss my mate and his little bike.'

Three days after the funeral, Margaret was cleaning out her father's house when she came across an address book. She flicked through it and stopped at the letter I, which contained a single word, 'Indian', and an American phone number. On a whim she called it. A man answered, his voice reverberating slightly. 'Indian Motorcycles. Can I help you?'

For a moment Margaret was silent, then remembered the purpose of her call. 'Hello, my name is Margaret. I'm Burt Munro's daughter and I am calling to tell you that he has died peacefully at home.'

'I'm really pleased to hear that, Margaret.' The unexpected sentiment hung in the air for a moment, somewhere near the middle of the Pacific Ocean. 'I'm sorry, ma'am, that came out wrong. I'm real sad to hear Burt's gone and everybody else round here will be too when I tell them. We already miss him. It's just that we figured he'd be awfully lucky to go peacefully. I am so glad he did.' There was another pause. 'I would like you to know that he made all of us here at Indian Motorcycles proud. Real proud.'

As Margaret hung up, her eyes were drawn to the glittering trophies, waiting to be packed in boxes. She was struck by how much more there had been to the life they represented. Her father, she thought, had always been a true individual and, like all true individuals, he had always been himself.

It was enough, she thought, more than enough.